10/9/04

For Linda—
with all best wishes
for a full of happy reading

Natalin Singa

Scraping By in the Big Eighties

American Lives    *Series editor* : Tobias Wolff

# Scraping By in the Big Eighties

NATALIA RACHEL SINGER

*Natalia Rachel Singer*

University of Nebraska Press Lincoln and London

Acknowledgments for
previously published material
appear on page 227.

Library of Congress
Cataloging-in-Publication
Data
Singer, Natalia Rachel.
Scraping by in the big eighties /
Natalia Rachel Singer.
p. cm. – (American lives)
ISBN 0-8032-4309-x (cloth : alk. paper)
1. Singer, Natalia Rachel.    2. College
teachers – United States – Biography.
3. Mothers and daughters – United
States – Biography.    4. Children of
schizophrenics – United States –
Biography.    5. Paranoid schizophrenics
– United States – Family relationships.
6. United States – Social conditions –
1960–1980.    7. United States – Social
conditions – 1980–
I. Title.    II. Series.
CT275.S521753A3 2004
362.2'0973'09048 – dc22
2004001018

Set in AGaramond
by Kim Essman
Designed by Dika Eckersley
Printed by Thomson-Shore Inc.

I do not see my life as separate from history. In my mind my family secrets mingle with the secrets of statesmen and bombers.
— Susan Griffin, *A Chorus of Stones*

The opinion that art should have nothing to do with politics is itself a political attitude.
— George Orwell, "Why I Write"

But how does a poet put bread on the table?
— Adrienne Rich, "How Does a Poet Put Bread on the Table?"

# Contents

# Acknowledgments

I am indebted to the U.S. Census and the National Law Center on Homelessness and Poverty in Washington DC for data on poverty and income distribution in the United States under Presidents Reagan and Bush. I also want to thank the following writers whose work, listed below, both supplemented this research and helped inform my thinking on the 1980s: Barbara Ehrenreich, *The Worst Years of Our Lives: Irreverent Notes from a Decade of Greed*; Benjamin Friedman, *Day of Reckoning: The Consequence of American Economic Policy under Reagan and After*; Paul Leonard, Cushing Dolbeare, and Edward Lazare, *A Place to Call Home: The Crisis in Housing for the Poor*, published by the Center on Budget and Policy Priorities in 1989; Haynes Johnson, *Sleepwalking through History: America in the Reagan Years*; Robert Scheer, *With Enough Shovels: Reagan, Bush, and Nuclear War*; Robert Lekachman, *Visions and Nightmares: American After Reagan*; Andy Pasztor, *When the Pentagon Was for Sale*; Michael Schaller, *Reckoning with Reagan*; Garry Wills, *Reagan's America: Innocents at Home*; Susan Faludi, *Backlash: The Undeclared War against American Women*; and Stephanie Coontz, *The Way We Never Were: American Families and the Nostalgia Trap*.

For "Voodoo Economics," I also relied on data provided by the sociologist Paul Starr, who contributed to an excellent retrospective of the 1980s in an article in the September 1990 issue of *Commentary*, "The American '80s, Disaster or Triumph? A Symposium," and the historian Arthur L. Tolson's September/October 1985 article in the *Black Scholar*, "Reaganomics and Black Americans." The chapter itself was inspired by Walter Karp, whose essay in the October 1981 *Harper's*, called "Coolidge Redux," laid out in detail the ways in which Reagan's new budget would transfer money from the poor to the rich and the Pentagon. As *Harper's* editor, Lewis H. Lapham, wrote in the preface to Karp's *Buried Alive: Essays on Our Endangered Republic*, "America lost one of its vigilant and resourceful advocates" when he died in 1989. "To read Karp is to read the blueprint on which the country raises up the architecture of its politics." Because, as this book goes into print, supply-side economics has been vigorously revived by George W. Bush, I also recommend that readers review other early critiques of the Program for Economic Recovery of 1981, among them "The Education of David Stockman," by William Greider, in the December 1981 issue of the *Atlantic*, and Bernard D. Nossiter's July 1981 essay and review in the *Nation* of *An Economic Analysis of the Reagan Program for Economic Recovery* by the Joint Economic Committee of the U.S. Congress, in which he tracked the paternity of supply-side economics not to the Kennedy administration, as its champions erroneously claimed, but a theory dating back to Jean Baptiste Say (1767–1832), which was vehemently discredited during the Great Depression.

In addition, I could not have written this book without reading and rereading the work of George Orwell, James Baldwin, Terry Tempest Williams, Joan Didion, Phillip Lopate, Susan Griffin, Rick Bass, Patricia Hampl, Tobias Wolff, and Alix Kates Shulman. Two fine memoirs about the 1960s – Margot Adler's *Heretic Heart* and Leslie Brody's *Red Star Sister* – gave me courage to tackle the 1980s. Lewis H. Lapham's political columns in *Harper's* have kept me sane for the last two decades; he is a national treasure, as is Patricia Williams of the *Nation*. I recommend all these authors to anyone interested in the essay in general, the political essay, memoirs that capture an era in American history, and the essay in which the political and spiritual intersect.

Dozens of people helped me bring this book into print. Among them I first want to thank Stephanie Higgs and Ladette Randolph, extraordinary editors, and agents Emma Parry and Byrd Stuart Leavell. Their work on my behalf has meant everything to me. Every writer also needs a cheering squad of fellow writers, and mine were Michael Steinberg, Bill Roorbach, Dawn Raffel, Bill McKibben, Robin Hemley, Deborah Tall, Robert Root, and, above all, Rosellen Brown, who is one of literature's angels in plainclothes. This book would still be in a box had it not been championed by these generous and talented people.

Thanks also to the monks, residents, and fellow visitors of Dai Bosatsu Zendo in the Catskill Mountains, who answered my many questions on three separate trips – in 1980, 1992, and 2000 – with good humor.

If I have butchered the tenets of Buddhism in this memoir, I humbly apologize.

Many thanks to Charlotte Ward at St. Lawrence University and colleagues, past and present, who read drafts of chapters and offered advice: Bob Cowser, Mary Hussmann, Margaret Kent-Bass, Elizabeth Stuckey-French, and Ned Stuckey-French, all of them fine writers and teachers of writing. Hearty thanks to Marina Llorente for help with Spanish and Roy Caldwell for help with French. Thanks, also, to the Office of Academic Affairs for a research grant that allowed me to go back to Washington State to retrace my old steps. I could not have made this trip without the assistance of Jan Wallace, Marianne Mears, and Wendy Feuer. I also want to thank the research assistants who helped with the first draft: Nimanthi Rajasingham, Noelle Everett, Rebecca Schmidt, and William Bradley. The sociologists Ron Flores and Donna Fish helped me locate data; their expertise and friendship were invaluable. Cathy Tedford, Laura Fredrickson, and Eve Stoddard listened to me talk through my ideas on long walks. Their support and wisdom are priceless.

Poet and friend Robin Behn helped me see how I was still trapped in the habit of the polemic, a theme that became central to the book thanks to her insights. The essayists Leslie Ryan and Diana Hume George gently reminded me that I was writing a woman's story. The artist Sara Krohn deserves credit for helping me coin the expression, "déjà voodoo," for introducing me to the Japanese marble paper method, and for reminding me not to shield my own "windows of vulnerability" as a memoirist. I am grateful to friends on both coasts who have allowed me to share their stories and first names: Claudia, Joe, John, Neal, everyone at the Salal Café, Dawn, Cindy, and Patti, along with her kind and generous family. To anyone else who makes an appearance in this book, I claim full responsibility for any mistakes I've made, any lapses in memory or taste. To protect their anonymity, I have changed the names of some people whom I was unable to locate.

My sister, Mira Bartok, deserves special thanks for her support and love. It is, after all, partly her story I tell in these pages, and her willingness to let me delve deeply into our family difficulties allowed me to speak with candor. This book is dedicated to her, as well as to our grandmother, whose anger in the face of injustice made us strong, and our mother, whose obsessions, however frightening, taught us what it means to persist. I want to thank my stepsons, Paul Grant and Benjamin Grant, for listening as I told some of these stories around the dinner table, and my father-in-law, Ian Grant, who read early chapters and generously supported the construction of my writer's studio. Above all, I am eternally grateful to my husband and best friend, Kerry Grant, to whom everything I write is dedicated. He is my best friend and companion in this life. I can't begin to find the words to thank him for his efforts here, but I intend to try for a long, long time.

# BOOK I
## Free Enterprise, 1980–1982

I say to you if you think we can live without federal help, God bless you. Some of us are on the brink of catastrophe.

Mayor Henry Maier (Democrat) of Milwaukee, on January 20, 1981

# Soul Work in the Age of Reagan

"Purple is the color of transcendence," a woman announced from her open doorway when she heard us gasping at the mailboxes, newly painted in honor of our arrival. The duplex Joe and I had signed a lease for was white with faded gray trim, but now the front steps, mailboxes, and porch were all this same eye-frying plum, the handiwork of our downstairs neighbors, apparently. "It's the color of the seventh chakra," a male voice explained. To our left on the front porch, a balding, blond man in his late twenties was sprawled out in a hammock reading a book called *Life after Death*. I half hoped he'd leap up to help us move in, but he stayed horizontal.

"We're Vicki and Glenn," the woman called up to us, almost as an afterthought, as though names did not matter in the world she inhabited, only colors, chakras, essences. A quick glance had already told us that purple was the color of the neighbors themselves: their gauzy shirts, her thick eye shadow and long, flowing Indian skirt, even the hammock.

Joe, in his usual Keds and jeans, hummed *The Twilight Zone* theme song, but I was charmed. I had always longed to lounge in a hammock (though preferably on a beach in Mexico), and I was inspired to see that Vicki, whose accent screamed Brooklyn, had morphed into some groovy New Age priestess out here in the hinterlands of Seattle's Ballard District. Having denounced the Midwesterners of my past and their color schemes – my mad mother in Cleveland (polyester stretch pants in red), our career-obsessed classmates at Northwestern (crew-neck sweaters in navy, gray, or pastel) – I could learn to like purple if it would help me mellow out. That was exactly what I'd moved out west to do.

Joe and I had set out for Seattle in separate driveaway cars: giant gas-guzzling Cadillacs that attracted scowls of disapproval from the other drivers lining up at those OPEC-embargoed pumps. I arrived first, when the blackberries were still on the vine, and Joe made it in time for my birthday in October. We could have gone together but depending on a guy on the road did not jive with my feminist notion of how to become a free spirit, so I depended, instead, on the kindness of strangers (to quote the subject of my senior honors thesis): in this case, two grumpy best gal-pals who sought out a ride-share passenger just to cut costs. I was pining for Joe by North Dakota, but given that neither of us had savings, furniture, cookware, or outfits appropriate for nine-to-five work, necessity dictated that we depend on the kindness of strangers through the first fall and winter. I loved the couple I rented with – an artist named Claudia who supported her unemployed philosopher boyfriend on her scandalously low teaching wages – but their daily battles about money were wearing. Joe was equally fond of the young marrieds he bunked with, but their colicky baby screamed half the night. We sought refuge from domestic discord on each other's lumpy foam pads, imagining our utopia à deux.

And so we'd hustled, toiling away at uncool desk jobs to come up with the requisite first, last, and security deposit, plus all the supplies for a love shack. Now, as we emptied our just-bought 1963 Buick Le Sabre station wagon (monkey-dung brown, with rust) I felt the weight of our new loot – the shiny pots, Pyrex casseroles, toaster, blender, the price tags still on – as the physical expression of those long months of tedium and pantyhose chafing. I was ready to let the transcendence begin.

It was March of 1980, and even as a Republican presidential candidate named Ronald Reagan was plotting revenge on all the able-bodied lazies living off big government, I was scheming to become one of them. I was twenty-two, a little young to be contemplating a sabbatical, but back then when our world seemed poised for nuclear war, contributing nothing to the fluorescent-lit, acronym-ridden, anesthetizing, military-industrial complex seemed like the most subversive but productive thing I could do.

The plan was to get laid off, go on unemployment, and become laid back, meanwhile training myself to write and publish the most important bildungsroman of the late twentieth century. It was a tall order, a seemingly incongruous mix of ignoring the call of hustle and material ambition while pursuing a lifelong dream with the focus of a pole-vaulter. But I was used to contradictions, and most of all, used to scraping by on next to nothing. I was kind of macha about it.

I hadn't always aspired to live on $330 a month, the maximum I'd be eligible to draw (I had checked). From the age of six I had done my homework, studied for tests, written for school publications, nabbed the scholarships, pulled all-nighters, read all assigned texts and recommend-eds, crafted to-do lists and five-year plans . . . until something shifted around the time my friends started hearing back from law schools and buying job interview suits. I began to feel that I'd somehow been duped by my liberal arts education, that all the Emerson and Thoreau and even *Zen and the Art of Motorcycle Maintenance* had been the lures into a club in which everyone wore the same uniforms and were lumped into the same marketing niche. Weren't we all, here on Island U.S., nothing more than buyers and sellers? And wasn't it, finally, death we were peddling: the Cold War products and by-products of mass extermination, and consumer culture's products of catatonia, complete with laugh tracks?

This crisis of faith in Team America coincided with a parallel crisis of self. While I was writing my tome to Tennessee Williams's tarnished heroines I made the realization that no amount of good grades or college prizes could fill up a certain bottomless hole. I had "baggage," as they said back then. Most of it had to do with my mother, a paranoid schizophrenic who read my every move toward independence as a rejection of her, and my father, who was off who-knows-where cobbling together a life as a writer and a painter that I romanticized and was looking to emulate, minus the alcoholism. In the wake of his abandonment, my mother, younger sister, and I had limped along on welfare and whatever handouts in the way of food and shelter my mother could finagle from her folks in Cleveland: our affectionate, leftie grandmother (whom we adored) and our violent, misogynistic grandfather (whom we had wished dead on so many occasions that when his cancer finally came, we felt like assassins). In my psyche, feelings of suffocation, guilt, rejection, shame, self-loathing and its compensatory arrogance competed for floor space with a wide-eyed bohemianism that only occasionally grew sharp with the awareness of the possibility of personal and collective doom.

Mostly I wanted, in Seattle, to become a more evolved human. I'd done the hedonism thing, but now I got up early and ate healthy, or tried to. I was reading literary magazines, novels by women and people of color I hadn't been exposed to as a student, and also books about history, philosophy, politics, and Eastern mysticism. Inspired by Doris Lessing's *The Golden Notebook*, I was hoping through my writing to find some link between the personal and the political, the political and the spiritual, art and politics, all the schisms and Manichean opposites that in our bifurcated cold-war world seemed unbridgeable. I was open to any text, classic or kooky, I thought would expand my worldview, from Virginia Woolf to Edgar Cayce, and all the occult primers Glenn was inhaling in that purple hammock. I wasn't sure about life after death, but life after Group Death (my nickname for my place of employment) was certain to be sweeter.

I had always been a dreamer and what got me to Seattle was a dream, literally. A few weeks before graduation I had found myself soaring like a condor over a map of North America toward the Northwest's dense green pockets of spruce and cedar. I was flying, then I was falling, and I woke up bracing for impact.

Joe did not call me a flake for reading my REM imagery as a summons. While his roommates began to dress for success he hung onto his red-flecked beard and shoulder-length brown hair. We had met in a Romanticism seminar our senior spring and decided that Romanticism was not just a literary movement: it was a lifestyle choice and it would be ours.

Together we were denouncing the values of our soon-to-be-labeled yuppie generation. We were rejecting late-century industrial capitalism. We were abandoning the industrial Midwest of our childhoods: the steel mills of Pittsburgh, where Joe had been expected to become a miner like his father or Protestant minister like his older brother, and Cleveland with its chemical factories and self-igniting river. In their stead we were embracing nature, art, funky cafés, and the time to partake in such havens.

Seattle was the perfect, moist setting to give succor to a young, romantic heart. A shopping expedition downtown through the endless stalls of produce and crafts at the Pike Place Market could take all day if you indulged yourself, letting your nose lead you from fresh crab to wild blueberries; to avenues of cheeses pungent with pepper or chives; to herb stands aromatic with lavender, sage, and myrrh. You could relive the Gold Rush era in Pioneer Square, whose dark, wrought-iron benches and handsome old saloons and shops had barely escaped the flames that demolished the city in the great fire of 1889. When your feet were tired you could sip lattés in the cozy café of Elliot Bay Books and gaze at the shiny new hardbacks feeling happily agitated: so much to read, so little time.

For nature lovers, there were countless mountains in the vicinity – the Cascades, the Olympic Range, Mount Rainier, Mount Hood, Mount

Baker, and more – the only rain forest in North America, and lovely city parks and beaches. Whereas I'd grown up near a junkyard of rusting cars, our new digs were just a jog from a place where salmon swam upstream to spawn.

I loved Seattle's coffeehouses, the cappuccino and pastries. I loved the neighborhood diners. A late leisurely brunch might offer avocado omelets, cinnamon rolls as big as box turtles, and primo people-watching. You could seat yourself at the splintered counter or at wobbly tables with sticky chairs, while big, hairy, slow-moving men in aprons served up cheap hippie fare and braless women with jangly earrings wrote down the recipes if you asked nicely. The drone of flies and bees dive-bombing the honey jars were perfect accompaniment to the scratchy old Traffic tapes and conversations about silversmithing or the Dalai Lama. You could work all this atmosphere into your novel.

Newcomers in their twenties were arriving every day, all with their big backpacks and clunky hiking books and chewed-up poetry volumes and dreams. There was still a pioneer mentality at work, the belief that you could start over, live cheaply and well, and become a calmer being than the anxious striver you'd been in the industrial wasteland you had fled. If you wanted to be a writer, there were several live reading series that brought in the famous but seemed to welcome all comers; if you wanted to be a painter, there were new galleries springing up everywhere and openings almost every night. There were so many plays and foreign films and art happenings and lectures to choose from that even though Joe and I went out several times a week, we were always pining for the amazing cultural moment we had missed. In fact, one cent of every tax dollar went into the arts: public sculptures, murals, poetry-on-the-bus, and free concerts and plays, the one catch being that most of the theatrical freebies took place during conventional work hours. Who *were* these lucky people who could catch the new Sam Shephard at the Tuesday matinée?

Well, a lot of these theatergoers were the unemployed and underemployed, we'd soon discover. Seattle's infrastructure was in flux. During the Boeing plant closings of the early and mid-seventies, people had left town in droves with bumper stickers saying *Will the last person leaving Seattle please turn off the light?* and leaving behind attractive middle-class houses that could be rented now for a song. The counterculture's influence was strong, the result being collectively owned businesses, food co-ops, women's health-care cooperatives, and a burgeoning alternative spiritual community – all this before the New Age was a cultural cliché, before the first Windham Hill record was even cut, let alone used as mood music to sell luxury cars on TV. As a girl who hailed from the land of white bread, these innovations seemed revolutionary. The *real* revolution of the baby boom – young people uniting to end an unpopular war, bring down a villainous president, declare equality among men and women of all colors and persuasions, and protect the spotted owls – well, that had all happened just before I came of age and I was sorry I had missed it. Now it seemed that the best way to help the planet was to lead a thoughtful, balanced life in a peaceful place. I wasn't satisfied with the social progress we'd made but I could live with this worldview, in a pinch.

Joe and I thought it was cool that when Seattleites asked us what we did they were usually referring to our free time. Did we know that a mile from our new home was a beautiful beach called Golden Gardens, where a path along blackberry-festooned railroad tracks led to the even prettier Karkeek Park? Had we discovered the joys of roller-skating around Green Lake? Were we ready to watch Mount St. Helens blow her top? Had we been to the Seattle Psychic Institute to hear of other future seismic events and to find out what we been "called" to the Northwest to do?

Almost everyone we met – from outdoors enthusiast to table-tapper – was engaged in something called "soul work." Soul work was a lifestyle and a worldview, a goal and the path itself. To engage in soul work was to apprentice oneself to an art form while also learning to bake organic bread, meditate and do yoga, get some form of daily aerobic exercise, learn the names of local trees, write down random thoughts and feelings daily in a journal so as to ferret out hidden motivations and unresolved hang-ups, read everything, and record one's dreams in a separate journal made of handmade paper and studded with inspiring quotes from Rilke, Yeats, Shakespeare, Goethe, Margaret Mead, Freud, and Jung.

Fitting soul work around a forty-hour-a-week job was simply out of the question.

After we'd unpacked the kitchen and cooked up our first utopian supper of black beans, avocado, and rice, Joe and I sat at our five-buck garage sale dining-room table and marveled at our good fortune. "To new beginnings," I said, clinking our Rainier Beer bottles together. We toasted every appealing detail of the apartment: the knotty branches of the giant monkey puzzle tree knocking against our leaded windows; the views of snow-capped Mount Rainier to the south and the Cascades facing the northeast; the converted darkroom that would be my study; the tiny cubbyhole in the living room (perfect for storing Joe's fermenting home-brews); the dark, cavernous bedroom so conducive to lucid dreaming; and above all, the miraculously low, $230-each rent.

"To the wilderness," Joe said.

He unfolded a map and plotted our upcoming hike through the Hoh River Rain Forest, where the ancient, moss-cloaked cedars and Douglas fir in the guidebook photographs looked as gnarled and enchanted as Arthur Rackham's trees in *Alice in Wonderland*. My sister was flying in soon for her spring break from the Chicago Art Institute and I'd managed to wrack up enough comp time at work to take her to the Olympic Peninsula for a four-day weekend. When Joe's miserly employers had told him he couldn't go, he simply resigned.

"To freedom," I said.

"To the end of devo jobs forever," Joe said. *Devo* was a word he had appropriated from the New Wave band by the same name, who per-formed in sterile white jumpsuits, with gas masks. Joe defined devo as "deevolutionary, dehumanizing, demonic" – all that we were rejecting. Joe's job, processing bank forms in a windowless cubicle on the tenth floor of an ugly, gray high-rise, fit the description to a tee. Having moved all this way to live near mountains, it was an abomination to be trapped inside a building that hid them from its employees while ruining every-one else's view too. After our wilderness excursion, he vowed, he'd line up something more humane.

I laid out the last details of my get-rid scheme to Joe as the moon rose. If luck had given me my devo job, luck would take it away.

Some background on the luck part: I'd cut things close to the bone when I moved to town, and after paying my first month of rent I had only thirty dollars to spare. I blew all of it on the only job-hunting outfit I could scavenge from the Bon Marché basement: black vinyl shoes with cardboard soles and a two-sizes too big polyester floral dress with a ruffled bodice like something a lactating Sunday school teacher might wear. The temp agency I visited that afternoon lined me up a typing gig the next morning at one of the nation's first HMOs – an acronym I'd never heard before – a sprawling brick complex called Group Health. The temp lady warned that my petty, supervisor-to-be was still complaining about the last "idiot" they'd sent, a graduate of Harvard Divinity School, but I figured that even if I only lasted a day, I could eat. I was taking things one grocery bag at a time.

My boss turned out to be a thirtyish, shaggy-haired man whose Wisconsin accent and slightly gooney name of Wayne Leloo put me at ease. What may have appeared to his former underlings as an anal-retentive perfectionism was a passion for the English language and a hatred for the jargon and peppy slogans of corporate-speak. He loathed acronyms and was appalled by the practice of using nouns as verbs. Our very department's name – Word Systems, or WS to management – was ridiculous to him. He longed, as I did, to write the Great American Novel, but the financial pressures of family life and home ownership had squashed his shot at it for the moment. We recognized each other as kindred spirits and by the end of the day he had hired me to work full time – not as his secretary, but his assistant technical writer.

Suddenly, literally overnight, I had landed a professional job with great benefits during a year of double-digit inflation and unemployment, a year when many young people with BAs were washing dishes. Everyone told me how lucky I was, but that didn't stop me from feeling sorry for myself when the alarm rang at half past six.

I, who had never even touched a computer, was now a writer of computer manuals. My task was to translate into human-speak the programming functions my colleagues described as they automated each area of the hospital, wing by wing. I didn't understand why they had to computerize their records at all; it seemed awfully devo. I was not good at this kind of writing and unwilling to work overtime to improve.

Wayne seemed grateful just to have someone around the office he could talk to about literature. He never once complained when I let my Word Systems communiqués pile up while I typed up my short stories on the company's dime, never took offense when I put my feet on the desk or when I renamed our place of employment. Perhaps if he had been a boss and not a buddy, he could have kept his job. That Christmas the management fired Wayne for "low productivity," putting me, the queen slacker, in charge of all in-house publications, with the caveat that there'd be no money for me to hire an assistant, and that I'd have to do all of my own typing because, well, I could. All this at my same assistant's salary, I might add.

Laden with guilt over my role in Wayne's demise and panic about my new responsibilities, I began to throw the *I Ching* (an oracular tool my first housemate, Claudia, had turned me on to); I was looking for the sage's way out. I kept getting image forty-one, Decrease, and the judgment, "Decrease combined with sincerity brings about supreme good fortune without blame." What I wanted was for my boss to decide not to fire me, which would hurt my future prospects, but to lay me off to save the department money. But how would I pull this off when I was the lone, overworked writer?

Then one day a salesman arrived wheeling in the ten volumes of a wonder-product with the laughably redundant name of System Development Systems, and I knew the road to redundancy was clear. I used reverse psychology on my boss. I sent him a memo excoriating him for thinking that this set of three-hole-punched forms that forced the programmers to document their procedures step by step could replace a human being. I also let it slip that WS could acquire the SDS for only 2K less than my yearly salary.

Management saw at once that the SDS would do a better job than a flawed human. The SDS didn't need vacations or health insurance. The SDS didn't call in comp time to take its sister on nature hikes. The SDS didn't sneak out for two-hour lunches at the collectively owned Cause Célèbre Café, then skulk back sullenly, longing to lose the suit and don a beret. The SDS did not think it was a sad and absurd indictment of the times that its initials, which now evoked regimentation and standardization, had once stood for a national student radical group. The SDS was simply glad to be of use and could, if reinforcements of its kind were needed, be cloned on the office Xerox machine.

I would not stand in the way of progress: I would allow myself to be replaced by an acronym. If hastening the dehumanizing trends in the work world would give me time to enrich my own humanity, so be it.

"Here's to the Great American Novel," Joe said, and we clinked bottles one last time.

We unfurled our foam-pad bed and hung above it Joe's poster of Che Guevara, whom he resembled, and my Arthur Rackham print of Alice in Wonderland, whom I resembled. We moved my desk into the slanty-ceilinged extra room, found shelf space for our books, hooked up the stereo, and put on some theme music. I chose Joni Mitchell, whose songs about the "free, free way" were to be my soundtrack in the months and years to come as I kept *trying* to become a free spirit (oblivious at first to the oxymoronic quality of this goal). Then Joe put on the new Devo album and we slam-danced around the apartment, jumping up and down on the bare hardwood floors, kicking around the empty boxes, commemorating our last gasp of Devodom until we remembered our purple-clad neighbors downstairs.

"Well, let's hear it for transcendence," I whispered as I turned down the stereo and clinked my empty bottle to his.

I had no idea what I was inviting into my life with that toast, and also how little, how very little.

# 2

# A Room of Blue Flowers

Mount St. Helens blew one Sunday morning in May, triggering an earthquake that jostled Joe and me from a deep sleep. The eruption coincided with my last week at Group Death. As I cleared shelf space for my successor, the SDS, clouds of sticky black ash traveled eastward. Many in Seattle panicked, hoarding water and groceries as though expecting Armageddon, but the wind patterns spared us until the ash made its second lap around the planet and was so diluted that it barely darkened the clouds. By then I was officially free. As I contemplated my future, newscasters replayed an interview they'd done with a lone, beard-to-the-belt-buckle crank named Harry Truman who had elected to stay on the mountain in the face of dire warnings, determined to live and die off the grid. Now, when I remember my departure from the American work force, I picture herds of elk and caribou running for their lives while a stubborn misanthrope rattles his tin cup and shouts, "Bring it on!"

To celebrate my liberation, Joe and I went camping on Orcas Island. We hiked up a small mountain, picked blueberries, napped in fields of mint and lupine, and saw American eagles swooping across the sky. Nearly every Friday after that we loaded up the Buick and took off: to La Push and the northern Washington coast and south to the jagged rocks at Kalaloch; to the coast of British Columbia near Port Renfrew where we rented scooters and spotted whales; to the Skagit River valley where we watched snow geese migrating to Siberia. We got naked in hot springs near Mount Adams; we scraped mussels from sea rocks and boiled them for dinner; we learned to cross-country ski. Once, while we were making love on a rain tarp in the Hoh River Rain Forest, the forest floor quaked as though with thunder and a herd of a hundred elk stampeded through, so close our hair riffled in their wind.

We met odd, interesting people on the trail, like the woman who told us about a commune on a tiny island off the coast of British Columbia. Everyone wove clothing on handmade looms with wool from their own sheep, grew their own vegetables, caught salmon, and gathered kelp from the beach beside their yurts. "We've found a way to live without money," she said. On Shi Shi Beach we encountered a colony of people who lived in trees. Some of these tree houses had artwork, stained-glass windows, and in one case – the thermodynamics of which escaped me – a sauna. Although we never traveled more than a day's drive from home, we returned on Sundays with the feeling that we'd voyaged far away to wondrous, exotic lands.

By then Joe had landed something at United Cerebral Palsy – minimum-wage grunt work, but he loved it. He came home with stories about the patients he wheeled through the hallways: the blind, bearded man who shouted, "Raymond Burr! Raymond Burr!"; the shy, married couple who asked him if he would "arrange them" for sex; the sad, soulful boy who pointed to words in magazines to compose poetry. Although Joe made two-thirds of his old salary, the hours were flexible and he adored his coworkers, who were all about our age and liked to go out after work to hear New Wave bands. I was glad that Joe was making friends. I didn't want him to get lonesome when I felt like being alone.

During the week, I tried to write. Joe got up at five for work and I tried to wake up with him, but sometimes I fell back asleep until nine. Then I'd bolt from bed in a panic, full of self-reproach for being a sloth.

My concept of the artist's life was very boot camp and monastic: Rise before dawn for journal work and meditation, swim a mile at the Y at seven, write all day breaking only for a salad, read novels and take notes on the reading. I wanted to relish each day and not be so product-oriented, but I was still my same old Type A-minus self: goal-obsessed and driven but apparently not driven enough.

Focusing on craft was new for me; in college I'd written in a white heat and had never worked line by line, word by word, comma by comma. And then there was the issue of finding a voice. I would read Nabokov's *Pale Fire* and try to imitate it, or Wallace Stevens's collected poems with their fake-flippant, learned lines like, "Hi! The creator too is blind." How do you find your voice when you've always believed there is something wrong with you, when self-invention and transformation have become your mission?

Write what you know, people say. I wasn't ready to tackle my mother, that woman in the stained red stretch pants with red lipstick smeared across her teeth; I could not reconcile my idealized vision of my future self – a published writer, looking calm and confident on the book jacket photo – with the despair and self-hatred I felt when I recalled the sound of my mother, a cigarette at her lips, hissing my name during one of her breakdowns.

I could not write about my father, although I did write him the letters I would have sent had I known his address: ten-paged, single-spaced essays in which I compared our writing styles as though we were literary cronies in the same league as the authors I was reading – Günter Grass, Saul Bellow, Gabriel Garcia Marquez, Doris Lessing – and I regaled him with boastful tales about my burgeoning outdoor prowess.

I thought meditation would help, but I didn't know how to do it. That spring a friend from college, a music major named Bill, sent me a copy of *Golden Wind: Zen Talks* by Eido Shimano Roshi, which Bill and his mother had helped transcribe. I regretted that I'd declined Bill's offers to teach me to meditate when we'd shared an apartment one summer. Now he was clear across the country, at a Buddhist monastery in the Catskill Mountains. Closer to home, Claudia practiced transcendental meditation, but she said I needed a mantra. I was leery of chanting out loud by myself: this was something my mad mother did, after all. And so, what I began to do instead, was to simply sit in my darkroom/study, close my eyes, and wait. Sometimes, I fell asleep.

One day when I was sitting like that, an image of my sister formed in my mind. I saw her in a sunny room filled with lovely blue petals. That evening I called to tell her about the meditation. She gasped.

"I was at the Chicago botanical museum today," she said, "and I walked into a greenhouse filled with blue flowers. There were hyacinth, aster, and begonia. They were so beautiful I wanted you to see them."

"I saw them," I said, amazed that I wasn't amazed.

What I took away from this encounter had more to do with art than the paranormal. I told myself that if I learned to listen I could access "messages" as sensory images. My stories would write me, as though I were just the secretary taking dictation, not the dictatorlike ego contriving where the stories should go.

It was around this time that I signed up for astrology classes at a metaphysical bookstore in the University District. Soon I was exchanging readings for tune-ups on our Buick and even a dinner for two at a romantic Queen Anne bistro. I was glad to pick up a skill that allowed me to live in a world without money.

By now my grandmother and my mother were hounding me about my joblessness. "You'll end up on the street," Grandma said. She had always wanted me to become a civil rights lawyer, or to marry one. A passion for social justice ran in her family, the Russian Jewish side. Her brother-in-law was blacklisted in the fifties as a union organizer for the longshoremen in Texas; his son worked in California for Cesar Chavez; his daughter had been a member of the SDS at Berkeley. Grandma had wanted to study law as a way to help the poor, but family poverty and then a shotgun marriage (in more ways than one) got in the way. She had always nurtured my scholastic ambitions, sending me checks for books and supplies whenever I needed them, and now I was wasting that investment.

My mother respected my desire to write, but she thought I should do it in Cleveland, in the creepy bedroom my grandfather's recent death had made vacant. "No one will ever love you like I do," she said. What if Joe dumped me, having milked the cow for free? What if I got knocked up? What if that fascist Reagan won the election and sent the poor people to concentration camps? Why wasn't I reading the *Daily Worker*?

"Don't forget there's a safety net in America," I said to her, a line she herself had always used in the face of my panic as a child when she lost a job or splurged on a pay-as-you-go piano instead of paying rent. I now visualized this safety net as a big, purple hammock like the one that Glenn-from-downstairs lounged in day and night. Besides, if things really got hairy, I could always live in a tree.

I talked a good line, but at night, in the hallucinatory landscape of dreams, my mother and I were marooned together in the one-bedroom basement dump where we'd lived in my high school years. It was a thin-walled, low-income complex that ricocheted with the sounds of neighbors' shouting and police sirens: the brick-and-peeling plaster embodiment of all I'd fled to college to escape, the 3D repository of all my fears of failure and doom, especially the part about bunking with Mommy Dearest.

Sometimes my mother's warnings took hold of me in daylight, especially her pronouncements about a coming sea change on the political landscape. The Iran hostage crisis and Carter's botched rescue mission had turned the public against him, and I wondered what other debacles would be forthcoming. Every time I read the news I would scare myself into heart-thumping terror about what lay ahead. It occurred to me that I had been constructing myself as Alice in Wonderland for far too long. I became obsessed with who had plutonium. Brazil was buying it from West Germany, I read in the *Nation*, and rumor had it that Libya, Iraq, Yugoslavia, and several unstable countries near the Persian Gulf would get it by '81. Then there were all these technological disasters. People were still talking about Love Canal and Three Mile Island, and I now lived within meltdown distance of the Hanford Nuclear Reactor, which had been built right on top of a volcano fault line. The acronym for the notoriously unsafe Washington Power Plant Supply (WPPS) gave way to the nickname, Whoops! There were DC-10 crashes in the news all the time, and recently, a train wreck outside of Toronto that had dumped so much chlorine gas into the city that two hundred thousand people had to be evacuated.

I began to write some of this stuff down in my journal when I was supposed to be writing fiction.

One day as I sat at the Pike Place Café watching ferries sail across the sound, I pondered the future we were sailing toward as a nation. My college friends in New York had been writing me about their budding careers in journalism and law while I wrote them lyrical mini-essays about my nature treks, and the disconnect amused us. But as I wrote one of them a letter that day, this East Coast/West Coast polarity – careerism versus lifestyleism – struck me suddenly as evidence that we were all like Berliners in the twenties, drinking champagne from each other's slippers while fascism was afoot:

> I am quite afraid about what is going to happen in the eighties. Many of our younger friends will be killed in war; conservatism – perhaps on the scale of McCarthyism – will once again reign; protest will be squashed; unions will be undermined; the nuclear industry will continue to boom and boomerang; and then there's the slow time bomb we've inherited from Industrialism – Cancer, the big C. The ERA and pro-abortion movements will be squelched by corporate-backed lobbyists with Christian constituencies; and of course the threat of N buttons being pushed continues to beckon. I am normally not so pessimistic and I have always felt that I could live my life independently regardless of which hawk was sitting in the red, white, and blue throne, but somehow today I feel like the ugliness has gotten so big and beastly that not even the Idaho potato farmer will be spared.

Of course the counter movements, particularly here in the North-west, are strong, and the grass roots activists continue to speak out against the proliferation of nuclear weapons, and I do believe our planet, like all forces in the universe – including people and volcanic mountains – is self-regulating, and that this one-sidedness will even-tually wear itself out, that the yin will take revenge on the yang, but nature has always employed disastrous eruptions and humans have manufactured holocausts to re-shift the energies and I fear that only through something devastatingly destructive can the earth become peaceful again. Perhaps the present situation stems from a Newtonian worldview gone haywire, a cold vision of the world as nothing but easily dissected compartments rather than a whole working organism. Having lost our relationship to nature and to the feminine principle in general we are spinning out of orbit without a grounding cord, with no vision of what moves above and below us. People are left with no purpose except the gratification of urges – sex and drugs and rock-'n'-roll for one person, or the nice car, big house, and family for the other. It's all the same in some way, isn't it?

I tucked this letter in my journal and never sent it. The next day, Joe and I went to Vashon Island, and when we got off the ferry and I first saw that green, misty, watery place – the fields of cows, the old roads and farmhouses with rusted weather vanes, the starfish in tide pools – I imagined another future in which Joe and I would grow our own food and haul our own water, bake bread from our own grain, and brew beer from our own hops. Gazing at blue water, cedar trees, and a cloud-fluffed sky, I felt ashamed for yesterday's pompous rant. Gloominess and pessimism and intellectual arrogance seemed like the toxic residue of a childhood I had to get over, something I had to transcend if I wanted to embrace the art of living.

Thoughts had power, I had discovered. Flowers could be transmitted halfway across the country without a florist; our mother's anguish and paranoia could make the same low-tech trek. If our minds could create or destroy, shouldn't we aim to think only of peace and beauty?

It would be unfashionable, in the 1980s, to look for economic reasons and political solutions for societal failings. Whatever our problems, they could be overcome by the power of right thinking. Sociological analysis was pontification of the obvious; socialism, my old family friend, was now an old shoe the dogs of history and empire had chewed full of holes. Pop psychology and a belief in spiritual transcendence would fix everything. All you needed to be happy was enough self-esteem and a daily bath of white light. It helped if you lived somewhere pretty.

And ultimately it was the beautiful Northwest setting that freed me from my writer's block.

I began to write about the hikes I took with Joe, the elk sweeping through the rain forest, the smell of burning cedar. These trees took me back to the Ohio River valley and my bike rides past oak trees and buckeye.

I wrote about the Pike Place Market, the sound of the seagulls, the fishmongers and their banter, the street musicians. This market led me back to the West Side Public Market where my grandfather shopped, its giant slabs of beef and perfect plums, the ladies in black babushkas filling their baskets, the spires of the Greek Orthodox church hovering near us like the Old Country, Macedonia, that never left my grandfather's voice.

I wrote about my grandfather's cousin Toda, the family mystic, who read our futures in the clumps of Turkish coffee. I wrote about my grandmother in her flowered sleeveless, shapeless shifts shouting at Richard Nixon and Spiro Agnew on TV – "Bastards! You bastards!" – her flabby upper arms shaking with fury.

By October I was fifty pages into a novella in which two old ladies, a Turkish coffee-clump reader and a socialist newsletter-reader, are doppelgänger twins. As I looked out the window of the Ballard apartment, I used the shapes of two knotted branches of the monkey puzzle tree to give me the central image I was looking for: the gray braids of my matriarchs, the sister strands intertwined like a double-stranded DNA helix. I let these women duke it out and refute each other's worldviews – spiritualism versus Bolshevik materialism – so that I could resolve this conflict within myself.

And so I spent the first installment of my sabbatical: writing in fits and starts in a converted darkroom; squirming on meditation pillows, hoping for enlightenment and falling asleep; snuggling up with Joe on the McCarthy-era couch through evening reruns of *Star Trek* on our Sputnik-era TV; hiking the wilderness on three-day weekends; writing down every dream. I sipped wheatgrass juice when I was virtuous, and chugged yeasty home-brew when I rebelled against my own regimes. I frequented discount card-readers and seers, seeking affirmation of future literary glory with the sheepish ardor of a teen buying porn. I was told I had spent my last lifetime as a well-to-do intellectual in Europe during Jefferson's visit, writing important texts about democracy and revolution, and that I had come back to complete that work. I accepted this reading as true, even though I wondered why psychics never seemed to tell people they'd been serfs, thieves, lousy dancers, or Adolph Hitler.

# 3

# When the Monks Wept

On the first Monday in November of 1980, I got off the bus of sleepy smokers I had boarded in New York City and into a car of Zen Buddhists. I was headed to the monastery in the Catskill Mountains where my friend Bill lived. I didn't tell him this, but I also wanted to find out if I was secretly a Buddhist.

The full-time residents and visitors of Dai Bosatsu Zendo were just finishing the grueling Harvest Jukai Sesshin, a weeklong period of unbroken silence and meditation and teachings designed to help the initiates accept the precepts of Zen. It wasn't quite over, so the people who met me at the station pantomimed their greetings. Unlike the car's driver, whose newly shaven head made him look like a big scary baby, Bill had still not taken monk's vows. His name was still Bill, and his longish, wavy hair curling up beneath his cap looked blacker than usual against the snow. Our quiet gave me the space to study him, to see how much or how little Buddhism had changed him. I was hoping he hadn't lost his sense of humor.

The monastery was near the quiet village of Livingston Manor on the property of the late Harriet Beecher Stowe: several wooded acres with a stream weaving through it and stands of pine and beech, the dry, near-transparent yellow tear-shaped leaves the only color against the snow. When I got out of the car I saw deer sprinting through the trees and heard mountain-cooled water rushing through stone. The zendo was a lovely Japanese pagoda with a white stucco façade and black trim. I felt like I had left America.

Then I heard the familiar scraping sound of someone shoveling snow. It was not-quite-sunset, and the residents of Dai Bosatsu were still engaged in work practice, as they called their chores: cleaning, chopping wood, dicing vegetables, mending the furnace, clearing walkways. I don't know what kind of unearthly spectacle I'd expected – robed monks in full lotus levitating in the clouds? – but it was certainly not the sight of a young working lad in neon orange with sweat beads freezing on his eyebrows. When Bill and I were housemates, we had arguments over whose turn it was to do the dishes. Our other work – his music lessons and rehearsals, my poems and term papers – had taken precedence, and we were unrepentant slobs. In the land of Zen, apparently, every task, every chore, was a form of meditation.

Northwestern's music program was rabidly competitive, and until his conversion Bill had been one of their stars. He'd been groomed for the fast track since early childhood with the requisite private lessons in New York and summers at Tanglewood. When I met him he was taking lessons with Arnold Jacobs, the principal tuba player of the Chicago Symphony Orchestra, and he seemed destined to land a similar spot.

My mother was a classically trained pianist who taught us to read music before we could read, but it was Bill who taught me how to *listen* to music, to hear it as language. I loved sitting in his room in appreciative silence while he played me his favorite records: Pachelbel's serene Canon in D Major, Mahler's bold Fifth Symphony.

When we weren't talking music, we did shtick. Bill brought out my inner goofball. We conversed in silly accents: bad fake Russian, bad Borscht Belt, bad Godfather, bad Miss America contestant. We sang Broadway show tunes, first as a joke, then for real. One morning at 5 AM we decided to have a parade. We marched up and down the quiet streets of Evanston while he air-played every instrument in our marching band and I did a princesslike, turn-at-the-wrist float wave. He tapped out fight songs and anthems, and I sang: "The Star Spangled Banner," "Over the Rainbow," and "There's No Business Like Show Business" in a hammed-up Ethel Merman. And it seemed to us at the time that there really was no business for Bill but performing music.

The summer of the nation's bicentennial, the summer we decided to do the unconventional thing and be platonic boy-girl housemates in an apartment near the Evanston Y, Bill joined a band. It was called Ezra Quantine's Memorial Ragtime Band, a nightclub act that played songs from the 1930s. This group was great fun to watch: total theater. They dressed in costume, the female vocalist in sleek vintage dresses, her hair in a chignon, the men in zoot suits and spats, their hair slicked back and parted down the middle. This was shtick too: their look and their raucous parodies of "Let's Call the Whole Thing Off" and the "St. James Infirmary" blues. While the nightclubs on Rush Street blasted almost nothing but disco, Ezra Quantine was the thinking person's alternative. I went to see them every weekend with my girlfriends. The band got so popular that they decided to tour, and Bill was faced with the first big decision of his adult life: drop out of college or quit the band.

Dropping out meant turning his back on his first love, classical music. You can't serve more than one master in the music world; there just isn't enough time. But it must have been intoxicating for Bill to finally call himself a professional and not a student, to stop training to be and start being.

Enter, stage door left, Buddhism, just when the world with all its temptations came rushing to meet him. That fall, when school started up again, I watched closely as Bill struggled to balance his life as a club musician with his life as a spiritual seeker. When he had gigs in town he was out all night playing in smoky bars, eating greasy food, and drinking until 5:00 AM meditation. He bought a black meditation pillow, chopsticks, and a Japanese tea set with his earnings. I suppose, in the end, the discipline of his musical training must have been excellent preparation for the rigors of zazen, but I didn't see it that way.

When Bill told me he was quitting the band and entering a monastery I was shocked. Here was someone with artistic success within his grasp, and he was chucking it, and for what? I had not yet begun to question the path of achievement and the only life I saw for myself if I didn't make it through college was a career of dead-end typing jobs like my mother's. Now Bill's only contact with music was to ring the zendo gong. I feared he was having some kind of breakdown.

But now, several months into my spiritual makeover, Bill's choice struck me as an act of sanity.

The other residents of Dai Bosatsu were mostly Jewish and Protestant twenty-somethings, lively and smart, positively aglow with the equanimity I attributed to monastery life. I liked them.

A tall, dark-haired, graceful woman from Stinson Beach was selected to be my silent teacher at meals – showing me how to unfold my napkin, to serve myself rice before sliding the urn to the next person, to rinse my oatmeal bowl in the communal water. She exuded the serenity and self-possession I was looking for. She led me into the zendo for meditation and taught me how to walk, how to bow, how to sit with my robes draped around me just so, how to arrange my feet so they wouldn't fall asleep, and how to sneak in a scratch or a shift in posture without being obvious. I was grateful for her instruction, because oh my goodness: this was work! I knew, sitting in that too-cold zendo for our forty-five-minute stretches, my back aching, my mind rushing like city traffic, that not only was I too soft and lazy for Zen Buddhism but that Bill had chosen a much more difficult, rigorous path than the one he'd been on when we met. He hadn't dropped out, I saw now; he'd simply chosen one exacting master over another.

After the session was officially over, it was party time. I had never been so relieved to switch gears in my life. We told stories, drank sake, and danced, then gave one another back rubs in a snakelike chain across the dining room. I could have stayed up all night with this crew but they had the morning to consider, and so did I. Bill had pulled some strings, and I had a 7 AM meeting scheduled with the abbot of the zendo, Eido Shimano Roshi, the beloved master, the big cheese.

In my borrowed black robe I walked into the master's room where all the teachings took place, bowed, and sat near the hem of his robe as though we were old friends. I took on the jaunty air of someone twice my age, a person securely established in the world, even though I felt unworthy and fraudulent.

I asked him if he had ever read William Blake.

"Tell me about this Blake," he said.

"Some of his lines seem very Zen," I said. " 'To see a World in a Grain of Sand / And a Heaven in a Wild Flower / Hold Infinity in the palm of your hand / And Eternity in an Hour.' Do you know this poem, 'Auguries of Innocence'?"

"No," said the master. "I would appreciate it very much if you would write it down for me."

Afterward I printed it as neatly as I could and then gave him a list of Blake's greatest hits, plus some Yeats, all the mystical ones, Walt Whitman's "Song of Myself," and a little Wallace Stevens: the snowman that ponders the "nothing that is not there and the nothing that is," which had always sounded to me like a Zen koan. I cringe now with the memory that I gave one of the great Zen masters of America homework.

Bill and I were talking in his room when we heard a knock on the door. Some residents were going to town to vote and wondered if we needed a ride. I had forgotten about the election. Bill had mailed in his absentee ballot days ago; it was the kind of thing he would never neglect. Even in the monastery he kept up with the *New York Times*.

Everyone I knew on either coast felt they had only two choices: to hang in with Carter, even though he was too middle-of-the-road, or to not vote at all. I was worried about the election, but it seemed to me that in the contest between a centrist and an extremist, only a centrist would win. Now that the party of Lincoln had been taken over by a fringe of sexist, judgmental, gun-slinging zealots, they were no doubt on a path toward extinction. I was no GOP sympathizer, but it was sad, really, to see the party whose wealth had built the great museums and universities and national parks and arts foundations be taken over by some yahoos who thought nothing should be free – not art, not clean water, not even the air we breathed. Maybe a new party would emerge from the rubble, or socialism would be revived. Until then, why dignify this race at all?

Not voting as a symbolic protest against the paltry choices on offer had a satisfying moral ring to it, but I'll never stop wondering what would have happened and what kind of America we would be living in now if the eighty million eligible voters who didn't vote that November had turned out in droves.

I woke up on Bill's floor to another knock on the door some hours later. There was a murmur in the hall. Bill and I went into a nearby room, where a circle of Dai Bosatsu residents sat listening to the radio. "Ronald Reagan is the president," someone said, and everyone in the room seemed to stop breathing.

This had to be a mistake. I found myself thinking of the Belltown Café in Seattle, a place Joe and I frequented when we could afford a night out. A *Bedtime for Bonzo* poster hung from the wall between the bathrooms and people would say, when they had to pee, "I have to pay a visit to Ronnie and the chimp."

Bill and I used to ask, "Are you for real?" when we weren't sure if the other's tasteless gag was really a joke. We got good at deadpan, announcing to the other grimly that the brain tumor was inoperable, or that a dozen overwrought students had just jumped off the library tower like lemmings. "Is he for real?" I whispered.

"No, it's true," someone replied. "Reagan won."

I looked at the alarm clock on the desk; I don't remember what time it was but I remember thinking it wasn't late enough for us to get this news. "Aren't the polls still open out West?" I had meant to call Joe that day from the pay phone. I missed him.

"Shhhh," Bill said. I turned toward the center of the room, where the monks began to kneel and bow until their foreheads touched the floor, their bald heads gleaming. Outside, the snow was falling more heavily now, covering the stands of birch and pine and hemlock with white. Earlier that day Bill and I had talked about building a snowman but we hadn't gotten around to it, just as I'd never gotten around to voting. I thought of the Zen concept of nothingness and, once again, of Wallace Stevens's "Snowman." I heard the sound of weeping and at that moment I didn't know who was crying: the monks, Bill, me, or all of us. I may have experienced what the Buddhists call nonduality, the awareness that we are all one thing: monks, me, Bill, the snowman, and maybe (I'm not quite ready to consider this but a true Buddhist would) Ronald Reagan. The election, the snow, Stevens's "Snowman" and our unbuilt snowman, the sudden possibility of a nuclear winter, our weeping: it all seemed connected and symbolic, but of what, I couldn't say.

Finally, I said to the monks, "Isn't it kind of un-Zen to be attached to an outcome? Isn't the world of politics all an illusion? Aren't you supposed to desire nothing?"

"Maybe," one of them said, "but we're still, like, American citizens. That doesn't change."

I've held on to this picture since that night: young men kneeling on a bare, wooden floor, their bare heads signifying worldly denunciation, my fellow mourners and strange ushers into the era when worldly goods would become household gods. The conjunction of these antitheticals would seem even eerier as the decade progressed. It's a tableau that will stay with me always: a dark, austere room, hushed voices, men my age crying, a feeling shared among us that our youthful optimism has betrayed us, that we have to prepare ourselves like sober adults for the worst. Would Reagan's "crackdown on welfare cheats" send the poor off to prison, like something out of Dickens? Did Reagan really believe we could win a nuclear war? Was this the beginning of the end? I wrote in my journal later that it was now the winter of our collective discontent, but I didn't know who "our" was anymore.

Neither did Bill.

Bill told me the next morning that the path for him was clear: he would take his monk's vows after all. He no longer belonged in the world outside the monastery.

I didn't either, but where could I go? Not here, as much as I liked the people. I had told everyone I knew that if Reagan were elected I'd leave the country. I'd move to Paris where I would trail in the footsteps of Ernest Hemingway and Gertrude Stein and argue about art in cafés with men with dark goatees. But of course, I hadn't expected him to win and I didn't have the money to leave the country. I barely had enough money to get myself home. I would have to declare myself an expatriate without a relocation scheme.

We were in Bill's room, and I was packing. My grandmother had funded my train trip as a birthday present with the proviso that I stop to see her and my mother on the way back to Seattle. I was more afraid of seeing my family, I admit, than of what would happen to the nation in the immediate future.

I looked at Bill again and for some reason, I thought of the night we'd made our own parade. I remembered how he'd teared up, as I had, when we sang the national anthem. Afterward, we'd confessed to each other what goody-two-shoes we'd been in high school with school government and our dreams to change the world into one big everyone's-equal-and-no-one's-hungry utopia.

It occurred to me that Bill was actually my most patriotic of friends. How else would you explain his secret passion for marching-band music?

It was as though he and America had been a terrific nightclub act, and they were breaking up.

I refrained from making any cracks about how fat his head would look without hair. At the moment I was all joked out.

# 4

# Voodoo Economics

MAGIC REALISM

It was George Bush who coined the phrase "voodoo economics." At that time he was Bush, the GOP candidate, and not yet Bush, the running mate, when he got stuck with the plan and had to see it through to its disastrous conclusions. Although the term was meant to attack what became known as Reaganomics and Reagan's use of what Senator Howard Baker dubbed the "magic asterisk" – footnotes attributing further savings in the future to unidentified savings in the present – I liked the occult-sounding ring to Bush's word choice, despite its racist overtones in his hands. One imagines Reagan conjuring effigies and amulets, straw dolls with needles, rattles and drums.

*Voodoo.* The infliction of harm on one's enemies seemed to fit many of the policies Reagan and his fellow millionaires in the Cabinet would make their own.

*Voodoo.* Black magic or faith healing: who's to say? The word suggested the plan's intriguing appeal to the irrational. If only you believed enough, it would work: those dollars would mysteriously trickle down to all of us like manna from heaven.

As 1980 came to a close, I was hoping to remedy my own finances. The problem: Joe and I had not accounted for the price of winter heating oil when we drew up our close-to-the-bone budget. Oil prices that year were sky-high. I needed some cash, pronto.

A woman I met at a party told me about a way to make some quick money without losing my unemployment benefits. The place was a notorious hippie sweat shop; it paid less than minimum wage and exposed its workers to heavy fixatives with no ventilation, but it was under the table and therefore tax free, and I could probably put in unlimited hours until Christmas. I would be assembling handcrafted jewelry boxes in precious woods for a young woodworking couple named John and Mary. I arranged to meet with them the following afternoon.

I have never been good with my hands, but I told myself this work would be good for my soul because I had only one earth sign in my astrology chart and needed to compensate for my egghead airiness. I even explained my deficiency to John and Mary as we sat in their kitchen drinking herbal tea and spacing out to the rhapsodies of the first Windham Hill album. They nodded with enthusiasm, as though that were the most logical reason to hire someone that they'd ever heard.

John and Mary were engaged to be married the following June. They lived in a nearby part of Ballard with John's mother, who had recently retired from a career of building bombs at Boeing. John was thirty and good-looking in a longhaired, bearded, scrawny sort of way. Mary was twenty-one, plump and pixyish. While he was aloof and critical, she had a tendency to seize her employees for long, soulful, breast-to-breast bear hugs. After our chat, the two of them led me into their workshop in the basement and introduced me to the capable crew, all of whom, it turned out, were lesbians making their way through the underground economic system, some of whom were doing the job full time. Most of them were training themselves to become carpenters, and I admired them for their dreams of breaking the gender barrier and for their comfort level around power tools. They were dressed, as I was, in flannel shirts, jeans, and hiking boots, and were friendly at first, but within a day or two of watching me in action, they began to eye me with cool suspicion. I would have been leery of me too.

The work seemed simple at first, and to everyone else it was. John and Mary did the hard part, cutting the wood to form each section of the jewelry box, working power tools and a lathe, and burning in delicate designs; all I had to do was to sand the bits of the box and glue them together, then cover them gingerly with varnish. My coworkers could do it blindfolded. After my mangling, however, the misshapen boxes, of varying wood thickness and bumpy with glue lumps, fell apart at the slightest provocation, usually just as John happened to walk by my station. And now I'm coming to the strange part of this story. Although John was a perfectionist and would chew someone out for the kind of microscopic flaws I was never capable of seeing, he'd smile at my pathetic boxes and pat me on the head. "Keep it up, dear," he whispered. "You'll get there." Sometimes he pulled his most talented gal off her favorite detail work to help me. This preferential treatment did not exactly endear me to the crew.

Even more bizarre was Mary's behavior. Although she was younger than I, and looked about twelve herself, she treated me like I was a darling five-year-old, sometimes begging to brush my long hair. One day, just when I was leaving, she sat me down for cookies and milk. "You've been to Scotland," she said mysteriously, then looked deeply into my eyes, and sighed.

I actually had been to Scotland the summer before my junior year of college. I'd attended a study abroad program in the north of England, then traveled to Edinburgh on a field trip.

"I don't mean in this lifetime," she said.

Slowly, as she refilled my glass of milk, Mary told me how she and John had lived in Scotland in another life. They'd each been the opposite sex and had been married to other people. John, as a woman, had been vain, self-centered, and manipulative; Mary had been rich and greedy. They'd become lovers, and then were stabbed to death by John's vengeful cuckolded husband. "We didn't know this until we met you," Mary said, "but we had a baby girl, and that girl witnessed our murders from a window outside the castle. Through a lot of spiritual work and nutrition we've removed the etheric swords from our bodies. But now it's our karma to remove the etheric suffering from our little girl's mind." Before I could stop her, she had braided my hair for me and tied it with a bow. "So here's some Scottish shortbread to remind you of our Scottish lifetime together."

I headed home as soon as politeness would allow.

This strange conversation resumed in another form on my front porch, where my downstairs neighbors were standing by the purple mailboxes, whooping with joy. "We're going to celebrate tonight," Vicki explained. "Glenn just found out he's eligible for disability!"

I had recently discovered that Glenn was confined to the hammock all day out of physical necessity, not choice. He had thrown his back doing seasonal inventory work stocking shelves in a warehouse. Moreover, as someone with only a GED, he was unqualified to do much of anything in the stagnant economy, and he was so depressed about his poor prospects that he avoided putting himself out there courting further rejection. None of the New Age books he devoured offered strategies for coping with the current job market. I was glad Uncle Sam had come through.

"Hooray for idle hands," I said. "I just got a three-month extension on my unemployment."

Somehow the topic of work got them talking about past lives and how much karmic debt to Vicki Glenn had wracked up through the ages. "I lost an arm in a factory accident in my last life as a man," Vicki explained. "Glenn was the foreman and he didn't turn off the machine in time. He was a sadist, and he watched me bleed. To this day I break out in hives when I'm around machines. I can't even use a lawn mower. Glenn's been doing it, and the landlord gives us a break on the rent."

Glenn looked down, still obviously feeling guilty.

Joe and I made jokes about our karma running over our dogma all evening, but when I went to sleep, I had nightmares: gothic romances involving daggers that turned into churning, limb-grinding machines. I woke up feeling exhausted and caught a cold that would linger for weeks. I didn't really believe John and Mary's fantasy about me, but I had grown up with a mother who projected me into all sorts of sick fantasies, and this love-child scenario wasn't good for my psyche. Their past-life regression somehow made me regress too. In their presence, I began to feel more and more like a clumsy child. My woodworking skills deteriorated even further. The moment John walked past me, nodding his head with fatherly devotion, the box I was holding would collapse like a house of cards.

One day when I went home early complaining of stomach cramps I knew I wouldn't be back. I slept well that night for the first time in weeks. Whatever psychic voodoo John and Mary had performed on me, its effects vanished at once.

I began to see that New Age thinking had seemed so liberating in part because it was so not-Cleveland. In the hands of my neighbors and my seasonal employers, however, it was just as rigid as any orthodoxy from Conservative Judaism to Fundamentalist Christianity to Free-Market Capitalism to Marxism. One day at the mailbox Vicki, who had been born Jewish, told me that she believed the Jews had agreed as souls to take part in the Holocaust so as to teach the world a lesson about racism and genocide, and that Hitler was being trained on "the Other Side" to come back as the most compassionate leader the world had ever known. I knew then that marrying spirituality – at least Vicki's brand of it – to my politics was going to be tougher than I thought.

That my job with my karmic parents was to construct square boxes, all of them identical, was not lost on me.


BEYOND THE SAFETY NET

Joe and I tried to pretend Reagan's first State of the Union address was just a scene from one of his cornball movies, but we'd never actually seen any of these movies and anyway, what he had to say wasn't funny. When he announced his plans for what he euphemistically called the Program for Economic Recovery, a tax scheme and budget that put eight thousand dollars into the hands of wealthy Americans and took four hundred dollars away from each household at the poverty level, I began to get nervous about my financial situation, which suddenly seemed emblematic of everything else that was tenuous in my life. I was still trying to write every day, but I was also spending more and more time writing columns of numbers in my diary: the modest numbers that meant the difference between making rent or not. As the former California governor, a multimillionaire, assembled his Cabinet of fellow multimillionaires, he kept talking about getting "government off our backs." I pictured these men in their California ranches riding horses named Buck or Champ all morning, then playing golf together all afternoon, their wives assembled under Tiffany lamps to gossip about so-and-so's weight gain or someone's trouble with her maid. That chummy personal pronoun "our" did not include me.

Growing up, I had never quite seen myself as poor, because my grandparents had a middle-class home on a quiet, tree-lined street, and even the basement apartment our mother moved us to was filled with books, the walls covered with my father's paintings of street scenes in Paris. In high school I juggled jobs to afford the same clothes the popular girls wore, and when I ran into a cheerleader at the checkout line at the A & P while my mother counted out our food stamps, I pretended I was there by myself, buying *Seventeen* magazine. My mother indulged us when she could, treating us to T-bone steak or shrimp at the beginning of the month, and when we were down to Saltines and made-with-water Campbell's soup I consoled myself with the thought of how svelte I would look in the cute, new outfit I had on layaway at Higbees.

Sometimes, of course, we had to supplement our diet at our grandparents' house. Everyone knew that this was how the welfare queens Reagan ranted about really got by: by drawing on their extended families when they needed to, because no one could really live at less than subsistence level twelve months a year. But what no one seemed to be saying, as the dependent poor were being made to feel increasingly like criminals, was that seven of the eleven million Americans supported by welfare in 1980 were children.

I began to think about all the other ways beyond immediate survival that the War on Poverty had sustained me in my childhood: the well-stocked public libraries, where I would go every weekend and get a sticker for each book I read; the school trips to see Shakespeare and hear Mozart performed by the Cleveland Symphony Orchestra, paid for in full by federal arts programs; the free Cleveland Art Museum, where my mother on her more lucid Sundays would take us to stare at Van Gogh's sunflowers and starry nights, and I would surreptitiously pat the guardian granite lion on the front steps as though he were my possession. Without all this I would have never caught a glimpse of the beauty to be found beyond the peeling walls of our cramped basement apartment, the enduring human values that ultimately saved my life. I would have never understood what Vicki and Glenn meant by the word *transcendence*. Without a decently funded, mostly crime-free public school with teachers who were still respected and valued by society, I would have never excelled academically. Without application fee waivers I could have never afforded to apply to college, and without government grants and scholarships and low-interest student loans, any college, let alone an expensive, private four-year university, would have been out of the question. I was the poster child for Johnson's Great Society.

But rising Pentagon costs to fight communism had to be paid for somehow, and Reagan sold his cuts in social programs with hardly a whimper from the Democrats in Congress. Although Reagan insisted these cuts wouldn't "hurt the poor," 70 percent came from programs that supported the poor. With one stroke of the pen, almost every social service that had sustained me or people I'd known was cut back sharply or disappeared. Unemployment insurance was sharply reduced, along with widows' pensions, disability benefits, Head Start, subsidized health, the arts and humanities, school lunch – who could forget the ketchup-as-a-vegetable controversy? – education, prenatal care, substance abuse programs, youth job training, you name it. Welfare payments went down 17 percent. Libraries had to shorten their hours and buy fewer books. Schools had to decide which to cut: music, art, athletics, or all three. Art museums had to establish or raise admission fees. After 1981, in spite of rising needs, no new subsidized housing was built by the federal government, and new tax laws encouraged landlords of existing projects to tear down their low-rent buildings, evacuate their tenants, and build luxury condominiums.

All of these cuts made it clear just whose "renewal" and "recovery" would be subsidized and whose would not. If one factored in the Social Security tax as well, by 1989 individuals earning between five hundred thousand and one million dollars a year would find that, since 1970, their tax rate had fallen 45 percent, while total federal taxes paid by the bottom 20 percent of all households would increase by 26 percent. As Walter Karp wrote in a *Harper's* essay called "Coolidge Redux," in 1981, "the torture of a thousand cuts inflicted on the poor is proposed as a means to recovery; the enrichment of the rich through tax cuts and credits is justified as a means to recovery; the restoration of corporate power to poison the air, the water, and the workplace is justified as a means to economic recovery."

The AFL-CIO union would be quoted in 1983 as saying, "There is no recovery for one of ten Americans still out of work. Worse, of the 10.7 million jobless, only 36 percent are receiving unemployment insurance compensation benefits." A *U.S. News and World Report* article in 1982 would show how only one year of Reaganomics added 2.6 million more people to the nation's poor. This increase would become less dramatic by the mid-1980s, but the gap between rich and poor would deepen. In 1980 the poorest 20 percent of Americans earned 5.3 percent of the nation's income; by 1990 that number had dropped to 4.6 percent. Meanwhile, the richest 20 percent went from earning 41.1 percent of the nation's income to 44.3 percent in the same decade. By then, the top 1 percent of the population would own almost 40 percent of the total wealth (factoring in property and stocks). In the same decade, while the poverty rate went up from 13 percent to 13.5 percent, the percentage of children living below the poverty line jumped from 17.9 percent to 19.9 percent. Think of it: one of five children were living below the poverty level and with significantly less assistance when it came to food, housing, education, and every other thread of the safety net that began to unravel under Reagan. By 1994 an editorial in the *Washington Post* would note that we were even worse than Bangladesh in terms of our economic inequality.

A big government that had funded public art, low-income housing, public schools, and higher education for all would morph into a big government that funded more police, more prisons, and a bigger military budget than ever before.

I still wanted to live in the world of the imagination and to bathe old wounds in white light. But I kept returning to the child I'd been in the welfare office with my mother, and all the other children I'd seen there. How would children born into similar circumstances now find the means to survive, let alone thrive as I had? The thought of all those wasted lives made me cry.

I could find no cosmic explanation, no spiritual paradigm, to affirm why, for example, 44 percent of all African American children in 1980 lived below the poverty line. Yet, if one viewed the world simply from the material-political standpoint of dialectical Marxism, weren't there intangible aspects of human life essential for survival – things like hope and faith and love – that got left out?

Reaganomics repoliticized me, returned me to my grandmother's anthem: "Bastards! The bastards!" Wherever I looked, there were reminders of what could happen if you lost your way, how far you could fall.

One cold winter night, when Joe and I were returning from a university production of *Waiting for Godot*, we got cornered at a stoplight by a woman with a long, brown ponytail like mine poking out of a green forest service cap, a thin windbreaker, and jeans. She was standing in the middle of the street, knocking on car windows, begging for money. "I just lost my job," she said, "I have nothing to eat and nowhere to stay." We were stunned. We had never seen a homeless woman before. Other than her inadequate coat, there was nothing unusual about her at all. We emptied our pockets for her and drove home in silence. I didn't have to look very far afield to see voodoo economics for what it was: a hex on the nonrich.

That night in dreams my mother and I were together again, only now we weren't inside the old basement apartment. We were camped out in front of it, on the street.

# Postcard from the New Economy

A NOTE TO MY SISTER, MARCH 1981:

Good news! Just as my unemployment payments ran out, I lucked into a job as a writer/editor for a small consulting firm called Word Masters Inc. The business is owned by a cheerful couple named Joyce and Bob who believe they can keep the values of the sixties alive by harnessing the humanistic aspects of the new technologies of the eighties. Their favorite word is *synergy*. While they pass for normal in the outside world in their power suits, they refer to the mainstream business establishment as the Other Paradigm. Believe it or not, it is company policy never to sign a contract when Mercury goes retrograde. Office conversations range from what we dreamed last night or where we hiked last weekend or which of our quirks have more to do with astrology than family conditioning. Everyone's an artist on the side. Everyone reads. My twenty-five hours a week at Word Masters Inc. don't feel like work. They're more like therapy.

Although the pace is sometimes hectic, we have pure spring water to drink, herbal tea, and soothing music piped in to keep us calm. We wear whatever we want when we don't have meetings with clients, which is lucky for me since I have lost weight from all my mile-long swims at the Y – hooray! – and can't wear my old suits from Group Death. In such a cool place, I am developing some approximation of a work ethic. I don't mind editing college catalogues, and I'm learning word processing. I can't believe how much I like typing on this newfangled thing. I'm still writing in the mornings, but a girl's gotta eat and I feel pretty damn lucky. It's getting scary out there, isn't it?

# The Come As You Are Not Party

One day in late winter, Joe and I watched a few minutes of *The 700 Club* by mistake. We were trying to find a *Star Trek* rerun when we came upon a televangelist screaming that Satan had taken over the women's movement. "Great toupee," Joe said, and we agreed that the man seemed like a character you might go as to a costume party, too out-there to be for real. I was thinking that a true disciple of Christ – someone who entered the ministry to serve humanity with kindness and compassion – well, a person like that might be offended by this TV guy's rage-red face and spraying spittle. He looked like my grandfather when he'd had a few.

I confess: this televangelist frightened me. He was my grandfather calling my sister and me "whooores," but he was also a pastor I'd once been subjected to in Cleveland. This man's sermon after the Kent State shootings that left four young people dead was a diatribe against hippies. Rock music had its roots in Africa, the continent of Satan. The true historical Jesus, despite artists' renderings, wore a crewcut.

Now Satan was convincing otherwise reasonable women to lobby for the Equal Rights Amendment, a Constitutional bill that would require good Christian women to become soldiers and men to . . . what? Wear dresses and take dictation?

"These guys are going mainstream," Joe said; "I shit you not." He'd heard about a recent Heritage Foundation gathering where a minister shouted, "We're here to turn the clock back to 1954 in this country." Paul Weyrich, one of its founders, was introducing a bill in Congress called the Family Protection Act, whereby federal funding would be denied to schools that issued textbooks portraying women in any but traditional roles, laws protecting battered wives from their husbands would be repealed, and federally funded legal aid for women seeking abortion counseling or divorce would be banned.

How could this be? How could a religious extremist be elected into the hall of lawmakers? Wasn't this against the spirit of democracy? Weren't the worlds of religion and politics meant to remain as separate as family holiday meals and school assembly? I had no idea that this mixture of right-wing conservatism and evangelical Christianity had been a force in America all along, a marriage best exemplified by the Scopes Monkey Trial of the 1920s. Nor did I know that Fundamentalist Christians were responsible for the insertion of the words "under God" into the Pledge of Allegiance and "in God we trust" onto American money and postage stamps just three years before I was born. Later I would also read that the Reverend Jerry Falwell had sent out voting cards to his congregation at the Thomas Road Baptist Church in Lynchburg, Virginia, a moment televised on the *Old-Time Gospel Hour*, and that Ronald Reagan paid a visit to this church shortly before the election.

Now, in much the same way that an older incarnation of the Christian right, the Ku Klux Klan, had downplayed their policy of lynching blacks and Jews and spoke, instead, of patriotism, morality, purity, and the flag, and the sexophobic Anthony Comstock, the zealous spokesman of the New York Society for the Suppression of Vice, successfully lobbied in Congress in 1873 to define birth control information as "obscene" (meanwhile collecting quite a hefty stash of porn), these fundamentalists were creating a strident language that eliminated nuance and silenced debate. To be against abortion you were "pro-life." If you were against women in the work force you were "pro-motherhood." To oppose women's newly claimed freedom to own their sexuality you could declare yourself "pro-chastity."

When Joe and I had moved on to admiring the abusive televangelist's wide lapels, my mother phoned to interrogate me about my sex life. "Did I ever tell you the story about the thirteen-year-old girl who had a baby on the same night I had you?" she said. "The poor little bastard baby?"

Actually, she told this story every chance she got, so often that I'd often thought of that poor little bastard baby as my first neighbor; after all, her mother had roomed with mine in the hospital. I also thought of her as my doppelgänger, my secret sharer, and I wondered if we'd recognize each other if we met.

"So what are you doing about birth control?" she asked.

"Chastity belt," I replied as I always did.

Oddly enough, after one of her phone calls I'd often come down with a nasty bladder infection and would have to swear off sex for weeks.

Our downstairs neighbors did not have sex. Although Glenn was clearly in love with Vicki, the two lived as brother and sister. They did not date other people either, and since they seldom left the house, together or apart, it seemed unlikely they would ever have prospects.

We'd been living above them for about a year when they revealed their nonconjugal status to us. Until then I had considered them living proof that opposites attract: she, almost forty, with her small, girlish body, long raven hair, and Brooklyn accent; he twenty-eight, with his plump face, blond hair wisps, bulging blue eyes, and local twang. They did everything together: gardening, shopping, cooking, and lounging on the porch reading books on ESP while listening to "If You Could Read My Mind," by Gordon Lightfoot, whom Joe called Gordon Clubfoot but I secretly liked.

Some weeks after Reagan's inauguration, we finally said yes to one of their dinner invitations. The vegetarian Indian banquet they prepared for us was sumptuous and it was enjoyable to eat it on the floor, on plump lavender silk pillows, while gazing at tapestries and beads and posters of unicorns and rainbows and listening to Ravi Shankar, the air musky with jasmine incense. But as I had begun to suspect during our mailbox conversations, our neighbors' insularity was both psychological and cultural: they had no interest in literature, history, art, government, science, film, the outdoors, or anything other than past lives and something Vicki called natural hygiene, which had to do with eating only plants and milk, wearing only silk or cotton, and avoiding contact with anything artificial, including Western doctors, medicines, contraceptives, even vitamins. We'd exhausted these topics by the mango and tea course, and if I hadn't stumbled into the wrong room on my way to the bathroom, I might never have found out anything as intimate about them as their sleeping arrangements.

I walked into a tiny room that was unremarkable except for the *Playboy* calendar hanging above the futon. Miss March's pink nipples swam toward me like tropical fish. There were *Playboy* magazines piled up beside the bed, not the books about UFOs I would have expected. The larger room next door featured a matching calendar – *Playgirl*. I had never seen one before.

When I emerged into the living room, my face probably flushed, Vicki guessed my mistake and felt the need to explain. "Glenn and I used to be lovers," she said. "But now we're just friends. We broke up five years ago."

"But . . ." I stopped, realizing that I already had been told much more than I needed to know. I glanced at Joe. He bent his head onto his hands to indicate his desperate need to sleep.

"I told you about the factory accident in our last life together?" Vicki continued. "Well, Glenn didn't have anywhere else to live, so I said he could stay and do all the guy things around here."

I was reminded again how Glenn did not exactly fit my stereotype of the handyman, but hey.

I thought, also, of an open house Joe and I had been to at a commune of Polarity Therapy practitioners who told us that they divided the household tasks along traditional gender lines because "women are naturally more nurturing, men are naturally the hunters." Their body therapy was designed to restore everyone's internal male-female balance, which had been thrown out of whack by a women's movement that, though "well-intended," had "gone too far": my first hint that some rogue strands of the left and the right were converging somewhere peculiar. Joe and I had passed on the complimentary "corrective" massage.

"I have *a lot* of past life karma with Vicki," Glenn said gravely, stroking her back, his fingers stained yellow with saffron, his eyes glossy. Vicki flinched. I understood at that moment that these nonlovers were the horniest people alive and also that they were stuck to each other like wet chapatis.

"To new friends," Vicki said, clinking our herbal tea mugs together, inviting us – imploring us, it seemed – to share their life of time-warped exile. Joe and I clinked back helplessly, knowing we'd inadvertently crossed a line.

We had been slow to accept our neighbors' overtures toward friendship in part because they had no friends and we were afraid they'd latch on like barnacles. My mother's phone calls were so intrusive and draining that I felt I had to protect myself from the demands of needy people. And now that I was back to working part time, I was reluctant to give up the mornings and evenings I had to myself, even when Joe wanted us to go out. I had become a bit of a hermit. In that way I'had something in common with our neighbors.

In my attempts to find a voice I was still trying to chisel away at my old peppy, goal-driven, Midwestern self and find out who was underneath, a process that made it a strain for me to even have a casual conversation. When the man at the corner store said something about the weather, I found it physically painful to do more than nod.

I did not want to be unkind; I was still searching for a spiritual teaching to make sense of the world, and I recognized that Vicki and Glenn were doing the same. "Judge not, lest ye be judged" was a Christian tenet that had always made sense to me, along with "Love thy neighbor as thy self."

Still, I would have preferred to love my neighbors from a healthy distance had Vicki not stopped me on the stairs a few days later with earth-shattering news.

"I'm pregnant," she said.

Had I misunderstood what separate bedrooms meant? "Glenn?" I asked tentatively.

"Are you kidding?" Without further ado she launched into the sad tale. It had all started when Vicki strained her neck from all those hours hunched over her word processor, perhaps in physical rebellion against such an unnatural technological advance: a machine, after all. She found a chiropractor in the yellow pages: a "square," she pronounced him, complete with short hair, a wife and kids, and a big house in the suburbs. There were photos of his family plastered around the office. "A practicing Catholic," she added. "Definitely not my type."

Yet there, week after week in his capable hands, obviously starved for affection, she began to fantasize. She appealed at first to his stomach, baking him pies and cakes and cookies. When that didn't work she began to wear slinky lingerie beneath her office attire. Then one day the good doctor gave her a *libidinal* adjustment, right there on the table. Now he was refusing to take her calls, and her neck was killing her.

"What a nightmare! Do you want me to help you find an abortion clinic? I'll go with you if you like." This tumbled out before I knew what I'd said.

Vicki glared at me, the purple veins in her temples pulsing like ticks. "I can't believe you would even say such a thing!" she cried. "With all those souls on the other side waiting to save the world!"

I was astonished. I had assumed that Vicki's purple skirts and embroidered muslin blouses were the markers of someone who was a liberal socially, even if she couldn't be bothered to vote. Until this point I had assumed that all New Agers were socially progressive, that only Jerry Falwell types and the Pope were anti-choice. My encounters with the

Polarity people notwithstanding, some months would pass before I understood that people who dealt tarot cards and carried crystals on their dashboards were not necessarily lefties; after all, we would eventually learn, Nancy Reagan regularly consulted an astrologer. Eventually all my assumptions about right and left, counterculture and mainstream, would break down. Perhaps the old cookie-cutter approach to politics was too shallow and this melding was a good thing, but nonetheless, Vicki threw me. *Whoa*, I thought, *Phyllis Schlafly in love beads. How weird is that?*

I tried another tactic. "But if the father isn't going to help you, how will you manage?" To be pregnant outside of matrimony, the financial and emotional burden of this: on this topic my mother and I were in perfect accord.

"He'll come to his senses," she said. "And anyway, I've got Glenn."

As late winter downfalls became incessant spring drizzle, psychics and card readers appeared at the house. Vicki recited affirmations, smoking up the building with aromatic candles and herbs. She baked more pies for her child's father, only now she slipped locks of her hair into the filling to draw him back by voodoo.

I suggested to Vicki that she augment her magic with a visit to an obstetrician, and perhaps to an attorney to sort out the paternity issues. "Careful," Joe said. "She's sucking you in." I knew he was right, but Vicki was losing weight and I was worried about the baby, that poor little bastard. She didn't even know her due date; apparently natural hygiene had never helped her keep track of her cycle. When she refused to go to a doctor, I found a midwife from the Fremont Women's Clinic, a move that ruffled Glenn's feathers because he wanted to deliver the baby himself, in her bedroom, without the intervention of any "outsiders." Perhaps he was just trying to insinuate himself back into her bed however he could.

Vicki was a terrible patient. Although blood tests showed her to be severely anemic, she refused the "unnatural" iron supplements and protein milkshakes I offered. She was unyielding in the extreme. It began to dawn on me that her rigidity resembled the fundamentalism that was becoming part of America's public face. "Health fascist" was what Joe called her.

Despite Joe's intentions, he got sucked in too. When the midwife finally convinced Vicki to eat more grains and iron-rich greens, Joe took them to our food co-op. But this co-op required its members to write down the prices per pound of produce, and Vicki and Glenn found this so stressful that they began to leave shopping lists for Joe in our mailbox. When the midwife and I persuaded Vicki to get some exercise, Joe drove us all to the Ballard pool, although Vicki and Glenn stayed in the baby pool clinging to the edge, overwhelmed by the commotion of people in lanes thrashing forward and back. Then, one sunny day in May, they called Joe to tell him their car had broken down. He drove an hour to the suburb where they were stranded only to discover that though their battery was indeed dead, they had their own jumper cables, and there were dozens of potentially helpful people at the garage sale where they'd just bought some baby clothes.

"These people are afraid of the world," he said.

When Vicki asked me to assist Glenn as birth coach, I couldn't refuse her. I believed they couldn't manage without me. I soon found myself attending weekly Lamaze classes with her and Glenn, visiting them every evening for practice breathing sessions, and being at Vicki's beck and call the rest of the time. Added to that was the responsibility of being Vicki's interpreter. The midwife, Miriam, was a feminist lesbian separatist; she hated the sulky Glenn, and she refused to deliver the baby on Vicki's bed if she had to stare up at a penis, even an airbrushed one. I had to coax Vicki to take down her *Playgirl* calendar.

Sometimes I would turn off the lights in the apartment to deter Vicki, but it was impossible to ignore the phone. When my mother called and I didn't answer, she wouldn't stop trying until I had.

"Did I ever tell you about the girl next to me in the birth ward?" she'd say. "She was only thirteen. Imagine getting knocked up at that age."

I felt, not for the first time in my life, like a prisoner in my own home.

When I was thirteen I did not become the teen mom my mother had scripted me to be; the bearded longhair I fell for was not some hippie sniffing for jailbait but Jesus Christ, who caught my young and yearning fancy at Baptist summer camp. I was there thanks to my across-the-street neighbor, Stephanie, who was the kind of girl who could make anything she endorsed, even Fundamentalist Christianity, look cool.

Stephanie befriended me when our mother, newly divorced, moved us from Indiana to Cleveland the same summer Barry Goldwater tried to yank the presidency from Lyndon Johnson. While my mother lay in bed chain-smoking in her underwear, surrounded by empty coffee cups and half-eaten baked goods, I fled to the order of our welcoming neighbors' home. Stephanie was pretty and petite, with gorgeous brown hair so long she could sit on it, a wardrobe of matching pedal pushers and ruffled midriff tops, and a menagerie of stuffed animals she was happy to share. Her family was comfortably middle class: the mother a real-estate agent, the father an industrial chemist who had studied classical violin. I wanted them to adopt me.

When Stephanie invited my sister and me to Camp Patmos one summer, it took some major persuasion to get our mother's permission. It was not just that we were Jews, albeit non-practicing ones. And it wasn't because my mother never forgot how Stephanie had spread a rumor through our first-grade class that if Johnson were reelected, he would make us go to school on Saturday and Sunday. The real problem had more to do with geography than ideology. I had woken up one morning with breasts, and our mother's spaced-out neglect had morphed into a puritanical obsession with my body and its comings and goings. Whenever I went out I had to give her the phone number of where I'd be. The only phone on the island was at a gas station two miles from our secluded outpost.

By now our mother had turned from slacker roommate to stalker. She showed up everywhere – the ice skating rink, girlfriends' homes, Friday-night dances at the junior high – convinced I was about to get pregnant. That I had yet to begin menstruating and was by design the least sexually advanced girl in my circle – *my* puritanical reaction to *her* disturbing displays of female dishevelment – did not factor into her theories; she took me to a doctor for a pregnancy test and painful pelvic exam. I wanted to go to that inaccessible-by-phone Christian camp just so I could get some rest.

The week at Camp Patmos was the first real vacation of my life. When we weren't singing hymns or making stained-glass portraits of Jesus we sailed, canoed, played volleyball, and hiked through a dense forest redolent with wintergreen and lemon balm. One midnight I crept out to enjoy the woods in solitude. The buckeye trees swayed, the mosquitoes hummed, the earth pulsed like a muffled drum. This music inhabited my body, my arms tan and lean, my thigh-length hair (it was now as long as Stephanie's) lifted by the breeze. There was no division between self and place, inside or outside, no *over there*. Deep in the foliage I felt the embrace of a loving force I'd never known in my mother's arms.

When I tried to describe this experience to a sympathetic counselor she explained that Jesus's love had awakened, calling me home. That night we were told in an open-air sermon that if we joined the counselors waiting in the trees and accepted the Lord Jesus as our personal savior, the joy of Christian fellowship was ours for an eternity. My conversion took less than a minute. My high washed away my anxieties about everything – the chaotic state of the world, my family's poverty, my tardy menses, and that morning's big upset: my mother had sleuthed out the gas station phone number and made the owner drive to camp, roust me from my bunk in front of everybody, and take me to the phone to call her back.

My sister took the plunge with me, and she lasted longer than I did. But when we returned home, it didn't take long for my old questioning self to spoil the party. On Sundays, I listened attentively to Stephanie's pastor's sermons but they seemed anti-youth, racist, and, well, ignorant in the extreme.

There was something inside this man that he had split off and disclaimed. A terror of something – the body? the inquisitive mind? – seemed to lie at the root of my new church's hateful admonitions. Where was creation? Mystery? Compassion? Rapture? The flesh made into word? Try as I might, I never once felt that joy that I'd known in the woods in Stephanie's church, nor in any other. Nor did I see how my fellow teens could be feeling it either as they sat around me in their uncomfortable pastel skirts and shirts and ties, passing notes and slam books.

In fact, the after-school Christian youth group felt to me like one big slam. One afternoon these new friends gathered on the couch of our shabby basement apartment. "Let's pray for Judy," they said solemnly. "Did you see all those hickeys?" My mother, in nondenominational collusion with any prurient force, lurked nearby in the kitchen, gathering ammunition.

When I left Stephanie's church, the Vietnam War was still claiming lives, and I was frightened by the violence flickering from the TV and by my mother's ever-intensifying fear of the world. When she began to lock my sister and me inside our apartment to "protect" us, and we had to climb out the bedroom window to go to school, we felt more like outcasts than ever. Surrounded by hard-partying, cynical seventies drones on one hand, and pious, backstabbing hypocrites on the other, I dreamed of a green paradise where I could romp in the woods writing poetry.

I still visited other friends' churches, but the only congregation that exuded the unwavering kindness and respect and love I craved was the secular one on the U.S.S. *Enterprise*. I did not watch the show religiously, but I tuned in for the same reason some people go to church.

I didn't give Fundamentalist Christianity another thought until the night, a decade after my conversion, when Joe and I were watching TV, looking for *Star Trek*.

Just as Jerry Falwell and Ronald Reagan would have approved of Vicki's opinions about abortion, her attempts to attract money and her child's father were not at odds with what the Trickle Downers were up to in 1981: they were as much an appeal to a hidden hand as any broker's invocations. Although the Wall Street Turks of 1981 were more likely to eat meat and vote Republican than the beaded, crystal-toting New Agers I knew, ultimately both groups espoused a belief in an invisible force.

This hidden affinity between committed capitalists and New Agers is what would eventually allow President Bush, the Elder, in appealing to philanthropy as a means to pay for axed social programs as Reagan had before him, to call on the "Thousand Points of Light" just as, at the end the nineteenth century, watered down Emersonian Transcendentalism was transmuted into upbeat business aphorisms to cheer up bankers and robber barons and affirm the exploitative American free enterprise system as the benevolent workings of nature.

But it would take me a long time to recognize these seemingly disparate forces as secret sharers; all I knew was that Vicki was causing friction between Joe and me. We had planned a summer just like our last one, with lots of backpacking treks. Vicki demanded I not go anywhere she couldn't reach me by phone: another bad déjà vu.

Until I became Vicki's birth coach, Joe and I had seldom quarreled. He was tolerant of my mother's middle-of-the-night phone calls and supportive of my writing and the financial sacrifices I was making to get better at it. When I realized my diaphragm was the source of my chronic cystitis, he converted to condoms without complaint. Then, on an afternoon in late May, one of those condoms broke.

Perhaps *because* this trouble seemed inevitable, a fate scripted for me since birth, I felt like the heroine of a Greek tragedy. Pregnancy was the physical embodiment of all my nightmares about confinement and suffocation. I lay sobbing on the couch, feeling sick, powerless, and doomed.

It was torture to attend birth class with Vicki and all of the other happily expectant mothers; there was no way, given Vicki's views on abortion, that I could tell her what was wrong. It was tough to keep my secret, though. I cried without provocation. My breasts swelled to painful proportions. I was always queasy. I hated my body, myself, my life, and resented how they all felt one and the same. When I looked into the mirror, someone else, someone like me but not me glared back. *Traitor*, she said.

The worse I felt, the more demands on me Vicki made. On top of twice-daily breathing practice she now required me to do daily massages, lead the three of us in guided relaxation ("You have a very soothing voice," she said), and to partake in forty-five-minute stints of communal meditation. She needed help puréeing several pounds of organic fruit and vegetables and freezing them to make natural baby food. And when she decided to blackmail the father into providing child support – writing him at his home address and threatening to tell the wife – she insisted that, as her birth coach and a writer to boot, I should help her craft a letter in coercive legalese. ("Aren't you worried about the karma of blackmail?" I asked her. "I'm more worried about his karma for abandoning his child," she said, and I winced at the memory of a father who had done just that.) All I knew was that at the time when I most needed to take care of myself, Vicki expected me to tend to her 24/7. It was an old drama I was reenacting, the story of my mother and me, and I felt powerless to change the script.

Early on the morning of the abortion I scrawled a hasty note about needing "minor surgery" on my "innards," left it in our neighbors' mailbox, and hurried with Joe to the car. Luckily she didn't see us.

That Joe and I were not ready to become parents was never a point of discussion. My childhood had ended in grade school when I realized that my mother was seriously ill and my father was gone and would never help us. I felt like I'd been an adult forever; I wanted to learn to be young. Joe still felt like a kid, but with none of the fringe benefits. His job paid minimum wage, and neither of us had health insurance.

But as much as I'd hardened myself against this situation, the moment I entered the clinic something inside me softened. As I sat down with a clipboard to fill out my forms, everyone I spoke to was respectful, understanding, and kind. And while I lay on the table waiting, I allowed myself to acknowledge, finally, that this uninvited guest bunking inside me was alive. I remembered how as a child, when Stephanie and Mira and I confessed what we longed to possess when we grew up – long before a room of my own and a book contract topped the list – I, like my sister, had wished for a loving family. I wanted a father and a healthy mother, but I also wanted to become the mother I never had.

For the first time in almost a decade, I prayed. I asked my unborn child to feel the love I would have had for it even as I said good-bye.

And I heard an answer. An answer that made me understand why the right-to-life people and pro-choice people – whatever you want to call each side – can't talk to each other. To acknowledge that what was leaving my body now was alive and had a kind of consciousness was to concede a point to the right, who would call me a baby killer. But to deny this feeling, to insist that this blob of cells in my uterine wall was not-yet-human, well, that required a kind of literal-mindedness and numbing that negated all the work I'd done to become more attuned to my feelings and the feelings of others. And yet, to call this not-yet-baby a baby and call this pregnancy termination a murder would be grossly inaccurate and also, well, unchristian. The tenet of Christianity I still believe could save the world is the mandate that we love *every* neighbor as thyself, reluctant mother included, if not above all.

As the procedure began I felt the last thing I'd expected: a whoosh of compassion that warmed me from my flushed face to my feet, which dangled from the cold metal stirrups. I felt understood by a presence much larger than myself, my politics, or anyone's theology. A feeling of forgiveness seemed directed at me, but also seemed to flow through me, from whom or what I had no idea. Later, when I lay in the recovery room and listened to the sobs of a woman in the next room, my first instinct was to want to console her. I felt no discomfort, just a mild cramping; those breathing lessons in Lamaze class had served me well. My isolation was replaced with something expansive, as vast as a love for the whole human race but even bigger than that. It was a flashback to what I'd experienced ten years before on that island in Lake Erie: an understanding that all of us – people, trees, lakes, mosquitoes, agnostics, and fundamentalists – are part of the same enterprise.

My mother phoned when we got home. I never told her what had happened to me but, interestingly enough, she changed the subject. I never had to hear about unplanned pregnancies again. From that point on, she wanted to know why I refused to give her any grandchildren.

Vicki phoned afterward to tell me it was okay if I had to take a day off from our routine; she'd survive. Then she asked me how my "surgery" had gone, spitting out the word like a cherry pit, and I knew that she *knew*.

I had thought I was perfectly fine but after five minutes at home everything had changed. Knowing that Vicki had had an inkling of my troubles and had still expected so much from me made me angry in a way I hadn't been in a long time. As insular as my neighbor was, as baffled by the contemporary world as she seemed to be, she'd found a way to get her needs met. But what had happened to me was also important: why had I gone through it alone? At last count, I had something Vicki didn't have: a boyfriend. But Joe had simply been my driver. He'd gone to work after he took me home, and I was astonished that he hadn't thought to get the day off or call in sick. I didn't want to have to *tell* him to stay home with me; I wanted him to know. Then, around midnight, he phoned from a bar; he and his friends from work were throwing a going-away bash for someone, *did I mind?* When I began to cry and he didn't change his plans, I moved beyond red-hot anger to something cold and colorless and irrevocable.

When Joe finally stumbled home at three that morning, drunk, I had already gone through the classifieds and circled the ads for cheap apartments. I was calm when I informed him I was moving out. He didn't try to talk me out of it, but he apologized; he said he had felt lonely and needed his buddies. "You never want to go anywhere anymore," he said. "I need people around more than you do." He was right. We held each other in mutual consolation, then watched, half comatose, the royal wedding of Prince Charles and Lady Diana Spencer on our black-and-white TV. Somehow it struck us as funny that while the whole world was fixated on marriage, we were divvying up our books and bowls.

A few days later we decided to celebrate our "amiable split" with a house-cooling party, the theme of which was Come As You Are Not. I don't know what inspired this idea (were we thinking of those *Star Trek* episodes when people encounter their evil twins on other planets?) but throwing a theme party to mark the end of a love affair strikes me now as something only I could have dreamed up to distance myself from my feelings of sadness and loss. I cringe now at the memory of turning a private matter into public theater.

Joe dressed for our party in a conservative navy jacket and tie he'd found in a thrift-store bin, a "Nixon Now" button on the lapel. I squeezed myself into my old size five homecoming dance gown and called myself

Betty-Jean Teen Queen, a virginal sweetheart from the Midwest. Joe's work friend, Nanette, the Deadhead dancer from Atlanta, went as a hoop-skirted southern belle; their friend Nick, the socialist punk rocker from London, went as a natty stockbroker. We had invited Glenn and Vicki, but to our relief they'd decided to pass. I still wonder what they would have worn: doctor's scrubs?

Eventually people started ditching their costumes. Those who hadn't brought a change of clothes borrowed ours. I guess the strain of wearing our doppelgängers on our sleeves was too much. But I actually *had* been a wholesome teen queen, a virgin until two weeks after high school graduation when I was deflowered by my first true love. I had banished this sweet younger self with the same ruthlessness with which I had banished all images of myself as a mother. And long before I'd stopped shaving my legs and started dressing like a lumberjack I'd been the girliest of girls. I had adored this ultrafeminine dress with its spaghetti straps and poplin jacket; I had saved my McDonald's wages for three months to pay for it. Now I'd worn it as a joke, then tossed it to the floor. But as I was cleaning up after the party, that heap of cloth kept reasserting itself in my vision, like the memory of an abandoned childhood friend. It was the kind of dress Stephanie would have liked. She would have looked really pretty in it.

I would think of Stephanie often in the years that followed, as the Christian Right kept trying to turn back the clock to 1954. When Ronald Reagan wanted to give tax-exempt status to Bob Jones University even though it practiced racial discrimination, I remembered that Stephanie's father had gone to school there. While extremists screamed bloody murder at women's clinics and exposed people's private peccadilloes on CNN, I'd remember how Stephanie's generosity had inspired me to become a Christian. And though I would feel childishly vindicated when the holier-than-thou embezzler Jim Bakker and the railer-against-fornication, prostitute-frequenting Jimmy Swaggart were defrocked and exposed, sometimes I would miss the era when people wore their politics and professed morals literally on their sleeves – the era before we all started talking and dressing alike. If I ran into Stephanie at a high school reunion now, I'm not so sure you would know who was the liberal. As I imagine our meeting, we'd both be wearing Ann Taylor suits, our shoulder-length brown hair layered like Monica Lewinsky's.

When Vicki went into labor not long after our break-up party, the baby was breech. By the light of the full moon, Vicki and Glenn and the midwife took an ambulance to the hospital. I don't know what was the bigger irony: that I only used my breathing lessons during my abortion, or that Vicki, who thought Western medicine was the work of the devil, had to submit to a Cesarean. Since only the midwife and dad stand-in could be admitted into the operating room, I went home and finished packing. I wasn't needed.

Some weeks later Joe told me that he had run into Vicki and her daughter, Lara, on our old street. "Glenn's out of the picture now," he said. "He started telling everyone that he was the father and she kicked him out. I went over and mowed the lawn."

"That was nice of you," I said. I thought I should go over too and volunteer my services in some way, but I just couldn't. I couldn't even go near the old house.

There would be times to come when I would be tempted to blame those secret sharer babies, Vicki's and mine, for thrusting me further along a solitary path that would grow increasingly lonely. But I knew that wasn't fair, just as I understood that Vicki was my secret sharer too, an extreme version of the isolated oddball I could become if I headed off too far by myself.

My hope is that motherhood gave Vicki membership to the community she never had and that her daughter has been well provided for. I hope that Vicki, with daughter in tow, has felt moments of unity, flickers of the feeling that people, trees, lakes, mosquitoes, agnostics, and fundamentalists are part of the same enterprise. Vicki was convinced her child was a wise old soul who was sent down to heal America. Let's hope, for all our sakes, that she was right.

# 7

# Postcard from the Street

The weekend I move into my new apartment my boss at Word Masters Inc. calls to tell me why she hasn't sent my last check. She and her husband have filed for bankruptcy. So much for the small family business and the entrepreneurial spirit of America. I'm screwed.

Desperation brings me to the ultimate Big Eighties operation: a corporate law firm that specializes in tax shelters, most often in the form of phony oil-drilling deals. My new boss is in his mid-thirties and has a stay-at-home wife studying to be a masseuse, a BMW, and a fanatical dedication to sixteen-hour work days, jogging, and B-vitamin injections ("for extra zip," he explains.) His initials are M.O.M., and when he writes us instructions he leaves out the periods. It's eerie to see notes from MOM taped to my computer when I've been screening out my own mother's phone calls for weeks.

MOM is reportedly vindictive toward anyone who crosses him. The rumor is that he once sued his own father – for what, no one dares ask. The typists whisper that he's already bounced a dozen attorneys this year. This happens my first week; suddenly the locks are changed and a lawyer named Art can't get into the building, can't get his files; this is how he finds out he's history.

Barbara, the heavyset office manager, calls me "Kid" and promises she'll look out for me. She offers to house me in her spare room if I can't make rent. Because it's obvious from the way she reaches her arms around me to show me how to type legal symbols that she has a crush on me, I'm careful not to cross her either. MOM, for some unknown reason, takes a liking to me too. When he hears me complain of a cramped neck, he offers to hook me up with his wife. When I'm tired, he hooks me up with vitamins. And so I make peace with my new job even if I'm suddenly part of the Other Paradigm.

It occurs to me that each job I've had since I graduated has had less prestige than the one before it. I don't even have the job security of your basic legal secretary; I'm the semipermanent temp. Still, I like my hours – two twelve-hour shifts on Saturday and Sunday at ten dollars an hour – which keep the rest of the week free for writing. Although I don't complain, I find it odd that my boss doesn't take out taxes or social security or pay health benefits for anyone, and that he has advised me to get myself incorporated so that I, too, can keep my wealth – such as it is – from Uncle Sam.

Several weeks pass and I'm used to my routine. I take the bus into Pioneer Square Saturday and Sunday mornings, treat myself to a Greek omelet and cappuccino, and work until ten o'clock at night. MOM is usually there, thumping his foot in his office while he recites dictation.

Then 1982 arrives, and with it another recession. Apparently my weekends-only job was only meant to get the firm through the tax-quarter crunch. "I'll call you when we have hours for you," Barbara says. "You're a freelancer, so enjoy it. You can work anywhere."

Meanwhile my mother keeps calling. She says it's obvious I can't support myself and there's only one thing to do: move back home with her and Grandma. "You're welcome to bring your typewriter," she says.

Joe suggests we pool our expenses and find another cheap place together even though we've both been out with other people. He now lives in a rundown rooming house in the University District. When I sleep there, I have to put on my shoes and Joe's robe to use the scary communal bathroom. The homeless woman we met last year – the one who got laid off by the Forestry Service – has taken up residence on the street out front. Sometimes we see her in the lobby trying to stay warm. One of my fears is that someone who shares the institutional-style kitchen with Joe will mistake me for this woman.

After I get off the phone with Barbara, I go downtown to apply for food stamps, then to Kelly Services to take their tests. They don't care that I'm a college graduate, that I've worked as a technical writer, writer/editor, and legal secretary, or that I've published two essays in the Sunday magazine of the *Seattle Post-Intelligencer*. They give me a quiz to determine whether or not I am capable of filling out a time card.

I am so demoralized that I go to the offices of MOM, sobbing. Barbara whispers that she's heard a rumor that firings are in the offing on the clerical side, and she promises I can come in full time when the next typist gets the boot. Someone's bad luck is to be my good fortune.

I decide then and there that I want out of all of this: the American marketplace, its disposable work force and heartless profiteers. I will join the Peace Corps. I look up the address in the office phone book, but on the way to pick up my application I realize I'm too distraught to make a good impression; maybe a swim at the Y will clear my head. I climb the hill up to Fifth and Seneca only to discover the Y is closed. Even this seems symbolic. Apparently Washington State has decided, against Reagan's wishes, to commemorate Martin Luther King, whose murder is yet another reason to feel ashamed of Team America. My logic goes like this: racial hatred = need-for-this-holiday = lockout. In other words, were it not for racism, I could swim. Were it not for racism, it also occurs to me, along with sexism, all the people with clerical and manufacturing jobs in America would unite as one lobby, and we'd all have job security. Tomorrow I'll write my sister an account of the day with a mini-essay on why racial prejudice and gender discrimination benefit Big Capitalism: how they keep us all fighting each other for scraps.

But for now, no analysis will distance me from *this* viscera: I need to pee, and when I swing open the stall door in the public bathroom by the Y a very drunk street person who's been leaning against it from the inside falls right on top of me and knocks us both to the ground. She looks Inuit and I'm thinking that in some other time and place she would be revered as a tribal elder. She bashes her forehead against the floor, and blood gushes out. I get her to sit and lean her head back against the wall while I find a pay phone to call for help.

After the paramedics have come and gone, I call Kelly Services from the same pay phone. "Has anything come in?" I ask. As traumatized as I am by this day, I just can't go home empty-handed. Actually, I'm in luck. They have something for that evening only a few blocks away in a bank tower, the place Joe worked when we first came to town. I head right over. It is only when I sit down to my computer that I notice the blood on my white blouse.

The bag ladies are circling closer. I look back on what launched me to Seattle, a dream of flying that I'm starting to remember more as a dream of falling.

A few days later I find out that Barbara is the typist MOM has been preparing to fire; her bad spin on the wheel of fortune will pay my February rent. I'm the new Barbara, but at two-thirds her pay. This is the second job I've gotten over someone older and vastly more qualified, but MOM, like my Group Death boss, has learned that if you nickel-and-dime your workers you can give yourself a raise. And I am learning that to survive in this brave new world, you will always have someone else's blood on your white blouse.

# BOOK II

# Brave New Worlds, 1982–1984

MIRANDA: O wonder!
How many goodly creatures are there here!
How beauteous mankind is! O brave new world!
That has such people in it!
PROSPERO: 'Tis new to thee.
  William Shakespeare, *The Tempest*

The themes are always the same. A return to innocence. The invocation of
an earlier authority and control. The mysteries of the blood. An itch for
the transcendental, for purification. Right there you've got the ways that
romanticism historically ends up in trouble, lends itself to authoritarianism.
  A San Francisco psychiatrist to Joan Didion, *Slouching towards Bethlehem*

Then the question becomes: Who is sane? Was Hitler sane? And is it not
possible for one whole culture to be insane by the standards of another?
  George Orwell, "Reflections on Gandhi"

# 8

# Shelter

I am not a democrat. . . . I am a dictator with a difference, a dictator with a heart of democracy
  Bhagwan Shree Rajneesh, *Notes of a Madman*

My first meeting with an Indian guru, and I didn't have a thing to wear. I laid out my paltry choices on the hotel bed. Morten thought I'd blend in better in the violet, but it was too hot for sleeves, and besides, I didn't want to be mistaken for a disciple. But such were the limitations of my wardrobe in 1982 that I could never pass for a reporter either. The violet A-line dress Morten liked was the most conservative thing I owned, which is why I'd worn it to my best friend's funeral in February, and why I would be wearing it again to my wedding in June, but I didn't know that yet; on this May morning, I was thinking that Morten and I were doomed. I slipped on my pale, barely tinted peach sundress and followed Morten to the car, wondering what strangeness lay in store for me.

The purple family was new to the followers of Bhagwan Shree Rajneesh. In India, he had required his disciples – called *sannyasins* – to wear orange to represent "the color of the sun rising" in the East. Since the summer of 1981, when the sannyasins had arrived in the desert of central Oregon to carry out Rajneesh's "experiment in creating a new human" – half contemplative Buddha, half zestful and lusty Zorba the Greek – Rajneesh had expanded the palette to include the colors of "the sun setting in the West." Maybe he was trying to prove there was nothing rigid about the Neo-Sannyas Movement now that it was registered as an organized religion (a formality to allow him tax-exempt status in America, he assured his followers). Maybe he was just bored with orange.

In one photo of me from this trip I look like I fit in rather well, eerily so, despite the near-whiteness of my dress. I have the same expression of wonder as the sannyasins who have gathered to catch a glimpse of Rajneesh driving past the vegetable gardens in one of his eleven Rolls Royces. (This was early in his collecting mania; eventually he would own ninety-three.) From behind the tinted windows of the car, protected from clouds of kicked-up dirt, Rajneesh's long white robe looks unnaturally clean. His wristwatch and cap flash diamonds. Because the photo is in black and white, it can't capture the contrasting colors: the merry ditch-diggers in plum jumpsuits swaying against gray-green juniper trees and sage; the tour guide in red silk gyrating her hips; the children in tie-dyes waving from the tops of adult shoulders. It can't capture the sound of the wind and the car and the collective hush, or the occasional utterance of "Oh." *Oh*, the most reverent of sounds, what Morten and I moaned, our arms and legs entwined in Tantric yoga poses, or the "oh" we sighed when, on the sixth day of a juice fast, our perceptions sharp as splinters, we stared out the window of my apartment to watch the moon float through the treetops like a scrap of paper from my abandoned novella.

My wonder, in part, was directed at these worshipers. What would motivate the same people who had stuck "Question Authority" bumper stickers on their Volkswagens to become (in their words) the "happy slaves" to the "the old man," a fifty-year-old spiritual leader who blithely decreed, "What I say, follow it" and then mocked that subservience and industry in these daily drive-bys? Were these former doctors and lawyers and therapists and professors *really* content planting soy beans, chopping carrots, building roads, leading tours, making beds, and installing new irrigation ditches twelve hours a day while their pampered leader flashed diamonds from behind tinted glass? And why were they in central Oregon? The back-to-the-land movement had been in full swing for a decade now, but what could motivate someone to start a "new Eden" on this ugly patch of desert?

In India the sannyasins' spiritual practice had been all about working on the self, body and soul, through psychotherapy, encounter groups, frenzied dancing, sexual experimentation, and meditation. In America, the land of the Protestant work ethic, the practice was about work, period. On the Big Muddy Ranch, outside of Antelope, Oregon – the site, interestingly, of a John Wayne movie – the overgrazed, eroded, rocky earth itself was to be transformed, revitalized, reharmonized into a fertile, communally farmed paradise using the most enlightened ecological principles *and* expensive technologies. Meanwhile the commune's increasingly aloof leader was bestowed with big-ticket drains on the environment: luxury vehicles, private jets, indoor swimming pools. It was a little like The Farm merging with *Silent Spring* and going to bed with *The Lifestyles of the Rich and Famous* and Ronald Reagan's "There'll always be a new frontier"-style capitalism.

A shift of wind and Rajneesh was gone, his followers embracing in gratitude for the shared sensation of being "awake in the Buddhafield," to quote the PR brochure. I suppose these three minutes of worship were also meant to be a stimulant, for it was three in the afternoon and the master's happy slaves had four more hours to go.

I turned to Morten and frowned. "So, do you think he noticed you, big guy?"

"Why are you always so negative?" Morten said.

When we'd met six weeks ago, I'd been charmed by his dreaminess, by his capacity to swoon. He wrote songs for me on the guitar and piano and taught me words in his native Norwegian – *skog* for forest, *elskede* for love. He consoled me in my grief; he almost convinced me that the dead were still around us, flashing signals, trying to help, and that my friend would never be lost to me if I knew how to listen for her. He helped me tune out my mother's phone calls. We meditated together. Time dissolved when we held each other. A lifetime of worries evaporated like sweat. Morten's moist skin smelled sweet, like jasmine incense.

Then one dawn Morten woke me to announce that Bhagwan Shree Rajneesh had summoned him in a dream. "I am supposed to be their top agricultural advisor," he said. As someone who had moved two thousand miles on the basis of a dream it felt unfair to judge him, but I cannot describe my panic at the discovery that the man I'd turned to for shelter from the storm was not exactly the sturdiest A-frame on the block.

I tried reasoning with Morten. I showed him articles describing the technical prowess of the Rajneesh people and asked how he was going to explain to the clannish and credentials-obsessed commune leadership that he, a young man who had never planted a bean in his life was going to, as he insisted, "teach the community how to be better farmers." As days passed and he did not back down I told myself that if he actually went to this place and saw it for what it was, he'd snap out of it. Now I, who had always done mock renditions of "Stand By Your Man" when friends sacrificed their principles for love, was standing by my man hip deep in sagebrush, still waiting for him to snap out of it.

The astonishment on my face in that photo is mostly directed at myself.

At least as a writer, with Morten as my photographer, I could pretend it wasn't weird for me to be here. And behind the reporter's cloak of neutrality I could quell my roiling emotions. I could try to see the big picture and put my personal crises of recent months into a cultural context.

I certainly wasn't the only one looking for shelter in all the wrong places. That year the Moral Majority, Seventh Day Adventists, Jehovah's Witnesses, disciples of Elizabeth Clare Prophet, and the survivalists who would later be called "home grown terrorists" by the U.S. government were all fortifying their strongholds, preparing for Armageddon. So were key members of the U.S. government. Fringe loonies and our national leaders were in cahoots in this bizarre and terrifying way. The new secretary of defense, Caspar W. Weinberger, believed in the book of Revelation's prophecies, as did the secretary of the interior, James G. Watt, who, though charged with the task of preserving public lands, promised to "mine more, drill more, [and] cut more timber" until the Rapture. He told a reporter for the *Washington Post* in 1981 that he got his marching orders not from legislation but from the "Scriptures, which call upon us to occupy the land until Jesus returns."

The fate of the earth, at least in America, was in the hands of people who disdained the laws they were appointed to uphold. This was Ronald Reagan's way of dealing with the inconveniences posed by democracy. He gave Anne Gorsuch Burford the task of heading the EPA, a woman who opposed government-mandated efforts to protect the environment. He chose a man named Peter Grace in the Commerce Department to work with Vice President George Bush to draw up plans to eliminate hundreds of regulations affecting the disposal of hazardous waste, air pollution, nuclear safety, and exposure to chemicals. Reagan would even declare that "the Constitutional doctrine of separation of powers" obliged him to withhold from Congress the documentary evidence of his efforts to give America "cost-effective" toxic waste dumps.

Worst of all, the press had recently leaked that Reagan was creating a civilian defense plan for a nuclear war.

A national disarmament march was scheduled three weeks from now in Central Park. I had long-standing plans to go with Patti, my best friend from college. Then she died, and our group of friends vowed to march together in her memory. But now my getting there at all depended on Morten and on what happened in this peculiar place.

How I got myself into this bind will take some explaining.

I can talk of life and death because they are one, and one can only talk of life if one knows death. . . . Death is where life goes on. Danger is beautiful, it is very beautiful.

Bhagwan Shree Rajneesh, *Notes of a Madman*

Patti and I met in U.S. Politics 101 on the very first day of classes our freshman year. I was just getting comfortable when she tapped me on the shoulder and asked if I'd move a seat to the right so that she could be on the aisle. "I'm left-handed," she explained, and then she settled in, asking me the usual questions about where I was from and where I lived on campus as she pulled out her day planner, her spiral notebook, and her battalion of writing implements. I can still picture her at my left, as she would always be from then on, her unscuffed Joan-and-David shoes crossed primly at her ankles, her notebook open, the pages crowded with her huge, cheerful, left-slanting letters, the subtopics highlighted for easy review. Patti looked like she knew what she was doing and had no doubts that she belonged in this elite institution, whereas I secretly feared I'd be found out as an unworthy gate-crasher and sent back to Cleveland on the next Greyhound.

I don't remember how we became best friends, but I can remember marveling at how easy it felt to trust her despite our surface differences. Her family was well off and happy: the first of its kind I had ever seen up close. We had near-opposite aesthetics, but over time we would meet near the center. While I clunked around in clogs, thrift-store Edwardian lace blouses, Indian batik wraparound skirts or baggy, Annie Hall tweed pants, Patti wore jeans, sweaters in solid, subdued colors, her hair cut in a neat brown bob. Eventually she'd wear dangling ethnic-chic earrings and lacy peasant tops, but she always looked tidy and elegant. We were the same height but she weighed fifteen pounds less, the weight I'd maintained in high school only by fanatical dieting. She had several pairs of size twenty-eight Levis, and I coveted them. When we shared an apartment I would sneak into her room when she was at class and try to squeeze into the pair on the top of the heap in her chest of drawers. She never said anything, but one day after I'd lost a few pounds she gave me the jeans. Then she told me not to diet anymore, that the lucky man who became my mate would "absolutely crave" my curves. Patti was the first person who made me feel that I did not need to launch myself on a self-improvement campaign to be worthy of love.

I have never met anyone more generous. She was tolerant of all her friends' quirks and gave insightful advice, always able to read in a glance when someone was hurting and to know what wise and compassionate thing to say. It was as though she'd lived a thousand lives and had access to the knowledge she'd acquired in each of them. In this one, however, Patti had found the kind of equilibrium many of us spend years trying to achieve. She never seemed to eat or drink too much, or throw herself at an unsuitable boy, or hate herself in the morning, and she never seemed to judge me when I did any of the above, which was often. Those of us who loved her always felt that she brought out our best qualities, that she knew what good we were capable of even when we ourselves forgot. But she wasn't pious or naïve; when it came to phonies and snobs, she was astute. One night, at a standing-room-only concert on campus, a woman in a white cotton midriff came running up, all flowing hair and flat tummy, to give Patti a hug, then scampered off. Patti whispered, "See the guy behind us? That whole little performance was for him. Normally she's too stuck up to talk to me."

When it came to each other's personal problems, we both trod gently. I knew that because of a birth defect – numerous benign tumors along her rib cage and arms, her right hand disfigured with scarred clumps and fused-together fingers – she had a phobia about being touched. This was why it took her until the age of twenty to become intimate with a man: an Israeli soldier she met during a semester in Haifa. Until then she seemed to derive vicarious pleasure from my escapades, whereas I read her shyness and fear of rejection from men as a dignified reserve I should learn to cultivate.

Patti never made me feel like damaged goods for having the family I had. "You and my dad are the two people I respect the most in the world," she would say. Her father had overcome poverty and (if memory serves me) an abusive father to become someone who owned a thriving business. He was the original self-made man. But what Patti admired most about him was how kind and generous he was to everyone, including his employees, who were all unfailingly loyal to their boss. On school breaks she invited me to her family's comfortable house in Mount Lebanon for refuge.

January of 1982 found us both in need of refuge. She was mourning the breakup with her Israeli lover and was disappointed that her master's program in nursing was not as stimulating as her history courses back at Northwestern. I was contending with my breakup with Joe, my unstable work situation, my mother's mad phone calls, and the fact that I was too distracted by all of the above to write. Patti proposed that we convene in her parents' condominium in Boca Raton if I could find a cheap flight. I felt such urgency about going that I was willing to dig into February's rent money to finagle the trip.

The tropical landscape of Florida stirred me – red bougainvillea, palm trees like giant sprouting pineapples, frisky pelicans and sandpipers. We dined that first evening on shrimp scampi and white wine, courtesy of that generous father of hers and his Visa card, who even got on the phone to say that dinner was on him all week. "You deserve this," Patti insisted, and I tried to believe her.

Every day after that we swam in the ocean, jogged on the beach, and went out to dinner. At night we lounged on the balcony trying to identify the constellations while we gave each other pep talks about the future.

On our last evening together we read each other's fortunes. She had been studying palmistry and she showed me the long, deep, clear line on the outside of my hand beneath my pinkie that foretold a solid, lifelong partnership with a man I'd meet some day – exactly when, she couldn't say. I brought out my new tarot deck and she shuffled. The first card I laid out for her was the card of death.

I was quick to tell her that this card was symbolic, that it was about, to quote our favorite Grace Paley story, "enormous changes at the last minute." This was good news to Patti, who felt that she'd been stagnating for months.

We were both tan and rested when we parted, both at peace for the first time in months. I wasn't sad because I knew I'd see her in June at the disarmament march and afterward, at our old housemate's wedding. We promised to make a January vacation in Florida our annual tradition.

Two weeks later, I was in MOM's office when the phone rang. It was Iris, Patti's older sister. She had called to tell me that Patti was dead.

"You're kidding," I said stupidly. I held the phone away for a brief moment, staring at it. All I could hear was a sound like a radio in between stations. From behind this static, I tried to listen.

After our vacation, Patti had gone home to get one of her tumors removed. This one was simply, as she said, "for vanity": the growth was beneath her rib and she didn't like how she looked in a bathing suit. I had known she'd be getting this done but she had insisted that it was a simple procedure and I hadn't even bothered to phone. But during the surgery her doctor discovered that the growth was huge – bigger than a man's fist. There had been a great deal of bleeding so they kept her in the hospital for almost a week.

The day before she died she had been bored and she had called my apartment dozens of times, profoundly disappointed that I wasn't there. Her mother had watched her twirl the phone cord around her finger while she dialed, and hearing this, picturing her trying to reach me, I was sick with regret. My mother had been telephoning so much that I'd decided to housesit for a coworker on vacation just to get some peace. When Patti died that night of a blood clot, I was asleep in a stranger's bed across town. I never got to say good-bye.

I remembered something Patti had told me during our last breakfast. Just before waking she'd had a dream that she was drawing blood from someone and there were air bubbles in the needle. "I knew I was going to give my patient a blood clot, but I couldn't do anything about it," she said. We had diagnosed this as a preparation anxiety dream since Patti had exams awaiting her, but now, on the phone with her sister, I wondered. Perhaps Patti had gotten a warning from her unconscious. Perhaps we had both unconsciously known the end was near which is what compelled us to find a way to see each other. Maybe there was something to the paranormal after all: Patti's dream, the tarot, weren't they proof?

Iris told me that Patti's parents had a ticket to Pittsburgh waiting for me at the U.S. Air counter at the airport, and I had to go home and pack. I remember worrying that I didn't have anything black. My new violet V-neck dress, with a dark navy sweater pulled over it for warmth, would have to do.

The enormity of what had happened did not register until I saw Patti lying in the open casket, her face smooth and serene. Like the rest of Patti's friends, I arrived at the funeral in shock. Afterward, Patti's friends and family gathered at her parents' house for the wake. Patti had always had a fantasy about having all her favorite people in the same place and now here we were, telling Patti stories. I talked about the time, our freshman year, when she walked into a crowded department store and carried away, in view of dozens of people and security cameras, a life-size cutout of Bruce Springsteen to add to her roommate's Bruce-shrine in their room. "Patti was no angel but she would do *anything* for a friend," her mother said.

Sometime that night I told everyone about the disarmament rally Patti and I had planned to go to, and we all decided we would meet in New York that June to march in her memory. We would keep Patti alive in this way.

Back in damp, cold Seattle, I was inconsolable. I was a space case at work and made stupid mistakes, the kind that could get me fired. I was sick every other week with some flu, and lay awake at night, too out of it to fully grasp how miserable I was. Having lost the anchor of the most solid and loving friendship of my life, I felt lost, airborne.

After thinking I was phasing out such things I threw myself back into the occult, plowing through the books about life after death that I associated with Vicki and Glenn. I tried to hypnotize myself into trances, hoping to find a way to contact Patti. I would stare for hours at a cup on a table, an album on my stereo, a book on the shelf, and will it to move on its own accord as some sign that the spirit world was all around me, something I could walk through like a doorway in my apartment. Once, a piece of paper floated off the top of my stereo to the carpet for no apparent reason and I lay in bed terrified, clutching the covers to my throat, wondering what chaos I was inviting into my life.

In March I went on a fast to empty my body of the sorrows I imaged as brackish liquids weighing me down. On the tenth day, I put on my violet dress and went to an open house at the astrology bookstore, hoping a reading would bring me some scrap of solace. It was the spring equinox, a time of new beginnings.

As I was making my way through the crowd, I bumped into him, or he bumped into me – a tall, thin, dreamy-looking young man with shoulder length blondish-brown hair, deep brown eyes, and a violet shirt the exact same hue and texture of my dress. "I am sorry to be so clumsy," he said. His Scandinavian accent was charming. "I am on a fast and I am dizzy."

"Me too," I said.

"Really?" he asked, amazed, and we both laughed. In our brief conversation I mentioned the astrology class that was starting the following Tuesday and when Tuesday arrived, I wasn't surprised to see him there.

I had never met a male person like Morten. Men drank beer, rooted for the home team, liked loud music, and had to be trained to be sensitive. Morten believed in making every detail of life a sacred thing. He was always stopping to admire flowers or birds, and the music he played for me on the piano and guitar was lushly melancholy.

I was ashamed of the place and the people I'd come from: the rotten egg stench of the factory fumes, the self-igniting river, the smoky air in my grandparents' house, my grandfather's stinky cigars, his habit of sitting on the toilet for hours reading *Reader's Digest* with the door slightly ajar, his crude and vulgar comments and insults, his misogynistic leer. I was embarrassed by my mother's slovenly ways, how she left her false teeth on the bathroom sink, how she wolfed down her food. I was repelled by my grandmother's arms, dimpled like cottage cheese, and her loud voice. I imagined Morten's family to be refined and polite and pictured Norway as lovely and unpolluted, full of evergreen forests and fjords of clean white snow. He promised to take me there someday.

I was also intrigued by the fact that he didn't work. His father – a rich industrialist in Oslo – sent him a thousand dollars each month. Morten was using this allowance to study something called applied kinesiology, which, as I understood it, was what chiropractors did. He had enough money to lease a baby grand piano, eat out almost every day, and attend meditation retreats. He had the time to compose music and take black-and-white photographs of Seattle haunts. He rented a room in a spacious Tibetan Buddhist household overlooking the Puget Sound, with beach access and even a darkroom. I hoped that some of Morton's ease and ethereal grace would rub off on me.

And yet his carefree attitude toward money nagged at me, given the limitations of my own finances. He was twenty-five, the same age I would be that fall. Far too old, I thought, to be living off Daddy. He was talented as a musician and photographer, and I thought he should be more ambitious about promoting his art, but it was against his nature to strive at anything. If he ran through his money in between Dad's checks he'd find someone to cook for him, or else he'd go on a fast, meditate more, and call this regimen a purification ritual. He didn't live in the world I knew, the world of unsatisfying day jobs, chronic anxiety, and long-range plans. That spring I was starting to think ahead to graduate school. Morten never planned beyond the weekend, and even then it was hard to pin him down. I wanted to spend the summer with him, but I wasn't sure if I could picture him taking the train to New York with me, carrying signs, shouting slogans, hanging with my college crew ("And what's your degree in, Mort?" "And what do you do?"). When I pictured us together at all, I only saw us naked on my little bed in the mother-in-law apartment, the rest of the world far off and unknown.


What is the first and last freedom? To be oneself, totally, utterly, without any consideration for any consequences.
Bhagwan Shree Rajneesh, *Notes of a Madman*

The word *Rajneesh* means "raja" or "king," and *Bhagwan*, his American followers insisted, means "holy one," although in India it also means God. This was one of the reasons Rajneesh was reviled by many in India as a charlatan. Indian gurus track their divinity through a lineage tracing back to the god Shiva or Vishnu, but Rajneesh had never sat at the feet of a guru. One can see why a self-made guru might some day be drawn to the land of the self-made man, and also why such a place, with its myriad material temptations, could hasten his downfall.

He was born as Chandra Mohan Jain in 1931, in a small village in central India, the ambitious son in a middle-class Jain merchant family. Although he did not embrace any particular religious path, the research psychiatrist James S. Gordon points out in his 1987 book *The Golden Guru: The Strange Journey of Bhagwan Shree Rajneesh* that Chandra Mohan Jain's early life was "shrouded in the kind of mystery and contradiction, the great expectations and great danger, that fill the early histories of other heroes, messianic figures, and shamans." The village astrologer predicted he would not live past the age of seven. His younger sister died when he was five, and he almost lost his life to asthma and smallpox, but when he survived the age of seven and his grandfather died instead, the astrologer reworded the prediction: every seven years he would face death in one form or another, until he died at twenty-one. Death became a motif for Rajneesh, a metaphor for framing his experience.

At fourteen, as he would eventually tell his disciples, he overcame his fear and resistance to death in an extended meditation. Throughout his adolescence he used his apparent fearlessness to goad the boys he knew to follow his example and jump off a high railroad bridge into the Shakhar River, always at night when they were most afraid. He was strong-willed, charismatic, and bossy, even as a child. He read Russian novels and studied magic and culled the scriptures of Buddhism and Christianity and Jainism even as he denounced them, promoting his own intellect and powers of persuasion so as to move beyond his narrow confines in a nation where social mobility was rare.

At age twenty-one, while he was a student of philosophy in Jabalpur, Rajneesh claimed to experience what he would later call "the last event of my personal history": his enlightenment. This, he decided, was the death foretold. From then on he insisted he was no longer just a man, but even as an immortal-human he enjoyed being a student, supplementing his reading with some Gurdjieff and Ouspensky and how-to books on hypnotism.

In 1960, he became a professor of philosophy. Six years on, he was asked to resign. All his talks on religion, politics, and sex, his attacks on Gandhi and socialism, and his defense of capitalism, science, and birth control were drawing audiences outside the university. His first followers were Indian businessmen who liked Rajneesh's idea that wealth was a precondition for the spiritual life. But Rajneesh would drop his old disciples as sexier, younger, richer ones came his way.

In 1971, a year after his ashram moved to Bombay, the Westerners began to arrive – hippies and spiritual seekers, then the leaders of the human potential movement, then the second group's clients. Disciples were given new names, told to wear orange and a mala (a beaded necklace, with a photo of Rajneesh) and were required to meditate at least once a day. That was it; this was all becoming a sannyasin entailed, other than forking over all your money.

At Rajneeshpuram, an American civil engineer in a long black ponytail explained to me why he was so drawn to Rajneesh. "When you read Ram Dass, he talks about meditating in a manure pile in India and being sick and isolated for thirty or sixty days, and that didn't appeal at all. So finally I sent for *Silence* magazine [a publication of the Rajneesh Foundation] and then you see people like this, they're laughing and holding hands and dancing and singing and I said, 'That's for me, time's a wasting,' so I wrapped up my affairs and a month later I was in India. I took sannyas immediately."

Since 1970, Rajneesh had been teaching something he called dynamic meditation, a whirling form of dance followed by silence. In Rajneesh's view, meditation for the typical neurotic, restless, Western mind, was like "sitting on a volcano." The Western seeker needed to release tensions by dancing ecstatically to loud music – something quite familiar to the hippies, after all – before he or she could be still.

Another reason for his popularity among the love generation was Rajneesh's stance toward celibacy: he didn't believe in it. Long before he was known as the Rolls Royce guru he was known as the sex guru. In fact, the first time Morten ever mentioned Rajneesh to me we were in bed. Morten was interested in "raising Tantric energy" from the lower chakras up to the crown of his head, to make lovemaking a form of meditation: something, he told me, that Rajneesh had lectured on extensively, evoking not only Tantric yoga but the teachings of Wilhelm Reich and his "orgone energy box."

In the ashram in Poona to which the followers moved in 1974 – a compound of clean, modern buildings and well-groomed gardens that contrasted sharply with the poverty nearby – disciples received "energy darshans" from their guru: multimedia events involving live music, flashing strobe lights, and frenzied dance, then talks by the white-robed, golden-tongued guru. He used his hypnotism training to mesmerize the assembled, his voice sibilant and rhythmic as he peppered his stories with allusions to familiar and beloved Western thinkers like Marx, Freud, Reich, Tolstoy, Timothy Leary, Herbert Marcuse, Norman Brown, and Aldous Huxley. But although Rajneesh admired these Western intellectuals, his goal was to liberate the seeker's body and the emotions from the intellect. One of the Rajneeshpuram tour guides, a slim, thin-lipped, blond former psychologist with an Oxbridge accent told me, "All psychology remains on the head level and the mind will always go on playing tricks forever and ever. The whole thing with Bhagwan is to relax the mind, and that's why Bhagwan has encouraged the therapy groups where a lot is involved in emotions and physical action, getting rid of the blocks in the body and all that kind of thing that people are so suspicious of because it's frightening, it's real."

To Rajneesh's way of thinking, the way to get rid of neurosis and more serious psychosis was to go *through* it. "To teach man I have to devise and use all sorts of mad games," Gordon quotes the guru as saying to his followers in Poona, "so that the accumulated madness could be acted out, catharted out, thrown out."

A week before our trip, Morten and I had been to a documentary film, *Ashram*, about Rajneesh's encounter groups in Poona, which was written and produced by a former sannyasin. Participants tore off each other's clothes, mocked, and assaulted partners, all in the name of therapeutic catharsis. A woman was almost raped; a man's arm was broken. Onlookers egged each other on like revelers in New Orleans shouting "Show me your tits!" to girls gone wild, or bloodthirsty classmates chanting "Fight! Fight! Fight!" when two hotheads duke it out in the schoolyard.

I was shaken by this documentary and hoped it would dissuade Morten, but he dismissed the film as propaganda.

The public story about why Rajneesh came to eastern Oregon in 1981 was that he needed a dry climate to protect his health. Rajneesh was a lifelong sufferer of diabetes, severe asthma, allergies, and back ailments. Indeed, his inner circle made such a fuss over Rajneesh's fragile state that visitors were frisked for evidence of anything that might exasperate his condition – perfumes, deodorants, even certain shampoos – and people who coughed in his presence were asked to leave. For someone fearless about death, he was awfully finicky.

The secret reason Rajneesh came to Oregon was to stay out of jail. He'd been charged with inciting riots by his attacks on Hinduism; he was in trouble for tax evasion and immigration violations. To avoid immigration problems in the United States a number of marriages between Indian citizens and Europeans were quietly dissolved so that both parties would be free to marry Americans. Rajneesh would set into motion his "Blueprint for the New Man" in the New World, thereby wedding East to West, for better or for worse.


Everyone can go mad except me because I am already mad. I have been mad for almost one fourth of a century, and if you all help me, I may make the century.
    Bhagwan Shree Rajneesh, *Notes of a Madman*

My mother always told me it was my obligation, as the elder of her daughters, to marry someone to support the family, preferably a Jewish doctor or lawyer. My beauty and intelligence would make up for our lack of a dowry.

One morning when I was in junior high, she tried to deface that beauty. I was heating up the iron to press my clothes for school and she begged me not to leave her that day. When I refused, she grabbed the steaming iron and tried to brand my face. She was stronger than I was, but my sister pulled a butcher knife from the drawer and threatened to stab herself if our mother did not stop. Somehow, we both got away.

Later that day I made a furtive call to the public mental hospital from the pay phone at school and convinced the receptionist to make an appointment for my mother. To con her into going, I had to tell my mother I wanted to see a psychiatrist for myself, and that's how I got her in the door. But she wouldn't take the medication; I had to chop it up in secret and mix it into her food. Each morning I packed each of us brown bag lunches, tuna salad or egg, and I slipped her pills in hers with the diced celery and carrots. If she had eaten her drug-laced sandwich, she would let us sleep that night. If not she'd keep us awake, accusing us of being part of a call-girl ring run by our school principal.

During my senior year of high school, our mother had another serious breakdown. She announced one evening that (1) I was not allowed to go to the prom, because it got out too late (although as a senior class officer, I was required to be there) and (2) that she'd changed her mind about college. Only if I found a school in Cleveland and commuted from home would she consider it. Then she ripped up all seven of my college acceptance letters and sprinkled the paper bits, like confetti, on my head. I would later have to consult a lawyer (at a free legal aid agency, which was easier to come by in the seventies) to find out if, at seventeen, I could legally "run away" to college.

It was in the midst of the letter-ripping drama that Mira and I found a handgun in our mother's underwear drawer. We did not let our mother know we had seen it, but then we called my friend, John, and asked him to drive over and pick us up. When he arrived my mother called him a Nazi, pulled the gun on him, and wouldn't let us leave. Mira and I ran into our bedroom, climbed out the window, called to John to run, hopped into his white Pinto, and called the police from his house. Our mother was hospitalized until after I graduated from high school, which is why I was able to go to the prom.

The summer after my first year at Northwestern she had another breakdown, only this time we were not on home turf; we were in Evanston, where I was spending the summer, having vowed when I left for college never to live at home again. One day that June my mother turned up at my door to "protect me" from my live-in "pimps" – Bill and our other male housemate, a music major from Bill's hometown. My sister had confiscated the latest gun, but she warned me to hide the knives. I was terrified, but all I knew to do was to send my roommates to stay with friends, where she couldn't hurt them. I believed I could soothe her, reason with her, then talk her into leaving. I filled the apartment with flowers and the music of Mozart. I even baked her an apple pie.

While I was at work the next day she went to my dean and signed papers to withdraw me from the university. She told him I was a drug addict and needed treatment. When I got to the apartment, I found that she had packed up most of my belongings and had called a cab to take us to the Greyhound station. She said we were going back to Cleveland where I belonged. I don't know what would have happened if I hadn't persuaded the police to intervene. I was only eighteen and I was committing my mother, without the help of my grandmother this time, to a state mental hospital notorious for being a snake pit. It was also the attending physician's first commitment case, and he was so paralyzed by the weight of his decision that he kept me up all night questioning me to see if I was lying, to see if I'd crack. When we'd arrived, my mother had insisted I was the one having the breakdown. The psychiatrist looked back and forth between us, trying to discern who looked crazier, and the more he did this, the more distraught I became. I begged him to check on my mother's medical records in Cleveland and it wasn't until he made the call that he began to take my claims seriously. I had to emphasize the gun, although I did not believe she would ever use it. Finally, by daylight, the doctor signed the papers.

"Please, walk with me," my mother pleaded, as the incoming nurse came to take her to the ward. We got to the barricaded door that separated the sick from the well, and from where I stood I could see that it was a horrifying place, with people shouting obscenities, leering at us through the window, and others tied in restraints. "Are you leaving me here?" she asked me with so much trembling in her voice that I have never, to this day, quite forgiven myself for doing what I had to do to save myself.

I turned and walked away.

Six years passed and that event still stood out as the most traumatic incident of my life other than Patti's death. And so, about a month into my relationship with Morten, when the phone rang one morning and I heard my mother say, "What a lovely city you live in," I felt like my life was over.

"Where are you?" I shouted.

"I'm in a motel on Aurora Avenue. Judging from the map, I'm only about a fifteen-minute walk from you. I'm on my way over."

"No!" I proposed an alternative; we would meet in a coffee shop near her motel.

That I could just refuse to see her did not occur to me. At least confronting her on neutral ground, I hoped, would give me some small sense of power. For reasons that still escape me, I told her that if she promised to be civil I would introduce her to the new boyfriend she'd come here ostensibly to "check out." I'd made the mistake of letting him answer the phone for me a few days before, and my mother had heard his accent and decided I'd taken up with an illegal immigrant who planned to ship her daughter to the fjords to sell her into white slavery. I promise I am not exaggerating. Perhaps I was hoping that Morten would protect me from her if they met, that he'd rescue me from my old life.

Morten was at the beach house packing up. Everyone was moving out, and he was going to store his belongings at my place while he visited Rajneeshpuram. After he came back – *if* he came back – he would go with me to New York for the rally. I had purchased my round-trip train ticket already and I'd made a reservation for him.

It would be an understatement to say that he was not excited about the prospect of meeting my mother, but I gave him no choice. I told him to meet me at Green Lake, which was halfway between his place and mine. I ran there to wait for him. It was a spectacular spring day in May, with young people roller-skating, families feeding the ducks and flying kites, and lovers smooching beside lilac bushes. In a setting like this it was difficult to grasp that my mother lurked five blocks away. I sat on a bench, irritated at Morten for taking so long to get there, my pulse racing. To calm myself, I asked Patti to send me a message telling me how to survive what lay ahead.

At that moment I looked up and saw, with complete astonishment, that a small airplane was skywriting a message across the expansive, perfect blue. "LOVE," the blurry white letters said. *Love!* I have never had a stronger sense of cognitive dissonance in my life. If I could have projected my mood onto the landscape the sky would have cracked open with thunder, the people would have turned way from one another in terror, and everyone would have run, screaming, for cover.

Just then, Morten sauntered up with his hands in his tweed jacket pocket, breezy and relaxed, like someone who had never known worry in his life. The message was simple: the love of this calm, sweet man could save me from my mother.

My mother had a formal, polite persona she sometimes put on among strangers, but today she got right down to business. From the moment she spied us from her booth where she sat, chain-smoking, she interrogated him, and I knew that bringing Morten had been a terrible mistake. Morten had no defenses against someone so aggressive. He told her far too much, far more, even, than he'd ever told me: that he had a student visa but had never actually completed a college course, that this visa had, in fact, expired. I don't remember how we got out of there. "We're screwed," I told him. "If she has her way, you'll be deported."

By the end of the day my mother called to say she'd informed the Immigration Services about Morten's expired visa and they were launching an investigation. That Monday, she showed up at my office in a beige trench coat. I slipped on the identical beige trench coat she had sent me for my birthday, and ran, overturning a chair as I bolted past a row of computers like some character in a cold-war spy film, stalked by a deadly double agent.

We ran and ran. She followed me along the waterfront, all the way to the Pike Place Market, chanting my name again and again. We surged through crowds like James Bond characters, knocking into carts, sending pears, plums, and tomatoes flying. Finally she caught up to me in front of the fish stand where I was slowed down by a group of Japanese tourists with cameras. There we began our strange, sad waltz. She pulled me by the hair, turned me toward her, and grabbed my shoulders like a man leading a partner in a slow dance. We were exactly the same height and although she was darker and more Mediterranean looking than I am, our resemblance must have been striking to any passersby. Then she wrapped her fingers around my neck and started squeezing. My mother, who was always afraid when I wore long winter scarves that I'd be strangled in a streetcar like Isadora Duncan, was strangling me, her first born, her baby. I flailed my arms. This was my mother. I know there were people in the market who tried to get between us, but I felt like there was no one else in the world, that she and I were the lone survivors of a holocaust and were doomed to spend our remaining days together, each struggling to remove the other's hands from her neck. Even now, as I return to this moment, I have trouble breathing.

After I broke her hold I fled into Pike Street traffic, knocked on the door of a moving bus, and rode off, literally, into the setting sun, not knowing where the bus was going or what I would do when I got to the end of the line.

What happened after that did not bode well for my relationship with Morten. I got off somewhere in Queen Anne and called him from a pay phone, crying hysterically. While my mother had been downtown stalking me, Morten had moved the last of his belongings into my sitting room. He sounded distracted and impatient. We were supposed to go to a potluck for our astrology class that night but I was in no state to shop and cook, let alone go to a party. But I was also afraid to go home, and Morten no longer had a home. "Be calm," he kept saying. "You are too stressed out!"

We met at a Safeway but he refused to make a single decision, from whether to bring strawberries or blueberries, or whether, once he saw me crying again, for us to skip the party. I realized only then that Morten had decided early on that my role in our relationship was to take care of all practical matters so he could be the romantic dreamer. That was the only song he could play.

We ended up buying some food just for ourselves and brought it to the beach outside the house he'd just moved out of. The door was locked, he'd turned in the keys, and we were going to have to sleep on the beach, but he seemed to think that we should just behave like two lovebirds on a picnic: why worry? My hysteria about my mother made him panic, which made me angry.

Sometime after midnight, we crawled through a window to get out of the wind. The new tenants were coming early the next morning and we'd have to be gone before daylight. I remember the break-in as a dream, the huge cold house empty except for the rented grand piano that Morten played for most of the night. I thought of my childhood, how my mother would pound out Chopin sonatas on a rented Steinway piano until the day the bill collectors took it away. There might be nothing to eat, or the apartment might be caked with cigarette smoke and dust, but she would play her haunting music.

I climbed back outside the window alone. There was a full moon and as I walked the beach in anguish, I remembered suddenly that tomorrow was Mother's Day. The very idea made me laugh bitterly.

Looking out at the water, at the Olympic Mountains in the distance, I felt the vastness of everything I couldn't control settle into my bones like a flu. I sat on a beach log shivering. Where could I go if my own apartment wasn't safe anymore? I loved that apartment. Even if I found somewhere else to live, my mother knew where I worked and would make more scenes. Seattle was ruined for me now. I couldn't stay. She would just keep coming back for me.

I went into the house again and watched my shadow move against the wall, against the silhouette of Morten at the piano.

"Your mother is like a black hole sucking us through," he said. "She almost broke us up tonight. But she is not our responsibility. She is not *your* responsibility. We can be free of her."

"How?"

"Leave her," he said.

"What do you mean?"

"Just go," he said. "Come with me. We'll go down to Rajneeshpuram, and then we'll go to New York. If the INS comes after me, we'll get married. We'll do what we want. She can't stop us."

It's not like I could honestly say I wanted to grow old with Morten and raise mini Mortens and Natalias together. But I didn't want my mother to win. And I wanted to go to New York. I couldn't think any further than that. And at least Morten was finally taking charge of a practical matter.

There was one catch, though. He had found out that day that you couldn't get to Antelope, Oregon, easily by bus. We would have to drive.

Would I cash in my train ticket and help him buy a used car some friends from astrology class were selling? We could drive the thing cross-country, camp the whole way, and have more freedom than we would on the train. Would I do this for him? For us?

The next morning I called an editor I knew at the *Seattle Post-Intelligencer* and tried to interest her in a feature story about Rajneeshpuram even though others had already been written. I needed a way to earn the money I'd lose by quitting my job, but perhaps even more importantly, going there as a writer would reassure me that I still had a toehold in the world I had come from. The editor said she would need it fast because of her vacation plans – by that Friday, an unrealistic deadline even for a seasoned feature writer – but that she would take a look.

We left that afternoon, even though we hadn't slept. On the run from my mother and the INS with Morten, I felt like an outlaw.

With the Buddha Velcroed to our dashboard that the car's former owners, Marilyn and James, bequeathed us for luck, we drove south, past Mount Rainier, and what was left of Mount Saint Helens, and through Portland, where roses were budding. Then we headed east across mountains and came to chalky buttes and barren stretches of cactus and sage I'd never imagined could be only a few hours' drive from the lush Pacific.

Morten suffered his first setback when we arrived at the visitor center that evening and were told by a tour guide named Sunshine that no, we couldn't "just crash" at the commune; we would have to stay in a motel in Madras, sixty miles away, the nearest town. We hadn't budgeted for this. I was angry that Morten hadn't done his homework but I didn't say anything as we searched for the cheapest place and went to sleep.

The next morning we learned that it would be impossible for us to speak with Rajneesh, that he had been "in silence" since 1981. The best we could do, if we were lucky, was to talk to Ma Anand Sheela, president of the Rajneesh Foundation International, his spokesperson. Morten should have accepted at this point that the whole trip was a wash. After all, he had insisted that Rajneesh had beckoned him there to have a private tête-à-tête.

By now Morten had explained to me what applied kinesiology was, the version he had studied anyway. First the practitioner, preferably the Sikh master who had taught him, would hold onto your arm while you asked a question. If you "tested strong," that is, you overpowered the

Sikh, the answer was yes; if you "tested weak," it was no. This arm-wrestling method has actually gained popularity over the years, and I even know a chiropractor who swears by it as a diagnostic tool, but I think you might as well use a magic eight ball or the Ouija board to get your answer.

Even more ludicrous was the notion that the sannyasins, with all their access to professional experts in pest management and agricultural science and botany, would welcome Morten as their savior. A study would soon reveal that one-sixth of the commune members had doctorates.

Morten refused to turn back. "Our link will just have to be telepathic," he said.

At this point I wanted to turn back, but I couldn't. I had put myself entirely in Morten's hands. By getting a refund on my train ticket and giving Morten the money, I had ensured that I had no way to get back to Seattle, where, for all I knew, my mother had already conned my landlords into gaining entry to my apartment. I had no means to get to New York. I had no source of income, only the prospect of the five hundred dollars the article might bring. I now had just as much invested in being there as he did.

And so we took the tour. We marveled at the many acres of perfect vegetables, and I hoped that Morten would see that his expertise would not be missed. We walked through the Magdalena dining hall where cheerful young men and women in purple made dinner to the beat of the Pat Metheny tape blasting from someone's boom box. We saw braless, pretty women in tank tops digging ditches and driving tractors; we saw handsome bearded men doing the same. Rajneesh seemed to attract good-looking disciples.

We marched on, marveling at the building that was to become the Rajneesh International Conference Center, now a city block's length of white scaffolding. Two years later there would also be a hotel, an airport, a casino, a city hall, a shopping center (which included restaurants), a beauty salon, a book and record store containing Rajneesh products, a disco, a post office, a boutique offering stylish clothing in sunset colors, a "Peace Force" (a.k.a. security force facility), and a bigger visitor center, even a center of "higher" learning: the Rajneesh International University of Meditation.

On we went, until we returned to the reception area where Ma Anand Sheela had agreed to a press conference with all the reporters present: about ten of us that day. She listed the commune's successes, to date, hoping for us to side with them in their bitter battle against the residents of nearby Antelope to incorporate Rajneeshpuram as a city. There were lots of interesting issues I could have asked about – church-state balance, land-use conflicts, the economics of collectivism, the INS investigations of sham marriages – but when it was my turn to ask Sheela something, all I could think about was how her piercing gaze reminded me of my mother's. I had nothing to say.

And neither did Morten. He had pretty much shut down by now. Except for the photos he took, I might as well have been there by myself.

It was time to go. At this point Morten and I had just enough gas money to get home. We didn't discuss anything and for all I knew, he was secretly planning to come back. There was nothing to do but drive in silence to my apartment and draw the shades and ignore the phone in case my mother with a team of Immigration officials in tow was still lurking in the vicinity, perhaps with a new handgun in her pocketbook.

We got back late on a Tuesday night, which gave me less than seventy-two hours to make my Friday deadline. On Saturday we would get married and then on Monday we'd leave for New York, hopefully with the five hundred dollars from the sale of my story. To add to the feeling of desperation, we had to fast until Monday because we were out of money. Morten's father's check for one thousand dollars was in the mail, and it would see us through our travels, but it would be, alas, the last of its kind.

When Morten had called him with all our news his father said, "If you're grown-up enough to get married, you shouldn't need me to support you any more." I was now Morten's sole means of support, and I had quit my day job.

And so, I set to it. I wrote nonstop, hardly sleeping, and produced a seven-thousand-word essay that vacillated between depicting Rajneeshpuram as a cult and as an eco-paradise in the American utopian tradition. It wasn't bad for something dashed off by someone under duress, but it was a rough first draft. The editor, who had always liked my writing style before, thought I needed to put it in a drawer. "You should rewrite it after you've had some time to think about it," she said. "You haven't really processed the contradictions in this."

But time was a luxury I didn't have.

Reeling from that disappointment, I focused on getting married. We hadn't heard from my mother but I was still convinced that at any minute, unless I saved the day, Morten would be deported. (Morten, I see now, was not the only one with a Messiah complex.) We were going to need a witness for the ceremony and trying to find one made me realize just how I isolated I had become since Patti's death. I called Claudia, my old housemate. "Marriage is a huge commitment, even if you don't think so now," she said. "And you're not responsible for Morten just because your mother is crazy." I knew she was right, but I wasn't ready to hear this. "There's no way I can support you doing this. You'll have to find someone else."

But who? Although I hadn't yet acknowledged this to myself, I was endeavoring to keep the marriage a secret. A lot of my friends from college didn't even know I had broken up with Joe. Joe didn't know I was seeing someone new either; I hadn't called him in weeks. The truth was, in my haze since Patti's death, I had let my old life evaporate.

We settled on Marilyn and James, the couple who had sold us their car. It made sense for them to be witnesses because they were our age, they had married after only a three-day courtship, Marilyn knew us from astrology class, and, well, they were the most "out there" people I knew. They were followers of the teachings of Elizabeth Clare Prophet, whose local church met on Aurora Avenue in the same stretch of urban sprawl as my mother's motel, the same street where we were to be wed. These folks believed their knowledge came channeled from ascended masters who floated above earth on something called the violet ray. James was a lay preacher in this church. What we were about to do would not seem outrageous and desperate to them.

On our way to Chapel of the Bells, Morten and I had an argument about car insurance. Insurance was optional in Washington State at that time but I wanted us to buy it before we set off for New York. "There you go again being pessimistic," he said. "It was *your* negative thinking that screwed up Rajneeshpuram for me. And now you want to waste money because of your fears. This is another example of how you refuse to trust the universe. I am not doing it."

*I* had screwed up Rajneeshpuram for him? I was ready to blame myself for a lot, including our need to be married in the first place, but this was beyond the beyond. I knew I should walk, no, run away, I knew I was quite possibly ruining my life, but at that moment I saw Marilyn and James smiling and waving to us from the street in violet cotton like ours, and I didn't know what else to do but get on with it.

Against all the odds and the dictates of common sense, dear reader, I married him.

An obese New Age priestess in a purple muumuu performed the

service. I'll give her credit for one thing: she could smell disaster when she saw it. "I prefer cash," she told us, and she almost refused to marry us when I wrote her a check for seventy dollars with Monday's date. "A lot of people in the New Age are getting together briefly to do some short-term karma clearing," she said to us, glancing toward Morten, who was poring over the menu of our choices for the day's ceremony until he arrived at Kahlil Gibran. *Short-term karma clearing?*

The ceremony itself was mercifully brief. I smiled ruefully as Morten and I took turns promising not to drink from each other's cup. Marilyn and James had anticipated that we wouldn't have thought about rings, so they had crafted necklaces for us with flowers from their yard, with lots of pinks and violets to match my dress and Morten's shirt. We changed our betrothal lines to "With this *lei* I thee wed," kissed, and I tried not to laugh. We emerged from the gloom of the building into the glaring sunlight with the leis around our neck like honeymooners in Hawaii. I was actually *married*. I couldn't believe it.

My mother would have had a heart attack.

But at that moment, I had no idea where she was.

Marilyn and James invited us to their place for cookies and punch to celebrate our nuptials. We got high on the sugar instantly; neither of us had eaten anything since our last meal at Zorba the Buddha Café in Antelope.

It was early evening when we left James and Marilyn's with our leis still strung around our necks, cookie crumbs falling from our hair. We were both in reasonably good spirits. I was starting to get excited about traveling cross-country with my new husband. Since I still didn't have a driver's license, I decided I'd let the car and its upkeep be Morten's baby. He had already proven his competence as a protector in the most profound way imaginable, by pulling me away from my mother, whose umbilical cord was still tied, like a noose, around my throat. If driving was Morten's only other responsibility, I would defer to him about the insurance.

No sooner did I have this thought when Morten pulled out without looking and sideswiped a woman in a vintage Buick almost identical to ours. No one was hurt but Morten and I would have to pay for the damage to the other car out of pocket, and it was bent up like a half-crushed can. Talk about instant karma! The bill came to one thousand dollars. Every penny of Morten's last allowance was going to have to go to this woman, which meant that my check to Chapel of the Bells would bounce after all and that we had no money to feed ourselves, let alone contemplate a summer of travel. In the meantime, I had to find a new job.

I kept waiting for Morten to apologize to me for getting us into this accident, to acknowledge I had been right about the insurance. Instead, he said, "Now you have seen what your negative thinking can do. It's powerful stuff." Somehow the accident was my fault too.

And so it came to pass that I spent my honeymoon typing. I found a job the next morning with a kindly yacht broker who had set up an office in his basement and needed someone to handle his leases. Instead of marching against the proliferation of nuclear arms, I would help the sailing set of Seattle have fun. I sent my regrets to my friends out East and got myself an unlisted phone number. I reluctantly joined my own cult, a not-so-utopian community of two. I dropped off the face of the earth.

Within days of our marriage, I didn't want Morten near me. In my view, we were already drinking far too much from the same cup. I had never intended to share my apartment with him for long; it was just a two-room suite, with a small sitting room, a larger room where I ate, a tiny standing-room-only kitchenette off to the side, and a small alcove surrounded by the windows facing the street with my single bed against one wall and the desk facing another. I had always found the bed to be small and cramped even when I was by myself. Having a man in it with me – the word *husband* still felt foreign – required bone-to-bone spooning, and I felt suffocated.

By now it was clear that Morten was going to be completely dependent on me financially. I had never considered this possibility. I had thought his father would help us, and that my marrying Morten would enable him to get a job. The problem was that in order for him to get his green card, I had to sign a form that guaranteed that for the rest of his tenure on American soil, I would be responsible for any debt he incurred, even if we were divorced. Morten would never be eligible for public assistance. I was to be his permanent meal ticket, his patron, *his* shelter from the storm.

This affidavit of support was the ultimate catch-22. If I didn't sign it, I would have to support Morten. If I did sign it, he could work and contribute to the finances of our marriage, as long, at least, as he wanted to. If he didn't, there was not a thing I could do about it.

Perhaps because Morten understood that whatever I chose to do, he would be looked after, he didn't pressure me either way. He seemed content. He played his guitar, he went to his kinesiology classes, he washed the dishes. Occasionally he would mumble something about trust, that I needed to stop projecting the worst outcome on our future together, but on the whole he was pretty chipper. All in all I think married life agreed with him.

And then I found out about his secret plan.

One day about two weeks after we were married Morten suggested we drive out to the country to visit some friends of his. Debbie was a fellow student of kinesiology. She and her boyfriend lived in a cabin in the woods near Mount Baker and I was glad to get out of the city for the day and relax, even though I was a little leery of anyone who shared Morten's passion for playing the human Ouija board.

When we arrived, Debbie's silent boyfriend stood in the kitchen serving us homemade soup and bread while Debbie shouted instructions. On the table where we sat drinking home-brews were piles of survivalist magazines full of ads for rifles and bomb shelters. While we were eating, Debbie went over the plan that she and Morten had discussed on the phone for the past couple weeks while I was at work. They were to start a utopian community in the Southwest, the location of which they'd arrived at through shared kinesiology sessions. Soon thereafter, Debbie, who had discovered (through kinesiology) that she was the reincarnation of the Virgin Mary, and her boyfriend, who was a recycled Joseph, would give birth to the new Messiah. Morten, being one of the apostles, had earned his right to join them; the other eleven would emerge over time, appearing by some kind of psychic homing device. Life would be good, and when the war of the worlds struck in 1984, they – *we* – would be spared. I wasn't sure who they thought I had been in the days of Nazareth but I sensed, with all the negativity I must have been emitting like an overcharged space heater, that they had me pegged for Judas.

"If we're going to make this thing work," Debbie said, "it's crucial we all brush up on our survival skills." Apparently there was only room for one artist in the bunch, and that would be Morten.

I would have left and walked home alone, but we were fifty miles from the city.

This should have been the last afternoon of my marriage to Morten but I must have needed one more lesson. What finally drove me away was a simple visual metaphor. When I got home from work a few days later, I looked at my desk, the only area of the apartment that I'd insisted Morten respect as "my space." On a nail on the wall above were our two marriage leis, the dried out petals now falling into the keys of my typewriter and onto the floor. On the back of the chair to my desk was his oversized, gray tweed jacket and beneath it, his Birkenstocks. Leaned up against the desk, his guitar. Beneath the flower petals, on top of my typewriter so dusty from disuse, were the papers from the Immigration Services, still unsigned. When I took in that tableau, that was it. I swept up the petals and threw all of Morten's things into the sitting room. I dusted the typewriter and told Morten he couldn't come near it. Morten sat on the bed staring at me. "But you never use it any more," he said. "Why are you so angry?"

I knew I was getting out of this, but I didn't know how.

What saved me, symbolically enough, was my writing, like the friend you try to ditch who refuses to desert you. Months earlier I had applied to go to a writer's conference that July in Port Townsend, a beautiful Victorian sea town on the Olympic Peninsula, two ferryboat rides away. Raymond Carver was going to be there – this was just when his story "Feathers" was back from the *Atlantic Monthly* in galley sheets – along with Gordon Lish and Jack Cady. I had sent in my deposit and forgotten about it. When I decided to go to New York I'd realized I would have to pass on the conference, but in all the drama that unfolded, I forgot to cancel. Then, when I received a letter about ridesharing opportunities from Seattle to the conference, I knew I was going.

I don't think Morten and I would make it into the *Guinness Book of Records* for the shortest marriage in history, but I doubt that even the priestess at Chapel of the Bells knew we would clear our karma in only thirty-five days. When I climbed into a Subaru with three strangers, I felt like a death row prisoner who'd just been given a midnight reprieve.


I want to create a home for the people I love. I do not want history to say I dreamed but could not make my dream a reality.
Bhagwan Shree Rajneesh, *Notes of a Madman*


In 1982, around the time that Morten and Debbie were deciding who would do what in the commune in New Mexico, Elizabeth Clare Prophet, or Ma Guru (as Marilyn and James called her) began to buy land in Montana, where her disciples would pay ten thousand dollars a head to live in concrete-and-steel bomb shelters stockpiled with automatic weapons. Also in 1982 Bhagwan Shree Rajneesh predicted that a nuclear war would take place in the Orwellian year of 1984, destroying the entire world except his ranch, after which he would be "the top Godman in India and the world." The Rajneeshees began to arm themselves.

When 1984 came and the world did not blow up, Rajneesh announced that AIDS was the disease that Nostradamus, the sixteenth-century physician and astrologer, had predicted would destroy two-thirds of the world. In the new era of Nancy Reagan's Just Say No campaign, the sex guru extolled the virtues of condoms and dental dams. Homosexuality, anal sex, and unprotected heterosexual sex were now grounds for expulsion from the ranch.

As the tensions between Rajneeshpuram and the outside world mounted – more conflicts over zoning, the town board, land use, and church-versus-state issues – Rajneesh began to make his drive-bys flanked with bodyguards, on foot and above in helicopter, all armed with semiautomatic weapons. Sheela, who conveyed all Rajneesh's announcements for him, was always seen with a 357 magnum on her hip.

In his three years of silence, from 1981 to 1984, he had left the matter of ruling to Sheela. I wonder if his followers found it ironic that it was in America, the birthplace of democracy, that the ashram became a military dictatorship. Among Sheela's most notorious attempts to bend democracy to her will was the 1984 "Share a Home" program. The ranch bused two thousand homeless people to share in the "abundance" of the Rajneesh way of life in return for their forced labor and, more importantly, their two thousand additional votes in local elections. These new recruits were housed separately from the commune members and treated like members of the lowest caste. Half of them departed within the first week. And that was the beginning of the end for the commune.

In September of 1985, when Sheela and a small group of supporters fled for Europe, Rajneesh denounced them as a "fascist gang" who had turned their Eden into a "concentration camp." Apparently Sheela had kept a hit list that included the U.S. attorney, an Oregon attorney general, and a reporter for the *Oregonian*, and she had managed a "dirty tricks" department to carry out nefarious deeds. In May of 1985, two women entered the *Oregonian* building posing as cleaning ladies with a plan to sabotage the computer system used by investigative reporters who had been conducting a twenty-part exposé of the commune. Sheela was responsible for a number of other serious crimes, including wire-tapping, bugging, embezzlement, arson, drugging the street people in order to control them, and – so eerily reminiscent of Jim Jones in Guyana – poisoning the people closest to Rajneesh: his personal assistant, doctor, and dentist. She was suspected of poisoning the district attorney and the entire water system in a neighboring area called The Dalles. She had overseen the culturing of the AIDS virus as a potential biological weapon. And she was responsible for a salmonella outbreak that made 751 people ill when her hit squad slipped the bacteria into the salad bar at a popular area restaurant on voting day to keep locals away from the polls: the first known case of homegrown biological terrorism in this country since the Europeans gave Native Americans blankets infested with smallpox in the 1400s.

Sheela was extradited from Germany by the FBI, charged, tried, and imprisoned. For one month, peace was restored to the commune. But then, as his final prophecy, Rajneesh said that the FBI and CIA planned to drop a nuclear bomb on the commune, but the sannyasins would survive if they hijacked the military jets at his command. He was bracing himself for his own brush with federal law officials. In October of 1985, Rajneesh and six sannyasins were stopped en route to Bermuda with four hundred thousand dollars in jewelry and fifty-eight thousand dollars in cash. Rajneesh was charged with thirty-five felony counts, all of them in connection to the violation of immigration laws. Among the charges were that he had conspired with a small group of sannyasins to "aid, abet, counsel, command, induce and cause" twelve sannyasin couples to enter "sham marriages." I wonder how many American spouses had filed affidavits of support. I suppose once you've signed your life's savings away to your guru, as many of them had, your mate's debts are small potatoes.

In a deal Rajneesh struck up with the U.S. attorney he paid a fine of four hundred thousand dollars and agreed to leave the country with the promise that he would not try to return for five years. By now he considered the entire United States of America to be his enemy. He took no responsibility for the commune's failure; among his last words to the remaining sannyasins in Oregon before they disbanded (according to "Gender, Discipleship, and Charismatic Authority in the Rajneesh Movement," an unpublished PhD thesis conducted at the University of London) was the assertion that Rajneeshpuram, "the first holy place in America" was brought down by a conspiracy of "red-necked Christian fundamentalists in league with a paranoid government." After sixty-one countries turned him away he was back in Poona with loyal sannyasins in tow.

Five years later he was dead of heart failure at the age of fifty-eight. By then he had turned to Zen Buddhism and changed his name to Osha, a Japanese honorific. When I visited India a decade later, I saw his old books in several stores reissued with his new name. The Osha Center's yoga and meditation classes are popular, I heard. The man continues to reinvent himself and even after death, he lives on. Perhaps his astrologer's prophecies came true.

Sometimes when I look back on my trip to Rajneeshpuram in 1982 I'm surprised I wasn't tempted to join them. The people we met seemed happy, dancing around the kitchen to Pat Metheny and planting corn; their affection for one another was palpable. I did not always want to be the aloof one in the corner taking notes; I wanted connection and community. I wanted to join hands with those who value the same things I do. Like everyone else, I wanted certainty and safety and shelter.

I'm not sure everyone remembers just how unsafe we *all* were in 1982. That spring, Thomas K. Jones, Reagan's appointment as deputy under-secretary of defense for research and engineering, Strategic Nuclear Forces, told the *Los Angeles Times* reporter Robert Scheer that the United States could fully recover from an all-out nuclear war. "If there are enough shovels to go around, everybody's going to make it." As reported by Scheer, the "shovels were for digging holes in the ground, which would be covered somehow or other with a couple of doors and with three feet of dirt thrown on top, thereby providing adequate fallout shelters for the millions who had been evacuated from America's cities to the countryside." In other words, our civil defense was to have the means to dig our own graves.

I, myself, did not own a shovel. When the time came, I would not be among the 90 percent of the population Jones predicted would survive. After the end, when the survivors dug through the rubble, I might be wearing the same violet dress that had seen me through death and love and now death again, but no one would know. I, like all those other unsaved souls who could not find shelter in any of the late century's demagogues, would dissolve, with so many flower petals, into ash.

9

# The Paradise at the End of the World

ETTA AND HER SISTERS

On the first day of my new life my lunchtime fortune cookie said, "The new path you have chosen is the correct one. Take it." I slipped the fortune in my near-empty wallet, grateful for any sign that this latest rash move wouldn't lead to more disaster.

I came upon another good omen as I made my way uptown: a woman in a long, embroidered dress emerging from a gypsy wagon swinging a long-handled wicker basket. With the Victorian houses and tall trees behind her, the ruby brooch clasping her shawl together, the rubied combs pinning back her long, chestnut hair, and the matching dangling earrings, she could have been the heroine of a Merchant Ivory film, but she also seemed contemporary in a romantic, neo-hippie way. Here was someone who seemed at home in the world but had still found a way to transcend the mass-marketed ugliness of our time. I wanted to know how this could be done.

I asked her if her horse-drawn wagon was for tourists. I could picture myself riding past all the historic homes, the rose-lined Chetzemoka Park, and up the bluff back to Fort Worden in time to say good-bye to all the writers as they packed up and left without me.

She laughed. "I'm just delivering my jewelry," she said, reaching into her basket and handing me her business card: a line drawing of a horse and buggy with her name, Etta, and her phone number. This carriage was just her mode of transportation, although it certainly added to the mystique of her wares. She made and sold her own line of exquisite necklaces, earrings, broaches, and bejeweled hairpieces, including the ones she was modeling herself; she had also designed the carriage, which was a cross between a Spanish gypsy wagon from the 1950s and an English delivery cart from the 1880s. She had obviously gone to a lot of trouble to live out this fantasy. As she rode away, I theorized: perhaps she had also spent a baby-boom childhood in the Rust Belt and vowed at some crucial turning point never to stack papers beneath the glare of fluorescent light. How had she pulled this off?

I was looking for an image of my future self to hang onto, the person I would become in Port Townsend. Beyond my need to flee certain elements I wanted to find a more satisfying way to earn my keep. "Right livelihood," the Buddhists call this: work that harms no one, including yourself. The job I'd just nabbed would pay less than the minimum wage, but at least it looked like fun.

It was the last day of the writing conference, the day I was due back in Seattle. After the final morning session I had walked to the lighthouse at Fort Worden, looked out at the seascape before me – the Strait of Juan de Fuca, the mountains in the distance, the vast blue-gray sky – and burst out sobbing. My ride was leaving in two hours and I decided that if I was *meant* to stay, I'd find a job in that time frame. I hitched a ride to town and a restaurant called the Salal Café was the second place I tried. If I could start early the next morning, I was hired. I said yes without hesitation and went out for tofu moo-shu on the last of the yacht broker's wages, celebrating the first day of the rest of my life.

The next morning I rose at 4:30 AM to walk to work. Until I found a home I'd still be squatting in empty rooms at the fort, thirty minutes up the coastline away from town: my most scenic commute, ever. That walk, which happened to coincide with high tide, put me narrowly between the green cliffs of town and the vast blue of the strait. I felt that I had fallen off the face of the earth, and I was glad.

Two ferryboat rides away from my troubles in Seattle, Port Townsend was a dreamy place to start over. The potential for collaborative self-invention roiled through the damp air, feeding on every appealing detail: the Victorian houses trimmed in lilac and aqua; the bright banners of upside-down fish waving with comic, festive flair; the cliffs of mossy rock and deep red madrona trees with drenched green leaves; beaches strewn with giant seaweed shaped like bullwhips for children to leap over; quiet uptown streets with sleepy dogs, beat-up cars, and gardens ebullient with roses, hydrangea, and rhododendrons.

I didn't expect miracles to happen here, to find love or fame or even a horse. I just wanted some small measure of peace and safety. In the meantime, I would settle for one day – my first shift as a prep cook – to pass without incident. It seemed possible.

Soon the United States would be spending nearly a billion dollars a day on nuclear weapons, each with enough power to annihilate tens of millions of people in an instant. During those last days in Seattle, it had felt to me like the world could end with the push of a button – a first-strike missile, perhaps, or a phone call from my mother. Here, in this small haven on the Olympic Peninsula where Etta rode through the daytime streets in her gypsy wagon, and others like her gathered at night to watch the northern lights or kiss and dance to Bob Marley in hand-woven shawls with Etta's rubies dangling against their necks, the arms race and my other life seemed to have taken place on a distant planet in a distant age.

Perhaps I should mention that when Etta read my tarot cards a few days later in her wagon (one of her sidelines), the card that defined me was that of a vagabond with all her belongings wrapped in a bandana-on-a-stick, grinning as she takes one step off a cliff: the Fool. This was probably an omen too, but I chose to ignore it.

BURNT

I did not get through the day without incident. On my first shift as a prep cook at the Salal Café on Water Street I witnessed the most incendiary event in twentieth-century town history. A poster in the remodeled Town Tavern has memorialized the date: July 12, 1982. It reads, with typical mock-tragic local humor: "The Great Town Tavern Fire: Port Townsend's worst disaster since the truck fell through Union Dock." The Town Tavern was directly across the street from the Salal. I would wonder for a long time afterward if this fire that ashed our window was also a sign, or if I, still under the dark cloud of recent woes, was simply bad luck for the town.

When I arrived that first morning I was greeted by a tall, thin, soft-spoken man in his early forties with blue eyes and shoulder-length, thinning strawberry-blond hair tied back in a ponytail. His name was Jeremiah, a name I'd always liked, and I could tell by his formal manner and aristocratic nose that he was not your usual fry cook.

"Do you like working with food?" he asked me as I awkwardly heaved up a giant pot of potatoes to chop. I forgot about the other potatoes that I'd left boiling and an acrid, smoky smell soon filled the air. He frowned and I felt like an idiot but in a few minutes we were scrubbing another batch together and sending it to boil. He sharpened my knife for me and gave me some pointers on technique. I picked up quite a lot from him that first morning: how to peel garlic easily by pressing it first with a large knife, how to slice oranges symmetrically – that would take some practice, for my orange wedges wanted to double as doorstops – how to distinguish between good lumps and bad in the muffins, and how to move quickly without losing my cool.

"It's not what you do in life that's important but how you do it," he said, a Zen line I would come to see in the months ahead as his all-purpose motto. Except on a few hot mornings behind the grill, Jeremiah was invariably thoughtful, calm, and self-contained. I appropriated this maxim to squelch my pangs of self-doubt about my unlikely career move when I took up correspondence again with my old college writing group and read their accounts of lunches with literary agents and editors at the Russian Tearoom.

"Port Townsend is a much better place to be a writer than New York," Jeremiah said when I listed some of my roads not taken. Jeremiah believed all the vital writing was now coming out of the West, and I respected his judgment. He was, he revealed shyly, the grandson of the famous literary editor Maxwell Perkins. He had left his fashionable home in Manhattan at seventeen, the year I'd been born, to make his way to California. He was not a name-dropper but I got the impression that he'd met everyone of the Beat and "mountain man" poet persuasion: Jack Kerouac, Allen Ginsberg, Robinson Jeffers, Gary Snyder, and more. Although he'd inherited a bundle he chose to live simply by himself in a tiny cabin in the woods, a small sea kayak his only material indulgence. After leaving three-fourths of his estate to his ex-wife and daughter, he had given most of his money to environmental organizations, and earned his keep doing the simple things he loved, planting trees as part of a reforestation project on the Olympic Peninsula and, since that winter, cooking breakfasts at the Salal. In his part time he was an editor of a collectively run book series called Empty Bowl and a literary journal called *Dalmo'Ma: An Anthology of Literature and Responsibility*, which published Northwest writers, many of whom, like John Haines, Barry Lopez, Sharon Doubiago, and Joy Harjo, were on the cusp of being nationally known. He invited me to attend the next staff meeting.

It dawned on me that what looked at first like an escape born of desperation might actually, as my fortune-cookie fortune promised, be the path itself.

By late morning Phyl Foley had come in to start her soup for the lunch shift: mushroom barley with sherry, which smelled delicious. I would be prepping all day, until the place closed at three, and then I would stay for cleanup, nearly a twelve-hour shift in total but I didn't mind. When breakfast was over, Phyl took Jeremiah's place, stocking her work area for the afternoon. The mother of five, she was earthy and irreverent and I liked her at once. I wanted her to be *my* mother and in the coming months she would do her best to oblige. Together we fell into an easy rhythm as we served up the lunch specials: steamed clams with garlic bread and salad, sautéed oysters, burritos, stir-fried rice and vegetables, and a multitude of hefty sandwiches, from homemade meatloaf to the surprisingly tasty tofu Reuben.

At half past twelve, early into the lunch rush, I smelled the burnt smell again and I wondered if someone had opened the back door letting in the odor of the scorched potatoes I'd left to cool. I was afraid people would think badly of me for all that waste. I was the new girl, after all, and I wanted to make a good impression. Within minutes people were running into the restaurant to use the phone. The news of the fire across the road hit town with so much shock and panic you would have thought it was the end of the world. For some people, I guess it was.

The Town Tavern – or simply, the Town, as locals referred to it – had been my first port of call during yesterday's job hunt. I'd gone drinking there with friends from the conference a few nights back and was told by the bartender that if you worked there, you automatically got a room of your own upstairs. The idea appealed to me as an efficient, one-stop-shopping way to run away. While the Town Tavern charmed the tourists because it conjured up images of nineteenth-century Western saloons, I liked it because it was an insider's watering hole, a place where local poets and wooden boat builders and artists came to talk shop and flirt and listen to Neil Young, who dropped in now and then when his boat, the *Ragland*, was docked in town.

The maroon brick building that housed the tavern was one of Port Townsend's important historical sites; it was commissioned by the retired pharmacist Nathaniel D. Hill and designed by Elmer H. Fisher, the Seattle architect who helped rebuild Seattle after the fire of 1889. At that time Port Townsend still harbored hopes for being the "Key City" of Puget Sound, and although the depression of the 1890s ultimately turned the area into a ghost town, the three-story brick and masonry buildings downtown and lovely Victorian homes in the Uptown District all remained intact, making Port Townsend an attractive place to stumble upon in the 1970s, when so many back-to-the-land homesteaders and crafts artisans like Etta (a navy brat, it turned out) and her husband (bank manager turned baker and yoga teacher) went in search of the rural outposts of their dreams.

Since 1973 the Hill building had enjoyed a lively history. That year a University of Oregon psychology professor turned up in town by accident, towed in by the Coast Guard after a failed sail to Victoria. He found the townspeople friendly and decided to buy the building and test out his ideas about community psychology by creating a nurturing place for people to drop out of the rat race and assess their lives. The system he implemented was based on bartering: in exchange for twenty hours of work a week tending bar or cooking or waiting tables, your basic needs would be provided for. You could arrive one morning, a traveler with an empty wallet, and by nightfall have a bed to sleep in, good food and draught beer in your belly, and a slew of new friends whose problems made you feel less freakish. If there had been an opening I would have installed myself there at once. If I had, I'd now be on the other side of the street watching my new life go up in smoke.

The fire started in an upstairs room: a cigarette thrown into a wastebasket. Before it was brought under control two hours had passed and the living quarters were trashed and the bar too damaged by smoke for business. The repairs would cost thousands of dollars and the owner, in typical, keep-the-faith hippie fashion, had no fire insurance. No one was hurt, but at least thirty people were suddenly homeless.

At one time or another the Town had housed most of Port Townsend's eccentrics, including our waiter and sometimes fix-it man, Henry, a tall, mumbly guy with a long, gray ponytail and enormous work boots that he tripped over as he walked. Although the words *acid casualty* came to mind when I met him, the rumor was that long ago he'd been a nuclear engineer in Florida until one day he had a crisis of conscience and decided to travel around America on a pilgrimage to purify himself. The Town was just the kind of place for someone like Henry to test out his new self-in-progress before the cement dried. A friend later told me that on Henry's birthday one year the Townies threw him a party and all shuffled into his room dressed . . . like Henry. The look then involved the signature oversize boots, hair pulled up into a severe bun, and a giant poncho like the one Mickey Dolenz wore on *The Monkees*. To find a dozen or more ponchos in the late days of the Ford administration was no small feat. He was thrilled.

Now Henry was trying to console his old friends.

Luckily, Phyl had made too much soup so we had something to offer the Town refugees. She filled me in on the backstory while together we served up bowl after bowl of mushroom barley, the scorched odor of the burnt potatoes from the morning blending in with the smell of smoke from across the street. Soon Salal workers and various customers were offering extra rooms and floor space to the Townies; I would have too if I hadn't been temporarily homeless myself. People were crying and hugging and shaking their heads with disbelief. I found myself feeling nostalgic for a life I hadn't experienced, for people I'd never known.

The outpouring from the town struck me as yet another reassuring sign. People donated tools, cash, labor, and good cheer as the remaining members worked around the clock to rebuild the Town. Although none of the upstairs rooms was habitable for another two and a half years, within weeks of the fire the tavern was open and people were dancing again to live music. In an already tight community, the fire seemed to bring everyone closer still. Many local businesses including the Salal held benefits to help pay the remodeling bills.

Although the Salal didn't house its workers like the Town Tavern did, it was also a collective, which is why it was named for the indigenous salal plant, an evergreen shrub bearing fruit in midsummer whose prolific underground root system struck the café's founders as an apt metaphor for the spirit of cooperation, grass-roots activism, friendship, and tolerance that coursed through the community as abundantly as Northwest rain. Jeremiah was one of the two founding members, the key coiner of phrases in the collective's bylaws, a document I would soon revere as our own in-house Bill of Rights. To become a worker/owner, all you had to do was kick in a hundred bucks and grab an apron. If you were strapped for cash, as I was, they could take it from your pay, smidgen by smidgen, over an outrageously long period of time.

The Salal's response to the plight of the Town refugees told me that I was in the right place at the right time; it gave me an instant identity as the member of a compassionate, civic-minded group. The place was so warm and welcoming that if I hadn't become a co-owner, I would have been a regular, coming in every morning for the same plate of eggs scrambled with Dabob oysters and parsley, loitering for hours, writing in my journal, flirting with the cute, bearded tree-planter at table three, and eavesdropping on the gossip. I would have left extravagant tips.

Strangely enough, the charred smell of fire seemed to follow me wherever I went, becoming a kind of motif. When I moved into the apartment

Phyl's eldest helped me find, I discovered why it came so cheap. It wasn't the Murphy bed that I first feared would spring back into the wall as I slept, like in some *Three Stooges* skit, the tiny bathroom with a shower that scalded me when my upstairs neighbor used the toilet, or the ringing of the tall fireproof clock tower across the street that had been telling the hour since the building was completed in 1892. My deliverance from high overhead came from the kitchen floor. There had been a fire in the kitchen and the owner hadn't bothered to replace the linoleum. It was bubbled up and black like the bottom of the pot of potatoes I had burned.

*Fire is the element of transformation* I wrote in my journal, still one to read upbeat, metaphysical symbolism into everything, even disasters that had nothing to do with me.


### BLOCKADE

The Town Tavern fire may not have signaled the end of the world, but the end of the world loomed large. One day I was sitting at the window in my apartment reading a flyer someone had given me when I first came upon the expression "window of vulnerability." That's when I realized that my out-of-the-way Witness Relocation Program refuge wasn't the safe haven I had thought. Port Townsend was only twenty miles from the naval base where the *U.S.S. Ohio*, a Trident submarine with first-strike capability, was due to arrive in August. The nuclear submarines were to be our state-of-the-art weapons of choice in "a preemptive strike" against the Russians; they were part of Reagan's deadly arsenal to close up our "window of vulnerability" to Russian technology, and although they were touted as a feather in the cap of "deterrence," their cumulative explosive power indicated that America was preparing to wage a "winnable" nuclear war. We had the power to threaten an "appropriate response" if anyone tried to mess with us (rendering from ten to sixty million dead in an instant, just to show 'em) or we could vaporize up to one hundred million in a "limited" nuclear war. The missilemen at ground zero, whose job it was to turn the key, would be, when dead, "rendered inoperable." This nukespeak was so akin to Orwell's Newspeak, its buzz words so like the "doublethink" slogans "war is peace" and "ignorance is strength" that I felt compelled to reread *1984*.

Eric Fromm wrote in the 1961 afterword to *1984* that one of Orwell's messages in his dystopia is that a democracy cannot continue in a world that "is constantly preparing for war, constantly afraid of being attacked, and preparing to find the means of complete annihilation of its opponents." Fromm points out that although Orwell had not anticipated thermonuclear weapons and their capacity to destroy all of a country's inhabitants in one go, his novel appeared three years after America had dropped atomic bombs on Nagasaki and Hiroshima. The flyer I'd just read explained that the total destructive power of the *Ohio*'s twenty-four missiles (each of which had several independently targeted warheads) was the equivalent of one Fat-Boy-over-Hiroshima blast per second for thirty-four straight minutes. I tried to do the math and imagine the destruction and genocide this would bring, but I couldn't.

The flyer had been penned by a peace group called Ground Zero that had formed to protest the installation of the Tridents. Part of their resistance work was to reclaim the language by translating the distancing jargon of these military euphemisms into the horrifics they were so as to galvanize the public. The other part of their mission was to perform acts of civil disobedience to block the *Ohio*. Ground Zero was part of an international peace coalition that was camped out near the site of the naval base at Oak Bay preparing to put themselves in the path of the submarine when it arrived. All of the protesters had been through intensive training on nonviolence, using the principles of Gandhi and King.

The Salal Café was donating food and other supplies to the protesters. I drove out to the encampment one afternoon after work with Phyl. She was heading to the settlement daily, sometimes with her four-year-old daughter, to bring soup, bread, salad, and messages from friends in town. We walked up to the beach, the nerve center for the movement, where people had already gathered to disseminate the big news: the *Ohio* was at the Panama Canal making its way north.

Opposition to the Trident subs had united a diverse gathering of people from both sides of the Pacific. There were scores of the predictable baby-boomer activists but also families with small children; religious groups from around Washington State; middle-class mill workers, many from British Columbia; an eighty-year-old woman who had just been voted Washington State's "Grandmother of the Year"; Japanese monks; and the twelve-person crew of the *Pacific Peacemaker*, a fifty-four-foot ketch that had sailed eleven thousand miles from Australia to help make people aware of the planetary scope of the cold war.

The Blockaders, as we began to call this assembly, were bracing themselves to take on serious physical, financial, and legal risks. When the Trident arrived it would be illegal to get within 1,000 feet of the 560-foot-long submarine. Those trespassing this buffer zone – which was the group's stated goal – could be fined ten thousand dollars, placed in jail for ten years, and have their vessel seized and forfeited. The struggle itself would be of David-and-Goliath proportions: a modest flotilla of fifty people in small boats and eight-foot, tublike prams strung together like ducklings following their mama to the largest vessel, the *Pacific Peacemaker*, taking on the mightiest submarine on the planet with its Coast Guard escort, one hundred government boats strong, some in high-speed Zodiac inflatable boats, many others in cutters armed with machine guns and water cannons.

This gathering of brave, hardy souls made me feel more hopeful about my fellow humans than I had in a long time. I still resented Morten for making us miss the disarmament march that June, and in a better frame of mind I would have joined the protesters. But as I filed for divorce and tried to sort out why I had married a benign version of my delusional mother, my peace blockade was personal: Me versus the frightening ambassadors of my past.

But that day with Phyl Foley I learned that you don't have to be out in the front lines to fight for your cause. Many people in Jefferson County supported the action by building boats, spreading information, and supplying meals. The people I met that day seemed unusually thankful for the food we brought, and I began to understand something important about revolutions. Sometimes an ordinary citizen can do her part to fight tyranny by an act as small and intimate as making soup.

STRANGE ANIMALS

Back in Seattle, Morten seemed to be coping well with my defection. I had paid the whole summer's rent when I left, and he was busking with his guitar at the Pike Place Market for food money. My mother was back in Ohio in a mental hospital. I had the space to process all that had happened that year, which was probably a good thing, but now and then, when delayed grief overtook me, I could see the benefits of denial.

As a correction to my solitary crying jags, I threw myself into my job. I loved everything about the Salal, from baking muffins to chopping potatoes, but mostly I was inspired by the collectivism. For the first time ever, I wasn't another expendable worker at the bottom of the food chain. Every member – dishwashers, cooks, and wait staff – had equal power and made exactly the same amount, less than three dollars an hour plus the tips, which we pooled and shared evenly. Every decision was handled collectively, from what brand of whipped cream to buy to how to resolve interpersonal conflicts, like the time when, during a stressful breakfast rush, a waiter exchanged some verbal salvos with the women in the kitchen and upped the ante by using the "c" word. When we were through processing this skirmish, a few of us holding forth on the destructive power of language and Phyl reminding us how gender inequities would undermine the strength of the collective, not only did he apologize profusely but we had negotiated a way as a group to be cranky without making enemies. Group process was our politics: we were Winthrop's pilgrims in the city on a hill; we were Emerson and Thoreau on Mount Katahdin, pondering where people and moose and trains might fit in the grand scheme of things; we were the Iroquois creating their grand confederacy; we were a hairy band of seventeen who had come together to put our ideals about equal representation into practice. In the two years I worked there I learned more about group dynamics and conflict resolution than in any other work setting before or since, which was great training for the collective body I would eventually join, the seventeen-member-strong English department of a liberal arts college.

I loved the Town Tavern refugees who joined the collective, especially Jenny, a woman with wild, Janis Joplin hair and an extravagant bent for storytelling that matched her flamboyant style of dress. She would wear several layers of the tapestry skirts she made herself in fuchsia, turquoise, and plum silk, matching velvet berets trimmed with hot pink satin or feathers and beads, a ring on every finger. She and Lizzy, the stepdaughter of the Montana writer Jim Crumley, often went dancing with me after hours at the Town Tavern when it was back in business. People called us the Three Muses.

I worked Tuesdays through Thursdays, from 5:00 AM to 5:00 PM. On Salal days, I did nothing afterward but bathe and collapse into the collapsible bed. On my four-day weekends, I jogged (my new eightiesesque sport) and wrote. Eventually I'd take Ashtanga Yoga from Etta's husband Gabriel, a ninety-minute class five days a week. Before the year was over I had sold my first short story. To celebrate, I got my ears pierced. Although I couldn't afford anything by Etta, I did buy myself a twenty-five-dollar pair of handcrafted earrings made by one of her competitors: amethyst stones inside silver half-moons.

Before long I was swept up into the literary culture of the town. For a village of six thousand, Port Townsend had an unusually high population of writers. There were two nationally known presses there beyond the more regional Empty Bowl: Graywolf and Copper Canyon. My first winter I ran a readings series in the Salal's new solarium, and I met poets and fiction writers from around the Pacific Northwest. They were kind and accessible people who showed me by example that you didn't have to live in Manhattan to find a national audience for your work. Many of them – especially the poets Michael Daley, David Romtvedt, Sam Hamill, and Sharon Doubiago – taught me that it was still possible in this cynical, post-Vietnam era to write lyrically about politics. Carolyn Forché was a friend to these poets, and her award-winning collection, *The Country between Us*, which savaged the U.S. government's support of the military dictatorship in El Salvador, inspired a poetry of witness that flourished in the Northwest alongside the region's more celebratory poetics of place.

At long last I had found my utopia. Our distance from the city gave all of us the freedom to live out our fantasies about right livelihood: to make jewelry and sell it from a gypsy wagon, build wooden catamarans, sing the blues, plant trees, or cook breakfast with a descendant of one of America's great literary figures while penning stories on the weekend. Every Thanksgiving we held a breakfast to benefit a local cause – a conflict-mediation course at the elementary school, the cancer treatments of a peace activist who had no health insurance – and in the afternoon, Henry would host a turkey dinner for all the Salal workers and their friends who had nowhere else to go. The Salal fed me even on my days off because after our shifts we were free to take home vats of soup, blueberry muffins, oyster stew, and bread. The economy wasn't exactly flush, but the locals banded together to keep each other in business. We ate at each other's restaurants, swapped edible flowers for basil from each other's gardens, gave astrology readings in exchange for massage, carpentry, and sewing. It was a good life, while it lasted.

Once while I was walking to work in the dark of 5:00 AM, I came upon a family of strange, thin-limbed animals with enormous owl-like eyes. I had no idea what they were and when I stopped to stare at them, they stared back. They seemed feline but marsupial, rodentlike yet tall. Years later, in a chiropractor's office of the upstate New York town where I live now, I'd see them again on a wildlife poster: meerkats. I thought I'd solved the mystery until I read the location of the photograph: West Africa. What were these guys doing in Port Townsend?

What were any of us doing in Port Townsend? There was no university, no major employer other than a pulp mill, and yet people kept arriving. I thought I had gone there to be a lone wolf but, instead, Port Townsend was the place I stared down unnamed animals from far-flung corners of the map, and they stared back.

PREEMPTIVE STRIKE

I was jogging one morning on the beach up to Fort Worden when I saw it: the ominous black shape of the nuclear submarine pushing through the chop of the Strait of Juan de Fuca.

On 12 August 1982, at 5:00 AM, an armada of one hundred Coast Guard and navy vessels ushered in the *U.S.S. Ohio* through a dense fog, attacking the Blockaders' boats long before these small vessels had a chance to violate the one-thousand-foot buffer. The Blockaders would later describe what was done to them as a *preemptive strike*. Most of the boats were immediately disabled; those who tried evasive action were hit with water cannons. One small vessel, the *James Jordan*, did get through the lines, within twenty feet of the *Ohio*. Pursued by the Coast Guard, a crew woman named Sunshine jumped into the water, attempting to throw herself in front of the submarine. She was prepared to die in order to stop it. When the Coast Guard cut the *James Jordan*'s gas line, the three members of her crew were left to drift at sea until other protesters rescued them. Michael Daley later commented about this moment in *Dalmo'Ma*: "It was at this point that we saw the Coast Guard's intention of leaving boats and people stranded or in the water in order to protect the submarine, relinquishing their responsibility to human life and safety on the water."

Seventeen arrests were made and three boats were taken under tow to the Bangor base, but the protesters felt they had made a modest victory of a kind. Quoting the legal briefs from the Nuremberg trials, they said that it was the moral obligation of every citizen to stop offensive military buildups in their countries. They had done their part to educate hundreds of people about the destructive power of the Trident subs, and they had fought back using the Gandhian nonviolent principle of *Satyagraha*, or "truth force," to demonstrate how love was more powerful than hydrogen bombs. The method was to let your truth worm its way into your opponent's heart through your essential goodness, forthrightness, and your willingness to let the only bloodshed be yours.

And that's when I realized what I would and would not do to resist the Orwellian nightmare of eternal warfare. March at a protest, yes. Write letters to Congress and sign petitions, yes. Find a way to nurture the doers, as Phyl did, yes. But jump directly into the path of a nuclear submarine? I had already put myself in the path of too many entities that did not wish me well. Moreover, the idea behind *Satyagraha* presupposes that your opponent can be reasoned with. But what if, as George Orwell asks in his essay on Gandhi, your opponent is insane? What, in the face of madness, both personal and political, is the "appropriate response"? I still don't know.

In Henry Carlisle's poem "Off Port Townsend One Month before the Arrival of the *U.S.S. Ohio*," there's a line about the submarine "staining the scenery," how it "slips through like grease." This poem evokes the feeling that flooded my heart that day when I first spotted the thing moving across the horizon like some misshapen whale, eclipsing all other vessels with its enormity, reminding me that in this place where I felt more alive and more suffused with Edenic hope than ever before, death, a collective death of proportions the world had never before had to fear, lurked nearby, a malevolent partner.

Carlisle's meditation on the threat of mega-death is a thing of beauty. The broadside version of it is its own paradox, a relic from a place in the world where wordsmiths flourished, where people would take time to make their own paper, swirling drops of ink into water onto the paper using the Japanese Suminagashi process, embracing an art form from our former enemies-turned-nuclear-allies on the Pacific Rim, and compose type, one letter at a time, to print one hundred or so copies of one poem: all in a time when we had to protect one another from those charged with protecting us.

# 10

# Postcard from the Asylum

### *The Nutmeg War*

I am at a bar with the Port Townsend Spanish Club conjugating verbs when a TV announcer describes a U.S. offensive. We know our government is covertly funding the civil wars in El Salvador, Guatemala, and Nicaragua, and we know we're in conflict with Beirut, where terrorists have just murdered 241 of our Marines. So why are we attacking this tiny British-colonized Caribbean island I've never heard of? We are all alarmed.

In his autobiography, *An American Life*, Reagan will declare Grenada's liberation from a "brutal gang of thugs" to be a "textbook success." Actually, to divert the public from our failure in Lebanon, we have bombed the unarmed. We have declared war on the inhabitants of an insane asylum, who are mistakenly killed by American shells fired on the basis of information pieced hastily together from tourist brochures, accounting for most of the few dozen casualties. And yet, 8,000 medals will be awarded – more than the number of soldiers serving – 152 of them Purple Hearts. In his autobiography Reagan will also quote one of his army helicopter pilots, who supposedly wrote him that if the Soviets had taken over, they would have controlled much of the world's supply of nutmeg, that key ingredient of holiday eggnog. "The Russians were trying to steal Christmas. We stopped them," Reagan will see fit to repeat to the world.

As ever, madness on this order reminds me of home.

When I was learning to cook, my mother taught me to make French toast with cinnamon and nutmeg. After she put me in charge, I ran the household like a little general, making sure we ate at set times from four food groups and had good table manners. I always used fresh spices.

When I read Reagan's fairy tale I picture my mother in the insane asylum on the island of Grenada just when the shelling starts. She flees into the gardens, a maze of lemon and avocado trees, cayenne pepper, and nutmeg, her nostrils alert to the scent of purloined spices. Armed with cooking pots and nutmeg graters, she is ready. She'll challenge any foe to democracy to a cook-off.

# In the Courtyard of the Iguana Brothers

Shortly before he was caught, Ivan Boesky drew up plans to convert his mansion in New York State into a replica of Monticello.
James B. Stewart, *Den of Thieves*

As above, so below.
Paracelsus

Among the many mysteries I would never solve in Mexico – along with how to distinguish the gecko from the iguana, or repel the advances of men – was the true story of how our landlord, Antonio, lost half his right arm. The version of events he advanced was that he had put himself in the path of a wayward firecracker that was headed straight toward a general's daughter. The gringo rumor was that he and a friend got wasted one night and played a game of catch with live hand grenades. I never asked Antonio myself. His alcoholic rages were legendary. Besides, my Spanish wasn't up to it, and the only words of English he knew were *money* and *dukes*, as in *The Dukes of Hazzard*, his favorite TV show, which came in dubbed on Wednesday evenings, the only time of the week the generator bringing power to our huts was guaranteed to work.

*Money* and *dukes*: these words were emblematic of what I was still running away from in America, and what I would be forced to confront even in the squalor of tropical exile. While the North of 1984 was all about real estate investment (even, suddenly, in Port Townsend), insider trading, hostile corporate takeovers, and the first zippy rock videos, the South had its own torpid, electronically challenged equivalent to the money-for-nothing-and-MTV mentality. This much was true: if you had American dollars, you could live like a duke (or duchess) south of the border – as long as you weren't obsessed with personal hygiene.

Twenty-four dollars a month got us a thatched-roof hut with a dirt floor, a saggy double bed, a hotplate with two burners, a table and two chairs, some aluminum cookware, and a rat that left bite marks in our papayas. Besides the rent, which was cheap even by Mexican standards, the main attraction of Antonio's was that despite his temper, he didn't care what you did as long as you kept him floating in tequila. You could be the ruler of your own kingdom, the CEO of your own shady business concern, or, in my case, a not-very-disciplined writer playing house with her new boyfriend.

Rumors about a cheap seaside courtyard like Antonio's had traveled all the way up to the Salal. As cold autumn rains fell, I heard a customer speak effusively of this unnamed, mango- and palm-tree-lined beach where I could wake to the sound of falling coconuts, breakfast on bananas from the vine, read from a hammock, and feast on homemade corn tortillas and shrimp, all without the presence of high-rise hotels, cruise ships, or any other evidence of American hegemony other than me and a handful of kindred spirits. After weeks of dark skies I yearned to see bright colors: purple bougainvillea, red hibiscus, blood oranges, the golden eye of an iguana.

I arranged a leave of absence from the café and stocked my backpack with books (*The Night of the Iguana* and *Under the Volcano*), natural cures for Montezuma's revenge, double-D batteries for my new electronic typewriter, a six-month supply of birth control pills (I wasn't looking but hey, you never know) and, despite a sudden windfall of $750 (my share of the sale of Grandpa's old rifles and gold) nowhere near enough travelers' checks. The herbs clumped in the heat, the typewriter wouldn't work (why? another mystery), and my literary models (penned by alcoholics) did not wean me from the romantic self-delusion I still needed to shed in order to write anything serviceable, but I did get some use out of the contraceptives with the aforementioned beau, who looked like a young John Travolta minus the hair grease.

I had always savored my mother's stories about my father's bohemian days in Mexico, where he started his one-and-only published novel in some cheap hotel room overlooking a lively outdoor market. When his pesos ran low, he caught iguanas and rattlesnakes in the wild and roasted them over an open fire. When he drank tequila, he swallowed the worm. Although my mother was, as ever, an unreliable narrator, I had wanted to believe her when she told me in a letter (to my post office box in Seattle, where she thought I still lived) that an old friend of the family's had seen him before he headed through Tijuana that fall to write and paint. I found myself rehearsing what I would say if I ran into him.

When he asked me about my life, I would give him the impression that I had transcended all of the material and emotional needs that had no doubt been a burden to him (or else why would he have left?). When he asked about my sister, I would not mention her worries; I would tell him how she and her Chicago friends assisted Guatemalans and Salvadorans in the underground amnesty movement. My father and I would toast my sister's courage, but he would reassure me that it was also an act of resistance to use the symbols of his ex-father-in-law's patriarchal authority on a trip the old gangster would have called me a *whooore* for taking.

These fantasies (my father spouting feminism? me tucking into charred snake?) underscore what I hoped would happen on the trip: that I'd become a fearless adventurer, the protagonist of some implausible picaresque narrative. Although the placard above the dashboard of the vehicle that got me to Mexico said, "Wherever you go, there you are," I was still hoping to become someone else: that free spirit I'd moved out West to be.

Ethan and I met en route to Cabo San Lucas on the Green Tortoise, the hippie answer to Greyhound. After the tour ended he went back to his brother's house in LA to financially refuel on a construction site and I took a ferry to Mazatlán and made my way slowly, by local village buses, to Mexico City, where we were reunited three weeks later on New Year's Day. We played tourist for a month – Oaxaca, San Cristóbal de Las Casas, Palenque, Chichén Itzá, Mérida – but we were impatient to set up base camp. We tried the unfashionable sides of Cancún, Tulum, and Playa del Carmen, but they were crowded with people who had the same idea, except that they could afford the pseudo-rustic rentals. Not even the sight, one evening over fajitas, of two boars mating a few feet from our table altered our gloomy conviction that we may as well have been back in California for all the middle-aged Americans flashing plastic, college kids on a cheap drunk, and ex-pats who claimed to live like the natives but knew no Spanish except *dos cervezas, por favor*. And we were no better: Ethan only knew the words for "love," "room," and "hot water," and I, having never moved beyond the present tense in my studies (something I tried to see as a Zen virtue) remained focused on "I am," "I have," "I want," and "I need."

Desperation thrust us two thousand miles west to San Blas, a small town between Mazatlán and Puerto Vallarta that had failed to attract major developers thanks to the pesky sandflies that swarmed the beaches at dusk, covering the skin of unwitting tourists with itchy, angry welts that took forever to go away. I had liked San Blas when I passed through it briefly in December, but I had not investigated the super-cheap beach huts I kept hearing about because the paradise in my mind featured daily, insect-free sunset strolls. It was easy to be picky when I still had money and had not yet encountered a Cancún conga line.

Ethan sprang for the plane tickets.

Which is how, that February, after interrogating several taxi drivers for the scoop on where and for how much, we found ourselves on the overgrown path five miles out of town that led into Antonio's property. "This is the place," we both exclaimed like the Mormons first beholding the Great Salt Lake. The *cabañas* were arranged in a horseshoe around a courtyard of hibiscus and bougainvillea, chickens and roosters, sunbathing geckos and iguanas, and the occasional roving dog. Bright-colored birds called down from the trees and coconuts did indeed fall onto the thatched rooftops. Only a hundred yards from where we stood was the pristine sandy ocean beach of my dreams (although you had to pass through a buggy lagoon and stinky garbage heap to get there) and behind us were hilltop jungle forests of deep green.

For plumbing we had to contend with a communal outhouse, a well, and a garden hose for "showers," but we weren't deterred: Ethan, a Catholic-turned-Quaker and avid outdoorsman, was big on "voluntary simplicity," and I was big on anything that kept down the price. There were only two foreseeable problems: one, that being this isolated would make it hard to get groceries, and the other, that we weren't isolated enough. Although communitarianism was still my bohemian ideal, we didn't exactly fit in with the neighbors.

We had already been warned that to get to Antonio, you had to go through Jim, a tall, slim surfer dude with a brown ponytail. Jim was the Duke of Campo Antonio, the master of ceremonies, the cruise director. His girlfriend, Marilyn, a small, cold, watchful blonde, was the Duchess. Bill, a shy man with sad blue eyes and a bushy black beard, was Jim's best friend and court eunuch (although Jim, being the consummate host he was, kept an eye out for pretty gringas to invite to his Help-Bill-Get-Laid parties.) The three were coworkers at a casino in Lake Tahoe, Jim and Bill as blackjack dealers and Marilyn a cocktail waitress. It was Bill's first visit to Mexico, but Jim and Marilyn were regulars; they had arranged their lives to spend six months each year at Antonio's and had, over time, acquired the seniority needed to snag the nicest place in the courtyard, a small, white stucco house with a functioning kitchen. Their status made it possible for Bill to jump the queue to the next best house, whereas Ethan and I would scrounge in one of Antonio's standard ramshackle huts *if* his gatekeeper decided we weren't duds.

We met him and the others that first morning. After we had gazed appreciatively at the beach we followed the sounds of laughter to an open window where three young people about our age sat rolling joints at the kitchen table. Ethan and I had been traveling without sleep for forty-eight hours, but when I asked Jim if he'd take us to Antonio, he laughed and said, "Relax. You have to wait until he's halfway through his first bottle of the day. Take a load off." We lowered our packs to the floor and joined them tentatively. We'd both intuited that being hyper over anything, even finding a home, wouldn't fly in these parts. "Some folks from Fresno just left," Jim said, when Ethan asked with feigned casualness what was available, "so you *might* get their hut, or the one next to it, but we've got some friends coming next week. So, do you like to party?" As Jim went through the complicated social calendar, we toked on command; Jim had made it clear that he had only derision for people who turned down his hospitality. People like Mark, a thirty-year-old Italian American from New York who was actually higher than Jim in the gringo chain of being because of his money and his friendship with Antonio but was too "antisocial" to screen renters.

"The guy's gone native," Jim said. "He speaks fluent Spanish," which was somehow another negative, and although he was a loner, he was friendly with the local *federales*, who often dropped by to drink shots with Antonio. He owned a car *and* a pickup; very few gringos owned vehicles at all. And he had been living in Mexico year-round for almost a decade, which was difficult to pull off since touring visas were for only six months. "If you need anything at all, Mark will know who to bribe and how much to pay," Jim said. "But if you want him to party with you, forget it. He seems to think he has better things to do." Weeks later, when I had something better to do myself, Jim asked me how much money I made from my writing. When I told him, he said, "You should find another hobby, man!"

Ethan and I were exhausted and stoned to the point of incoherence when Jim took us to meet Antonio, a tiny, toothless, wizened man who looked seventy, was maybe fifty, but had the high voltage energy of a frisky teen. He poured us tequila shots, waving around his stump merrily. After we had offered our stash of liquor as a deposit, we were in. Despite my worries about getting along with the Campo royalty – antisocial being a word so often applied to me – I felt incredibly lucky to live anywhere, let alone a rustic beach hut with a hunk.

Not that everything was hunky-dory with said hunk. There were moments when Ethan and I were fighting that I had visions of one of us leaving the other on the side of a road. We both knew we had no future together: I couldn't see myself settling down with someone who had never read Shakespeare or studied history, and he wasn't sure if he could handle someone so persistently "negative" about world affairs. He'd set out on this trip in search of a life-changing epiphany about the career path he should take: something, he hoped, that would get him away from construction work, but would not require any college. He had never planned to stay in Mexico this long and he blamed his lack of clarity about his direction on me. Even his passion for me scared him; he hated the loss of control. He was not so even-keeled as he'd seemed when we first met; his daily meditation was actually an attempt to find an equilibrium that seemed always out of grasp. And whenever I asked him what he was so mad about, or why he had suddenly stopped being affectionate, he accused me of being needy, which became increasingly true as I felt lonelier in his company. Being financially dependent on him didn't help.

Our travels had annihilated my budget. With three months left until I was expected back at the Salal, I needed a minimum of five hundred dollars to see the season out. Obviously, hitting up family or borrowing from Ethan were not options. I was going to have to ask someone else for help, but who?

I consoled myself with the thought that by North American standards, five hundred dollars was *nada*. This was the year Ivan Boesky would make sixty-five million dollars in profits from a single merger deal, the year *Newsweek* would proclaim the "Year of the Yuppie." I still did not want to join my fellow baby boomers on the fast track, but that didn't make it any less demoralizing to know that some of my crowd owned Manhattan apartments in buildings with uniformed doormen while I was scrounging to afford a twenty-four-dollar-a-month hut with holes in the roof and a rat.

I settled on borrowing the money from my old friend from high school and college, John, the one my mother had once pointed a gun at. As teenagers together when he drove me everywhere in his white Pinto – the getaway-mobile – our friend Sandy always imitated me by saying, "John wouldn't mind driving me to Mexico." Now that I was actually *in* Mexico and in trouble, John – who was now a well-paid entertainment lawyer in West Hollywood, a city he'd helped incorporate – seemed like the best person to turn to. I would call him from San Blas when Ethan and I went on our first grocery run. And that was where we were headed, on a mission to get me solvent enough to forget the business of America for three more months, when we came across a trio of American would-be businessmen who would make me realize that such escape was impossible. The men I would nickname the Iguana Brothers made me understand the permeability of borders in a personal way.

It was already sweltering when, just after dawn, Ethan and I set out on the five-mile walk to town. The driver of a rusted pickup with Florida plates asked us if we wanted a ride, and I regretted our decision when a fat man about our age backed out to make room for us, revealing some hairy butt crack. He introduced himself as Chris, asked us our names, and sat with us in the bed of the truck, smiling in a kindly, almost reassuring way, but I remained on alert. He was guarding a giant white gunnysack that moved even when we didn't bump over potholes. I felt the contents of the bag squirming toward my knees and I thought I heard a faint groaning. Something inside it was alive. Acutely aware of my bouncing breasts and the guys in front checking me out, I moved closer to the passenger side so that if I had to jump, I'd be able to roll onto the dense undergrowth and not the middle of the road.

When we got to town Ethan and I made evasive maneuvers. We weren't frightened of Chris, but the driver had the erect posture, mirrored dark glasses, and buzz cut of a CIA man while his friend riding shotgun, a dark-haired, slit-eyed, skinny smirker, put me in mind of a snake. "We should shop together," the driver said when he noticed the direction we were walking so quickly. "We have to watch each other's backs so we don't get ripped off. It's a jungle out there." The latter was literally true – how this region got into the guidebooks – but when I laughed, I realized he wasn't making a joke. His was a script from a movie where people dress in camouflage. Then he began boasting of his exploits in the actual jungle, where he and Chris and Snake Man had spent the last month tracking snakes, geckos, and iguanas. "We're going to sell them to pet stores and theme parks."

"Is that what was rubbing against our legs in the truck?" Ethan asked in the fake mellow voice I now recognized as his San Blas persona. I could see the driver assessing him: *Pussy*, his eyes seemed to say. *I could take him*.

"Payload." He then explained how the "profit margin potential" for this enterprise was unlimited because the critters came to them free of charge – the word *poaching* was never used – and by camping out, and eating light, their "overhead" was practically nil. "What's so innovative about us, and makes us attractive to the customer, is we've eliminated the middle man. We deliver the product directly and can vouch for where it's been. We're insiders. Who can beat that?"

I have forgotten this guy's name but years later, when his unpleasant memory came to mind, I dubbed him El Gecko, partly in honor of his payload. By then I had learned that geckos, unlike iguanas, have suction cups on their feet that allow them to climb, which make them literally upwardly mobile. By then I had also seen Michael Douglas play Gordon Gekko in the movie *Wall Street*, a character that was supposedly inspired by the real-life Ivan Boesky. "If you are not inside, you are outside," Gekko says to his young protégé as he counsels him to use insider information to buy up shares in companies targeted for takeovers.

"Imports are *in* now," El Gecko continued. We did not ask the inevitable – how he planned to get his payload across the border, or whether it had ever tried to bite them or escape.

Ethan gave my hand a tug and we attempted our own escape. We entered the covered market: the stalls of whole chickens and cow halves swarming with flies, peppers in every shade of red, green, and yellow, perfect avocados and tomatoes. The locals stepped out of our way as the five of us marched through, Ethan and I in front, trying not to seem like we were running, the Iguana Brothers close on our heels. "I'm an alpha male," El Gecko actually said over the din of vendors hawking meat, and I began to suspect that this man, boasting about his hunting prowess and business acumen into the privacy of my inner ear, was launching his own hostile takeover.

My fears were confirmed when El Gecko put his hand on my shoulder and asked for a taste of the mango and banana smoothie I ordered at the *licuado* stand. Ethan glared at me as though I had invited this forwardness, and I wondered what a spectacle we were making, five young gringos marking our respective territories with barely masked hostility and prejudices we had imported from El Norte.

We managed to get away when Chris announced that he was hungry for a sit-down breakfast at a restaurant. "You boys are starving me to death," he said, which prompted El Gecko and Snake Man to ridicule him for his "big fat lard ass" and accuse him of eating up their "overhead." Chris did not deserve this venom, but I was grateful for the distraction. I pulled Ethan into a nearby bakery and then we slipped into an alley, feeling like we, too, were in a movie where people dress in camouflage. We spent the rest of the morning as we would for days to come: jumping through the bureaucratic hoops it took to get cash.

To make an international call in the small-town Mexico of 1984 you had to get squatter's rights to one of the booths in the phone shack, hoping one of your fifty attempts got through. No one I knew ever made a connection on the first visit. You just kept coming back, maybe half a dozen times. Then, once you finally made contact, there was the tiresome business of waiting in the telegraph office. This entailed second-guessing when it might actually be open and then standing in a long, slow-moving line for two hours or more only to learn that the money had not arrived, all the while hating yourself for becoming the vocal champion of America's efficient infrastructure and fighting your growing paranoia that the man behind the counter had not only pocketed your dinero but was laughing at you.

When everything shut down for the siesta, we took a taxi to our hut and slept off the morning's troubles. Sometimes we'd catch a ride back to town for an afternoon go-round with the bilingual Mark (who was not that antisocial, we discovered), but often we just stayed sacked out in our bed or at the beach, waking now and then to the sound of Jim and company surfing or a local man in a sombrero clomping along in his burro. I tried to motivate myself to jog or write in my journal but with humidity, birth-control bloat, and the *mañana* culture oozing through my body like knockout drugs, I felt like a three-hundred-year-old tortoise.

Now and then, as a special treat, we dined out. Half a mile down the beach was an open-air café called Las Roches, where the proprietor greeted us by hacking two coconuts from the branches above us with a machete and drilling in straw holes for us to drink the juice. After this aperitif, we jumped off the rocks into the ocean. The man's entire family prepared the meal – a grandmother with gray braids grilling corn tortillas, children carrying out our beers, their mother chopping garlic – and because this place was *exactemente* the unspoiled *ramada* I'd set out to find, I stopped worrying if the children ever did homework or played with other children. Our feast of locally caught shrimp, frijoles, sliced onions, tomatoes, and tortillas cost less than two dollars each, including the coconuts and cool Tecates with lime. Despite my panic about my rising debt to Ethan, I felt like a low-maintenance duchess.

Before sundown, when the dreaded sandflies came out, we returned to our hut and, as Jim and Marilyn suggested, burned coconut husks on the dirt floor to keep the insects away. Then we zipped ourselves inside our mosquito net, made love, and played cards. Only after all this would I try to write.

I never understood why the portable electronic typewriter I'd bought just for this trip wouldn't power up down here – with electricity, on batteries, *nada*. After our victory at finding a home, discovering I wouldn't be able to type was a serious blow. I still managed to produce two stories set in Cleveland, and some notes about the market life in Mexico, but everything was raw and unpolished. If I had worked every day I would have revised more, but I was worried Ethan would get bored. Whenever he sighed extravagantly at the phone shack, or scratched his sandfly bites, or spoke longingly of his childhood home in Maine and how its cool temperatures made it easier to think, I put aside what I was doing and took his hand.

When I had traveled by myself before Ethan could join me I had been stroked and groped on almost every bus. I could not even buy bottled water without getting catcalls. In Mexico City, just as New Year's Eve was beginning, two men had tried to pull me into a black sedan full of their empty liquor bottles. I don't know what would have happened if I hadn't been rescued by an old *abuela* with gray braids who appeared on the lawn where one man was just opening his car door to try to yank me inside. The woman shouted at the men like they were children, wagging her finger as she would to two little boys torturing a baby iguana or using the name of the Virgin in vain. After we got away I took a cab to my hotel where I stayed up all night quaking in fear as men outside the bars of the cheap hotel room ushered in 1984 with drunken laughter. By the next morning, when I dragged myself to a taxi stand and made it to the airport to welcome Ethan, I had begun to think of him as my savior.

While I had waited for his plane I called my sister to wish her a happy 1984. When I made a joke about Big Brother listening in, she told me it was indeed likely that her phone was being bugged. She was in shock because an important figure in the amnesty movement, a folk singer she'd seen perform, had been deported back to El Salvador where the Reagan-backed secret police interrupted his concert and, in front of the audience, amputated his hands. I gasped and wept at this story. The threat of male violence was everywhere. As she spoke, I cracked my knuckles and swallowed hard, trying not to think of what the men in the car might have done to me.

Every part of life in Mexico – getting to town, shopping, negotiating the telegraph office, eating out, hosing off in our yard (with Ethan holding a towel around me), and fending off El Gecko – was less hassle with a male companion. Although I had set off on my trip full of pluck and bravado, I no longer believed I could remain in Mexico without a bodyguard.

Which is partly why our domestic rituals became more important to me than my writing, why my curiosity about the world outside our hut faded away. When John told me on the phone from Hollywood that he was satisfying his need to nest by painting the walls of his new condo cobalt blue, I could almost relate. I loved trying to see what I could make on the hotplate with yams, beans, garlic, and tomatoes. We even had a dog, a blond little puppy that followed us home from the beach, rolled on her back on our dirt floor, and demanded to be petted. She ate our table scraps and slept beside the bed, guarding us, I hoped, from the rat. I was discovering something about myself I hadn't known in the years I was climbing out the window of my mother's basement apartment – that I am, at heart, a homebody.

We could have seen more of the area with Jim and Marilyn, who invited us to join them for alligator boat cruises and picnics on remote islands. We wanted to be friendly – I hoped, in fact, that I'd become a regular at Antonio's, that I'd learn the geography and something of the culture – but their invocations to "party hearty" bordered on bullying. I think they finally gave up on us after we gagged up their prize peyote onto their white vinyl kitchen floor – "You two better stick to milk and cookies," Jim laughed. Dozens of their friends from Tahoe came and went, the courtyard pulsing with the music of Jimmy Buffet, Men at Work, and UB40, and we began to feel that even in exile, we were in exile.

The Iguana Brothers, we decided, were stalking us. El Gecko, in line behind us at the telegraph office, announced that he was waiting for money too: a business loan from one of his "financiers." When he heard me tell Ethan that I was going to fast to cut my expenses he decided to let us in on "another little secret" that kept down his "overhead."

"It's something I picked up in the military. The food was so bad I couldn't stand it, but I found a way to go for weeks just eating one meal a day."

"Yes?" I asked. Ethan thought by being polite I was leading El Gecko on, and we would fight over this later.

"I don't go to the bathroom."

In other words, El Gecko was, by design, full of shit.

"You'd be amazed at the discipline I developed in the army," he added, giving me the once-over, implying, perhaps, that he could delay the outflow of other bodily functions too, if given the chance.

The Iguana Brothers were at the market when we were at the market, the fried fish stand when we were at the fried fish stand, the highway in their pickup when we were huffing it on foot. At least we were safe inside our hut. But then one afternoon in late March, something terrible happened. The Iguana Brothers penetrated the courtyard.

We were naked, in bed, when we heard a loud knock at the door. We thought it was our new next-door neighbors, a hippie couple from Spokane who often dropped in to borrow rice or offer us something tasty they had fried up on the hotplate. Usually if we didn't answer right away, they got the hint, and once, as a joke, they cranked up their boom box with some mood music for us. The knocking persisted. Finally Ethan wrapped himself in a towel and swung the door open with undisguised irritation. El Gecko entered, taking in with a glance our disheveled bed and me in it, bare shoulders above the sheet, and plopped himself right next to me, pulling at the mosquito net with his weight. He didn't explain his presence; whether he was there to rape me, or just wanted a chat. I told him with the fake courtesy that had become my San Blas persona that I was sick, and "not to be rude" but I'd feel guilty if I vomited on his khakis. Ethan told me later that the whole time of this encounter he was scanning the room for a makeshift weapon. We would fight over this incident too.

To our horror, the Iguana Brothers had become our neighbors.

What happened was this: Chris, fed up with his buddies' insults, had jumped ship. One night while El Gecko and Snake Man were out, he took off with the truck and the large tent the three of them shared. Now the two remaining Iguana Brothers had to sleep in the small pup tent that housed their critters. Still trying to minimize their overhead, they tried this for a few nights, and I must admit I took some delight in imagining the menagerie of reptiles squirming over their sunburned bodies. They had made their bed and now they could lie in it, literally. That's where I would have liked the story to have ended except that Jim, ever the host with the most, encouraged them to sack out at Antonio's in the one remaining hut, if you could call it a hut. This ruin had huge holes in the roof and an abundance of rats, but it was roomier than the tent and gave them something to feed the snakes, who moved sluggishly now, and were dying by the dozen.

Our paradise now reeked of decomposing reptile flesh.

When my money finally came we took a vacation from our vacation, hoping the Iguana Brothers would pack it in while we hid out further south. They did, but not without waiting to say good-bye. The day after we returned we were in Mark's truck on a grocery run with half the courtyard when we saw them hitching on the highway with all their gear. They and their payload were off to the border while they still had some living payload left. Ethan and I sighed as they climbed in. "*Vámanos?* A woman like you could help us get rides," El Gecko whispered to me, looking down my tank top, and I pretended not to see or hear. Every now and then I felt a snake or an iguana behind the cotton rubbing against my leg, but it was a small price to pay for the knowledge that we were finally free of these creeps.

I have no idea how they got across the border, how they got through customs with the quivering white bag. Although it was unlikely that El Gecko retired to Miami before the age of fifty as a millionaire, as was his oft-stated aim, I would not be surprised if he made his mark in some other sleazy enterprise that was in keeping with the spirit of our age.

But Ethan and I would soon be contending with an object lesson of our own – this, about *our* greed.

Someone new moved into the hut made vacant by the Iguana Brothers. He was the only nongringo who ever rented from Antonio in our time there, an itinerant worker who picked grapes and oranges in California in the summer, apples in eastern Washington in the fall, and wintered in his native Mexico. At the moment, he was earning his living whittling broomsticks from the fallen branches of coconut and mango behind our huts and binding the straws together with Dos Equis caps and twine.

The finished products were funky and handsome; they might have sold for thirty bucks in the ethnic-chic stores of San Francisco or Manhattan, and Juan was charging a dollar.

We coveted those brooms, thinking they would make great gifts for our friends and family up north. Ethan, being from a family of ten, was in the habit of buying in bulk. "We'll take a dozen," he told Juan without consulting me (which we would fight about), and without considering how we would carry them and our backpacks in and out of cars and buses in the weeks to come. Juan, delighted, became his own one-man cottage industry. Whistling songs and carving away with his knife from dusk to dawn he had completed the job before we could cut back the order.

When he was finished, Juan offered us a small token of his gratitude. "Para ti," he said to me, his eyes gleaming. In his outstretched hands was a dead iguana that he had cut open, a female. Inside her abdomen were a dozen small eggs, blue and slick. I could see from the way he held the carcass so reverently that the iguana eggs were a delicacy and that this gift was a sign of his high esteem for us. Perhaps we would have gotten to know our neighbor better if I hadn't been so squeamish; my father would have swallowed the raw eggs without hesitation, invited Juan in for shots of bourbon, and written him into his novel, trading on the man's kindness in this way. It was our Last Supper at Campo Antonio, our last chance to bridge the gap with the locals, and we missed it. As acid churned in my stomach, I thanked Juan profusely, then carried the dead iguana inside our hut.

"Deliciosa," Ethan said when we ran into Juan later that evening. He had cooked the eggs up and fed them to the dog, who sucked them down with *mucho gusto*. After weeks of eating our leftover mashed yams, this was undoubtedly the best meal of her life.

I liked thinking that this pregnant iguana had escaped from the Iguana Brothers' gunnysack. Her life may have been cut short but at least she died more or less in the wild. For our part, there was something poetic about this justice, about being offered the spoils of our enemy in the outstretched hands of the one person we thought had a right to live off the bounty of this land. But I know I'm idealizing our neighbor, making him into a kind of noble savage when that's not what I intended at all. The problem is that even without a language barrier there could be no escaping the paradigm that we, the gringos, were the ones buying and he, the native, was selling, which is why he probably looked at us and thought whatever the Spanish is for "payload." If we had to be ugly, more-is-better Americans, I'm glad we helped a nice man pay his bills.

By now the mosquitoes had hatched in the swamp and I was beginning to think longingly of the cool spring days in the Pacific Northwest, the blooming rhododendrons and lilacs and cherry blossoms. And as luck would have it, we did not have to hitch to the border with all the brooms. Mark had to renew his six-month visa and Ethan and I were glad to accept his ride. I have a vague memory of everyone in the courtyard turning out for our departure – Jim and Marilyn and Bill, their visiting friends, Antonio, Juan, but all that I can bring to mind are the tears I shed for the puppy as she ran beside us in the road. I had looked into bringing her with us to Port Townsend but there was no way to do it legally. It had been cruel to let her depend on us, and now I had yet another thing to chastise myself about.

I was afraid that when I looked back to my time at Antonio's I would not remember the ocean and all the beauty, but only the Iguana Brothers' invasion, my quarrels with Ethan, and my worries about money, which only magnified my ongoing quarrel with America. I had no idea how I'd repay my debt to John on three dollars an hour, and all I had to show for the trip was the journal and the two Cleveland stories, which could have been written anywhere. I didn't have a realistic understanding yet of how long it takes to write two publishable stories, so I felt like a failure. Ethan felt like a failure too. He blamed me and the brain-frying Mexican sun for keeping him as confused about his life mission as ever. In six months I would turn twenty-seven. How long could I live in this day-to-day way? I was sick to death of the present tense.

We drove through the Sierra Madre Mountains in silence, staring out at desolate buttes and dry hamlets where grandmothers sold warm Fanta and children sold peso-packets of Chiclets gum and mangoes on a stick. Outside, it was one hundred degrees. Mark put on the air conditioning and kept the window closed but at the end of each day our skin was caked with dust. It got into our underwear and in between our toes – emblematic, I would ponder later, about how the outside always gets in, no matter how isolated you are, and reminding me how I was, in the most elemental way, dusty and dry myself.

America did not exactly welcome us back. The customs agents at the border went to town on us. They strip-searched us, examining every dust-coated orifice for drugs. They tore apart our dusty backpacks, questioning us about everything: the useless typewriter, Ethan's film cases, even his contact solution. My gummed up herbal remedies for diarrhea were a project for the sniff dogs while agents pulled apart every inch of Mark's car. I worried that he might be carrying some pot on him since people were so loose about such things at Antonio's but, thankfully, his car was clean.

Several hours later, when customs finally let us go, I asked what it was about us that aroused their suspicion. Ethan was still as well-scrubbed as a matinee idol, our plumbing situation notwithstanding, and I had braided my long hair and put on my favorite embroidered sundress. Mark had short hair and glasses and was wearing a clean white shirt and khakis. I'd assumed the three of us would breeze through.

"The brooms," the man told us. I laughed. Did he think we were part of some witch's coven?

"No, it's just that they're made from tropical woods. Everyone knows you're not allowed to bring them in. We figured you were using them as a decoy for something worse." I half hoped he would confiscate them and lighten our load, but I guess he felt guilty for giving us a hard time. We were stuck with them and, for the time being, with each other, and this slapstick would continue.

The three of us were replaying our ordeal with hilarity at the Holiday Inn bar in Nogales when Mark made a startling admission. For the last several years, he said, lowering his voice to a near whisper, he had made his living smuggling sacred Huichol artifacts into the States. It was a very lucrative business. He'd intended to bring his latest acquisitions on this particular border crossing, and he had already packed them in his duffel bag and put them in the car when he suddenly changed his mind. He took them back in the house while we were arranging our brooms and we were so preoccupied we never noticed.

In other words, Mark was also an Iguana Brother, another insider trader, another modern-day conquistador out to haul away everything that wasn't nailed to the ground. The only difference between him and El Gecko was that he was good at it.

"And you were going to smuggle this stuff with *us* in the car with you?" Ethan said. I was afraid they would argue, and I was too tired to contend with more friction. I just wanted to finish my drink and go to sleep.

"You guys were going to be my cover," he said. "I was wondering if they were starting to get suspicious of me and I thought the two of you, with your sweet and innocent faces, would get my loot through."

"Sweet and innocent?" I don't need to go into how I fancied myself quite the world-weary traveler by now, and a bit of a sexpot, or how I had also believed that Mark was just a nice, generous neighbor with no ulterior motives when he insisted on paying our hotel and dinner bills.

"Oh my word," Mark said. "Didn't you know? Everyone in the courtyard called you John Denver and Rebecca of Sunnybrook Farm!"

I realized then why Mark felt he could share his secret with us. He knew what I had only just admitted to myself, that our time at Antonio's had been the kind of adventure neither of us had it in us to repeat; he knew he would never see us again.

There was a lot more that we had failed to notice, and Mark decided it was time to fill us in. About the man who ran the fried fish stand with his daughter, how he had been raping this girl since she was barely old enough to walk, and was now forcing her, at seventeen, to bring up their baby and live with him as his second wife. About how the *federales*, who visited Mark late at night after they drank shots with Antonio, got a cut from his smuggling business and provided him with the names of crooked archeologists.

"Since you're telling us everything, what really happened to Antonio's arm?" Ethan asked. We'd heard other rumors that put our landlord in bloody, fight-to-the-death barroom brawls.

I don't remember what Mark said. It's possible that I excused myself from the table and went to bed, that's how uninterested I was. I have never liked hearing stories about drunken stupidity and male aggression. I thought back to a night early in our residency when Antonio invited us over to watch *The Dukes of Hazzard* with him: the highest honor to be bestowed on a Campo Antonio resident. He hooted and slapped his stump against his knee at every car chase while we sat motionless and mystified. Neither of us had ever seen this show in America. We had no idea who the characters were, but I guess we weren't supposed to care. What stayed with me was the feeling of bewilderment, like we'd heard a punch line, but missed the joke.

There had been a whole life around us, as corrupt, Dionysian, fecund, and dark as any writer could ask for, and I had tuned it out as though it were just another dubbed episode of *The Dukes of Hazzard*. Tennessee Williams and Malcolm Lowry and my father had written their Mexican courtyards into their work, but I had seen ours as one big distraction.

So how *does* a writer remain engaged in and still critical of the current time and place? I had set out on my journey believing I could and should escape the phallic culture of Ronald Reagan and Rambo and Donald

Trump by locking myself away in a hut in a landscape where life could be stripped down to the elemental: food, water, sex, bug repellant. To avoid the predators on both sides of the border, I had chosen to live with blinders. Rebecca of Sunnybrook Farm wasn't off the mark. As George Orwell wrote in an essay about Henry Miller, "Inside the Whale," "Exile is probably more damaging to a novelist than to a painter or even a poet, because its effect is to take him out of contact with working life and narrow down his range to the street, the café, the church, the brothel and the studio." My range, as a woman, was much narrower than that.

And I also had to acknowledge that I was an Iguana Sister myself, wintering on a beach where children served shrimp because it was the one place I could *almost* afford another sabbatical. What's more, the mindless hedonism I had detested in Jim and Marilyn looked a lot like mine on the surface, only with fewer books and more libations.

But exile comes with a cost, even if you're going for it on the cheap. If you are only looking for some R&R, the naïve outsider's oblivion may be soothing, but as a writer who hopes to make accurate observations about the world she lives in and her place in it, this kind of isolation is not – and I choose the following word thoughtfully – profitable. And if you're not careful, all that you've kept remote and foreign will rise up like a snake escaping from a gunnysack and strike you in the back.

## BOOK III
# Mourning in America, 1984–1987

Most of the material that you were dealing with had no connection with anything in the real world, not even the kind of connection that is contained in a direct lie.

George Orwell, *1984*

[Reagan] is the ideal past, the successful present, the hopeful future all in one. He is convincing because he has "been there" – been almost everywhere in our modern American culture – yet he "has no past" in the sinister sense. He is guilelessly guiltless. If, to recognize that miracle, one must reject historical record for historical fantasy, fact for parable, it is a small price to pay. . . . Indeed, he has made pretending the easiest thing to do.

Garry Wills, *Reagan's America: Innocents at Home*

In the eighties the symbiosis between Reagan and television raised new questions. Was it possible the predominant values of success, winning, fame, and fortune that television transmitted into American homes had begun to manifest themselves in the character of the country? Were Americans becoming what they saw? . . . Did their repeated exposure to fictional happy endings create an appetite for more of them in real life and make it more difficult for them to face life's realities?

Haynes Johnson, *Sleepwalking through History*

# 12

# Postcards from the Campaign Trail

### HIGH FLYING IN TINSEL TOWN

Ethan and I, weighed down by dusty backpacks, clutch the handcrafted brooms we've schlepped on the bus from the border. Me: deep tan, peasant skirt and purple tank, unshaved legs and armpits, sun-bleached braids; Ethan: purple shorts and Quaker camp T-shirt, hair slicked back with sweat. We haven't bathed in three days. We wait for John at his law office: cobalt blue carpet, brass doorknobs, flowering fig trees, a receptionist with pearl-pink nails.

Enter John: double-breasted blue. "Look what my friend and her boyfriend flew in on!" he laughs, twirling our gift to him like a baton. All the secretaries and attorneys turn to stare.

John is "out" in this office so he can act as he pleases. At twenty-six, he is vice president of the local ACLU and soon-to-be mayor of West Hollywood, a city he helped incorporate. He's a local hero for his work on rent control. I'm so proud of him I could hop on that broom and do a lap above his head. But I'm ashamed that I have no means to repay my debt to him, and that I stink.

Ethan has warned me that the woman he belongs with sees every glass as half-full.

Ronald Reagan is running his reelection campaign with the question: "Do you feel better off than you were four years ago?"

### CALIFORNIA DREAMING

Ethan and I make popcorn in his brother's Orange County kitchen. Enter Jim, the brother, and Monica, Jim's girlfriend. They are excited about a movie they just saw about a man who falls in love with a mermaid, elated also that one of Jim's clients gave them tickets to watch Mary Decker go for the gold. Los Angeles is hosting the Summer Olympics and people are pumped with a patriotism that reminds me of high school pep rallies. Everyone's suddenly a jock. Last year I ran the 7.5-mile Rhody Run in Port Townsend, but Monica and Jim are in training for a marathon.

Monica: tall and movie-star stunning, long, slim legs, coffee-colored skin, an infectious smile. She's twenty-six, like Ethan, me, John, and Mary Decker. Jim is nine years older, with Ethan's same caterpillar eyebrows and surface friendliness. Monica answers the phones in Jim's real estate office while she studies to get her broker's license. They met at a Scientology meeting. The words *advancement, self-help,* and *getting clear* pepper their speech; *can't* is a big no-no. Monica tells us how she grew up poor in Oakland, her father a janitor, her mother a maid.

Monica suggests we do affirmations to coax along the future lives of our dreams. The future has been a sore subject for Ethan and me.

"I want my prosperity to grow in tandem with my expanding consciousness," says Jim. He really says this.

"I want to be a spiritual healer and live close to the land," Ethan says.

"I just want to write and publish my books," I say. "And get a good teaching job."

When it's her turn, I'm shocked by Monica's reply, then surprised at my own reaction: "I'm going to live in the biggest mansion in Beverly Hills," she says in the kind of voice Ethan reserves for his lofty truisms about why everyone should compost. "And have lots and lots of maids."

I don't miss the hut, but after Mexico, all the gadgets in Jim's vast kitchen, the waste of water, the unused space: they feel obscene. But why do I expect Monica to be less materialistic than her boyfriend? To transcend the need for what she hasn't had?

I want to ask Monica how she'll vote in November, but I'm afraid of her answer. Later I will read that 93 percent of the African American vote went to Mondale, but 60 percent of the under-thirty vote went to the seventy-three-year-old Reagan, and I'll wonder which pull, race or age, earned her allegiance. Our fellow twenty-six-year-olds will be largely to blame for the cuts in social spending that put 25 percent more people on the streets every year of the 1980s, including mentally ill people like my mother, and some out-of-work janitors and maids.


THE ANARCHIST OF GRENADA HILLS

Ethan and I line up behind my Great-Aunt Judith and Great-Uncle Bob at the Hilton's All-You-Can-Eat brunch. Judith: sixty-four, plump and effervescent in a turquoise pant suit, silk scarf patterned with poppies, clip-on turquoise and silver earrings, frosted red hair, lipstick that leaves poppy-colored kisses on her mimosa glass. Bob: slightly younger, thin and circumspect, a scientist. He dotes on Judith, does all the cooking, buys her pottery and tickets to the Caribbean, and I wish Ethan would watch and learn.

"So, whadd'ya think of that Reagan?" Judith asks him as we all dive into the pastry tray.

Ethan votes Democrat and calls himself a witness for peace. He tithes, gives 10 percent of his money to charities like Greenpeace and Habitat for Humanity. He is also caught up in the decade's pressure, modeled by Reagan himself, to be upbeat. In today's epiphany about what he should do next, he suggested we co-edit a newsletter called *The Good News* in which only cheerful, inspiring missives would be printed.

"I'm not a fan," he says quietly, "but maybe he's good at heart."

"I'm still mad at that Hinckley," she says, loud enough to attract attention.

"You mean the guy who tried to assassinate the president?" Ethan asks, the straight guy in her routine. She is playing him like a pro.

"That's him," she says. Around us the good people of Grenada Hills wait beneath fake ferns to select prune Danish or apricot. All eyes are on Great-Aunt Judith and she is milking the moment for all it's worth.

She smiles, leads us to our table. "I CAN'T BELIEVE HE MISSED!!"


THE HIGHWAY TO ARMAGEDDON

Ethan and I get picked up in Santa Rosa by a mild-mannered, born-again evangelist who holds forth on the prophecies from the book of Revelations. He tells us that the "lake of fire" predicted at the end of chapter 20 is nuclear and that he is building a bomb shelter for his future family. He knows he'll be one of the 144,000 souls that will go up with the Rapture, but he has to protect the wife and kids "just in case."

In 1985 when Gorbachev with his wine-colored birthmark becomes the new Russian leader, I will think back to this driver's lecture on the Beast's strange markings, how said Beast is fated to "make war against him that sat on the horse, and against his army." Our driver says Ronald Reagan is supposedly the savior "on the white horse" who is destined to lead us out of the rubble of Babylon. When I hear this, I am tempted to mention the schools, highways, trains, bridges, and public housing buildings turning to rubble under our savior's care.

Ethan tells the driver to keep the faith.

The more affluent the locale, the harder it is to get rides. We wait for hours in pouring rain; even with my wool poncho under my rain parka, I just can't get warm. Northern California is a shock after Mexico and LA.

I am near tears when a woman circles back to pick us up in her Saab. "I don't normally pick up hitchhikers," she explains, "but there was something about you standing there with your long braids falling in your face, so wholesome looking," she says to me, smiling at the rearview mirror, "and your all-American good looks," she says to Ethan, who rides shotgun beside her. "You both have a biblical look." She turns back to me. "Your name isn't Rebecca is it? I'm getting an *R*."

*As in Sunnybrook Farm?* I've *got* to do something about the braids.

Our driver takes us to her apartment so we can have hot baths and a good night's sleep. I am so grateful I can barely speak. She has to go to work, but she trusts us completely and leaves us with keys, a map she sketches to a grocery store, and a whole shelf of tapes "channeled" from the disembodied spirit who directed her to pick us up.

After we recover from the shock of Marin County prices, we repair to the futon in her guest room where we listen to tape after tape, lectures about the soul, about how to transcend anger and fear and how to attract money and abundance. The woman's calm voice sooths us, enchants us with its optimism, and Ethan decides to join this organization. Maybe, he hopes, he can channel too.

I wish I could join him, I really do. I want to sound as content as the woman on the tape. And yet, I can't reconcile the world she abides in with the one that gave us the Holocaust, apartheid, and today's American-trained soldiers raping and murdering peasant families in three Central American countries while we drift to sleep.

THE GREAT WHITE WAY

So what are we, anyway? Magnets for every religious freak in California? Is it the braids? Or has America gotten so violent that only evangelists are brave enough to pick up hitchers? Today's driver is a disciple of Elizabeth Clare Prophet, James and Marilyn's guru, whose members chant "I AM, I AM," like drones to block out the world's darkness. This reminder of the Morten era throws me into a funk.

At a road stop over pie and coffee, our driver reads to us from *The Great White Brotherhood in the Culture and History and Religion of America* the lines that explain why America is great: "America is the land created as a repository of freedom that millions of souls might realize their potential to become one with God. It is the place where freedom of religion, freedom of speech, freedom of the press, and freedom to assemble provide the foundation for the individual pursuit of cosmic consciousness."

"Have you ever asked yourself why it's a great *white* brotherhood?" I say.

"Sweetie," Ethan whispers.


FEELIN' GROOVY AT BIG SUR

Our next driver is agnostic, and I'm relieved to be the recipient of a kindness not inspired by religious fervor. We three camp together at Big Sur, hike through forests, and gape in awe at cathedrals of moss. Ecstatic, I hop over rocks into Ethan's arms and miss, falling into a dense, waxy overgrowth, bloodying a knee.


MORNING IN OLYMPIA

Sara, who worked with Ethan at Quaker camp in Maine, lives with her boyfriend, Jesse, a fellow forestry student. Sara and Jesse: rosy-cheeked, fit, relaxed, friendly, with identical shoulder-length blond ponytails. On the foldout couch in the living room, Ethan and I wake up to the sound of our hosts tickling each other and giggling.

Ethan and I begin each morning continuing the fight we started at bedtime. A tone of voice or facial expression can launch a round of accusations. The issue at hand is the future. One minute Ethan says he loves me and wants to live together, the next he isn't sure. He's afraid that when he finds out what he wants to do with his life, I'll hold him back. And yet, because I'm his best friend, he needs to share with me every passing thought, forgetting that the woman he wants to pick apart with cool dispassion with his buddy is said buddy. When I react with visible hurt and sadness, he gets angry, wanting to disclaim responsibility for causing me pain. When I can be that patient and loving best pal and confidante he wants, he loves me. When we resolve a fight, we have wild make-up sex.

On this morning, still furious, Ethan rolls away. I try to coax him toward me without him touching my legs, where the poison oak rash has started.

The more urgently I reach for him, the more resolutely he turns away.

## THE ITCH YOU CAN'T SCRATCH

Ethan and I wake up on my friend Neal's waterbed in Seattle. I have bronchitis, a high fever, and poison oak. It's in my ears, between my toes, on my face, on every inch of my skin. The Calamine lotion leaves pink smears on Neal's black sheets.

Ethan reads my unhappiness as a rebuke. Convinced I am blaming him for feeling terrible, that I expect him to perform some miraculous healing, and equally convinced that we create our own realities by our thoughts, he says, "You got sick just to see if I would take care of you."

Actually, my friend Neal is taking care of us both. I met him in the ride-share to the Port Townsend writers' conference two years ago. He brings me hot soup, tea, oranges, more Calamine, cough syrup, and novels; he brings Ethan take-out Chinese, cookies, and Tylenol. Ethan has a migraine that no amount of meditation will touch.

I would like to have an out-of-body experience right now, to float above the quarreling couple in the waterbed and out the window to Discovery Park where egrets defend their territory against blue herons. I'd like to fly above this whole planet, above Wall Street tycoons and the people I saw living in Maytag boxes outside Mexican border towns, to the limits of the galaxy where Pluto, the planet of doom and gloom, is wreaking havoc on us all if you are to believe the day's astrologers. Maybe if I could fly off for just a minute I would find compassion for this girl whose skin is covered with pustules, who feels ashamed of the phlegm she spews into a steel bowl.

I wish I were a snake and could shed my own skin.

## THE YOUNG WOMAN WHO LIVED IN A SHOE

Port Townsend at last. Ethan and I repair to my crooked little house with its slanty floors and skewed walls dotted black with seeping moisture. Ethan, with his carpenter's love of right angles, is shocked.

Poor Lizzy, who has been living there all winter, apologizes for the dent she made one night when she got dumped by her boyfriend and hurled the chocolate cake she had just baked for him at the wall.

"Pretty hard cake," I say, fingering the groove.

I knew this house was a dump when I rented it and sublet it to Lizzy, but it was only one hundred dollars a month and I wanted to have a place to come back to. At the time I thought I would want to live in Port Townsend forever. But rents doubled in town after the realtors from California arrived, and I had to make do. "This house can be pretty depressing," Lizzy warns me, and for the first time I notice that even Lizzy's cologne and the rhododendrons shedding petals outside cannot camouflage the smell of mold.

## INDEPENDENCE DAY

Ethan and I enter the blue-and-white Victorian by the Bell Tower, one of the prettiest houses in town. We're here to celebrate the Fourth with Salal Café coworkers, poets, boat builders, peace workers from Ground Zero, and journalists, many of whom are doing amnesty work in Central America. We stand near the guacamole bowl on the widow's walk overlooking Water Street and the red sandstone Victorian office buildings, the Strait of Juan de Fuca, the wooden boats floating past, the hint of islands. I lived in this house before I left town. I loved it so much I set a story here. I'm glad to be back, but I'm a little worried about Ethan fitting in. Most of my friends at the Salal have given Ethan the thumbs up – "I like your import," Cindy said – but Bill took me aside and whispered, "Does that guy ever stop smiling?" The host of the party is a brilliant Harvard grad with a scathing sense of humor and a melancholy that his daily ninety-minute jogs cannot cure. Ethan has never heard of Carolyn Forché.

"Don't look at me like that," Ethan whispers.

"Like what?"

"Like you're insecure and you want me to reassure you at this party."

Now this is a bizarre thing for someone to say at a gathering where he is the stranger. I walk away and for the first time it occurs to me that perhaps I'm reacting to *him*, to his instability and the crazy-making nature of his projections. I've been blaming our problems on childhood baggage, global unrest, and the stars.

## MY MOON IS STILL IN CLEVELAND

Which is why I made this appointment with David Pond to get an update on my astrology chart. I want an explanation for why I shift from sorrow to joy to panic in reaction to Ethan's changing moods. Yesterday Ethan gave me an ultimatum – we move to California or Boston, or we break up. But the relationship isn't my only problem. I feel raw, troubled; it's like the anguish of our times, of this violent age, is moving through me. I've lost my protective outer coating. My ozone layer has been shot full of holes. Yesterday, after I talked to my sister about the orphaned Guatemalan children she teaches art to, I sobbed for hours. Whenever I see a homeless person I think that it could be my mother. David explains that Pluto and my progressed moon are doing something to my twelfth house, bringing intense emotions and identification with the underdog. Plus a configuration with Uranus and Saturn has put my "security in the hands of the demolition crew," making me feel out of control. This is not a good state of affairs for the daughter of a mad woman.

David explains the central lesson of my emotional life: "The paradox for you is that you will never get what you need directly from someone else. You have to reach inside and nurture yourself. You never got to play the little girl and never will. But if you focus as though you already have what you need, you'll get what you need."

I am astounded at how easily I can pull this off if I fake it. When I pretend to feel cheerful and loving, Ethan rubs my feet.

But years later, I will view the astrologer's advice through a gendered lens, thinking of all the women who have spiritualized their pain and anger to make nice.

In screwball comedies, when Katherine Hepburn throws a tantrum, Cary Grant or Spencer Tracy always tells her she looks beautiful when she's angry. I know that's a patronizing line, meant to belittle her fury so as to contain it, but I would have liked to have had it said to me once, just once.


WHO'S NUMBER ONE AT TABLE FIVE?

I need two full-time gigs to get the money to move to Boston, so my friend Jacqueline puts in a good word for me at Lanza's, the new Italian place where she works. After happy hour people come in from the Uptown Tavern next door where the TV blares the Olympics day and night. The buzz tonight is how Mary Decker got tripped "by some bitch named Zola" and deprived of her big moment. I will read later how the crowd "booed lustily."

"We're number one!" the Americans shout. Yes indeed. In 1984, we are more in debt than ever. We lead the West in infant mortality, violent crime, percentage of the population in prison, and contribution to greenhouse gases. Plus the gap between rich and poor is the highest it's been in forty years.

Tonight my number one concern is whether or not I'll be fired. I lied and said I had experience serving wine, and even though Jacqueline and I practiced with a bottle of Chilean red yesterday, I am so nervous that I go to the people I'm serving, set the bottle of Chianti right on the table, and completely demolish the cork.

"You fuck up a good bottle of wine and you bought it," the owner tells me, so furious he is shaking.

This is the memory I'll always return to as the moment shitty day jobs got old.


BORDERS

Tomorrow I turn twenty-seven. I have been asleep or have feigned sleep on this bus for the last three days, rousing myself only for meal stops, and sometimes not even then. I have absorbed the smells of the other passengers: their cigarettes, sweat, liquor, fried food, and the sour odor of their collective sorrows.

Before I left, I sold my stereo, my kitchen utensils, and my futon. I mailed my books and winter coat to Ethan, and stuffed all my other worldly goods inside my blue Kelty backpack, the same pack that got me across the country in 1979, through Mexico, and up Highway 101 to Port Townsend again. Before I left Seattle, I visited Joe. He told me how he once took the bus cross-country and met every kind of vagabond, petty criminal, drunk, druggie, and sad sack known to the Western World. "People who ride the Hound shouldn't be allowed off," he said, trying to cheer me up with his special brand of humor.

A long Greyhound journey is a descent into the man-made arteries of America. For travelers from abroad, students with backpacks, it can be a celebration of the vastness that is North America. For Americans without money, it is a flight from one place of disappointment to the next. The tattooed man out on bail traveling six states to see his estranged daughter smells like he bathed in whiskey; the young woman with the black eye keeps her head low at rest stops, hoping her boyfriend hasn't picked up her trail. With each mile I shrink lower in my seat myself, hoping no one will tell me another heartbreaking story.

I see my flight from coast to coast like this: I went to the West to mend, discover Nature, find a voice as a writer, and grow a soul. Now that I've OD'd on soul-speak, I'm going East to come to terms with the material world. I guess I've always been a type A-minus person, but was only pretending not to be.

Ethan would have preferred Marin County, where he could hook up with the channelers, but I told him that if I hear one more simplistic, apolitical New Age platitude I'm going to hurt someone.

Have *I* become the kind of person who shouldn't be allowed off the bus?


PEEPING SEASON

Ethan and I have a fight the day I arrive: what did I expect? Although I'm happy to be on a fall foliage jaunt to a gorge where the trees are aflame with red and yellow, he places the record albums I bought for our apartment on the windshield of the truck where they melt in the sun. He doesn't even go through the charade of offering to replace them so I can say "Don't worry, honey, that's all right."

The next morning he goes to a Quaker service, his new Sunday ritual. While he is gone, I read his journal. He mentions a woman he has met at this church and writes: "She wore her hair pulled back neatly in a bun today and I gasped, she looked so beautiful."

I've ditched the braids and my thick, hip-length hair is wavier than ever. No amount of bobby pins and hairspray would contain this mane in a bun.

When we fight that night, no matter how much I apologize for reading the journal, he will not forgive me for this "psychological rape" even though he left the book open on my side of the bed.


OFFICE COUP

I am on a tour of Biotechnica International, a genetic engineering firm a fifteen-minute walk from our apartment in North Cambridge. I just got hired as a secretary in the marketing division. My job will be to type letters, reports, and create overhead transparencies with diagrams of what "Bacillus subtilis, Streptomyces, and Escherichia coli" and certain strains of yeast can do to improve industrial products like sweeteners, pesticides, antibiotics, animal health products, chemicals, and whiskey.

I keep thinking of that scene in *Sleeper* when they clone a man's nose and I have to cough to keep from laughing.

My salary is eighteen thousand dollars a year: four times what I made in Port Townsend. I have lived for so long among organic farmers and artisans and poets and science-illiterate mystics that I feel like Rip Van Winkle waking up after twenty years. I've never even seen a fax machine.

My coworkers and bosses seem to like this eccentric transplant. They let me leave early on Tuesdays and Thursdays to teach aerobics at the Y – my new sideline – and I can type my short stories on the word processor and use the phone to track grad school applications, as long as I let them read my stuff. They are okay with the fact that I'm just passing through. It is no secret that I don't fit into the business world.

The other secretary in marketing is Deb, a gal with lacquered platinum hair and a thick Malden accent. We are four days apart in age. After she trains me on the Wang, I train her to give back rubs, and we swap them every afternoon. Her boyfriend, Dominick, who calls six times a day, teases us and calls us "lezzies."

Deb tells me it's time to think about shaving my legs. She takes me to T. J. Maxx for pantyhose and pumps and suits with giant shoulder pads.

The first time I type a memo, I refer to our CEO as the Chief *Executing* Officer – with no intended irony. This becomes the big joke in the office. When the various vice presidents pass my desk, they throw their hands in front of their hearts and fall to the floor as though they've just been gunned down by a firing squad.

THE BAG LADY OF HARVARD SQUARE

I have just gone shopping for cookware with my first paycheck. Ethan has given me two weeks' notice, as though living with me were a job. I have two weeks to stock myself with the essentials before he takes his things. He himself is already gone.

I am still uncomfortable with crowds, traffic, noise, and the dizzying sight of too many stores. I may be an East Coast person now, but my inner landscape is still one of Pacific beaches, madrona trees, rhododendrons, and egrets. Before I can board my bus, my heart starts beating so hard and fast I think I'm having a heart attack. I haul my pots into a phone booth and look up "Massage" under the yellow pages. Maybe if there's a massage therapist on this street who can see me, I might get calm enough to go home. I don't know how I'll make it otherwise.

Eight answering-machine messages later, I practice the breathing I learned as Vicki's birth coach so I can leave the phone booth. After an hour on a park bench, where I get mistaken for a homeless woman and urged by a cop to move along, I head out. I want to say, *Yo, Pig Man, do homeless women buy Paul Revere?* Later, a friend tells me I had all the symptoms of a full-fledged panic attack. I did not know such a thing existed.

At home a care package from Claudia is waiting for me. There are photos of us together in Seattle, a smiley creature she crafted out of clay with Day-Glo acrylic paint to cheer me up, a magic grow-frog, and a montage of medieval angels crafted into a card. Her note reminds me that she grew up in "chilly old Bean Town," and that I should call her for survival tips.

On the phone, we revisit Ronald Reagan's patriotic, retrospective "Morning in America" reelection campaign: its rosy recap of the last four years interspersed with clips from the Olympics, the crowds shouting "USA!" like it was staged as one big infomercial for America, Land of the Winners. "It was surreal," I say. "I'm glad Ethan took his stupid TV. I tried to watch one of the debates but I couldn't take it." Reagan was showing the signs of undiagnosed Alzheimer's disease when he squared off with Walter Mondale, but America let him win anyway because he still looked good on TV.

Claudia is appalled that I can see the reelection from any kind of remove. "When I found out he won in forty-nine states I just cried and cried knowing we live in such a dysfunctional country."

Although 55 million people voted for Reagan last week, 76 million eligible voters didn't vote at all. Including me. I forgot. Being in a bad relationship kind of saps the old civic energy, I guess. Maybe the other 75,999,999 Americans were in bad relationships too?


GO FOR THE GOLD

It's a snowy December noon and I just bombed the GRE. Instead of studying, boning up on how to compute the area of a circle, I have been recovering from you-know-who, who made up with me at Thanksgiving just long enough for the lateness of my period to send me into a tizzy. Now he's gone again. So here I am with fifteen minutes to spare until the literature exam, trying not to resent the college kids in ski jackets on the pay phone calling friends and doting parents for rides while I, the

Number One Idiot of the Western World, phone my doctor to find out the results of the kind of test that doesn't get you into graduate school.

Self-pity would be a crime right now: I *chose* to ditch the pill for condoms again; I *chose* to travel three thousand miles on the Hound to be with a guy who has never read Shakespeare or history and uses peppy slogans to cover up his fear of . . . what exactly? Depending on his mood, he's told me that I'm too deep/intellectual/negative/emotional/intense. Ethan's right about one thing: I haven't exactly been a barrel of laughs. But why does it seem like the whole culture is regressing back to high school when the popular kids were good-looking athletes, upbeat and dim? I always thought the reward for growing up was that the smart people finally got to be in charge.

Even the doctor's good news on the phone won't help me now. I have forgotten the difference between negative capability and the pathetic fallacy.

### YMCA!

Here I am in the big gym, teaching aerobics with a concussion. I was leaving Biotechnica for the Y when I fell on the ice, hit my head hard enough to black out, and had to wobble onto the bus seeing double. Now the room is a blur of Lycra, my timing is off, and I want to puke. After class, I will. Still, the show must go on. It would be unprofessional to cancel on short notice.

I wonder how I'll write about all this someday: *1984, The Year of Hard Knocks.* It's like I've been hazed into a club, the eastern chapter of the Tough Broads Association. Years later, when I am a professor and my students want extensions on papers because they are too upset about this or that, I will grant them the time but think privately that they *could* get a grip if they *had* to, if their survival depended on it. This year's turmoil has given me more compassion for the people who travel on Greyhound, but has also made me a little fiercer about everyone else.

Afterward I cab it to the emergency room for X-rays, thankful that I have health insurance. But then I hear the bad news: after a concussion, to avoid the possibility of falling into a coma I'll need to find someone to stay awake with me, to keep me talking. The trouble is, who can I impose on? I have only lived in Boston six weeks. So, like a fool, I phone Ethan, figuring I've lost a lot of sleep over him so he should return the favor. "Can you come over?" I say. "Or just talk on the phone?"

Ethan thinks I've made up the head injury as a ploy.

I call my friends on the West Coast. John, who is always up late, takes the last shift. He's disappointed about the breakup with Ethan. "He *was* a hunk," he says ruefully, but then he reminds me that every time I started dating a new guy in high school I said, "He's the one."

If Ethan were a character in one of the stories I write, the scientists and secretaries at work who read my fiction would ask, *Why is this girl wasting time with such an asshole?* America hates victims, and that's why I forced myself to lead aerobics grinning like I did when I performed can-cans at the high school pep rallies on mornings after my mother kept me up all night to make me confess that I was a call girl working for the Mafia.

Ethan's cruelty is therapeutic. It releases me from moping and returns me, for better or for worse, to myself. I start to read the newspaper again, and to make friends at work. I will never call Ethan again, although a year later, when I'm in grad school, he'll phone me to report that he and his girlfriend, the Quaker gal with the bun, are headed to California to become healers and live close to the land.


WHITE RAGE IN THE BIG APPLE

I refuse to let 1984 end with me in bed with a messed up head, bitter about some guy; I'm determined to write myself into an upbeat American success narrative. So a day later I get myself on Amtrak to see my college friends in New York. I stay at Cindy and Dawn's new apartment on the Upper West Side and we whoop it up at a friend of a friend's New Year's Eve party. My head still hurts but I dance and make merry. It seems like the right thing to do.

The big talk this evening is Bernard Getz, that white guy on the subway who got so enraged at the black kids who hassled him that he tried to take them all out at once with his handgun. We all argue and I'm one of the only people who thinks what Getz did was utterly wrong and unjustified. The assembled think that I'd know better if I got mugged. Apparently I'm *still* Rebecca of Sunnybrook Farm.

Everyone at the party is my age, twenty-seven.

This conversation shocks me. Is this how the well-educated people of my generation are going to read the growing divisions in our nation? By *attacking* the symptoms, literally, and refusing to think the root causes of inequality and crime have anything to do with us? I'm tempted to leave and go to bed.

But hey, it's New Year's Eve and my favorite Talking Heads song is playing: "Burning Down the House." There's a cute guy in the corner coming over to dance. It's not quite midnight, and if I squint beneath the strobe light, my champagne glass looks half-full.

# 13

# Girls Having Fun

Such a life required much exaggerated self-esteem. It engaged gross quantities of hope and despair and set them wildly side by side, like a Third World country of the heart.

Lorrie Moore, "Agnes of Iowa"

### KISS AND TELL

I didn't watch Krystal Carrington kiss Rock Hudson on the mouth on *Dynasty*, but after he died of AIDS I began to wish I could unkiss some of the places my lips had been. Hudson's death in 1985 inspired his old pal, Ronald Reagan, to get some basic information about the disease more than five years after AIDS had been identified and thousands of Americans had been infected. "I have always thought the world might end in a flash," he said to his former doctor, Brigadier General John Hutton, "but this sounds like it's worse."

I called John in California and asked about his health. An old friend of ours from the dorm was dying, and half his volleyball team was sick. "I'm like a virgin," he said, humming a certain song. "You should be too."

"You've been talking to my mother," I said.

Now that my mother was back in my life, AIDS had moved to the top of the list of disasters waiting to befall me, higher even than getting struck by lightning, run over by a car/truck/bus, swept away in a hurricane, electrocuted by a toaster, murdered by a new Boston Strangler, or hit in the head by a random flying object – an icicle, baseball, meteor, or grand piano. I grew weary of the subject, partly because the disease scared me too, but also because I resented the way the words "promiscuous" and "single women" and "high risk" were being yoked together in public discourse, reifying old rules. It's not like I wanted to have orgies with bisexual IV-drug users; in fact, as a correction to the Ethan debacle, I'd sworn off dating until grad school. But my New Year's Eve resolution had been to lighten up, to dare to eat a peach. I was now a girl who just wanted to have fun.

At lunch over spinach-ricotta-stuffed calzones, or salads when we were "good," the other secretaries and I conferred on shoes, bad boyfriends, and our weight. Our bosses were making history, creating the first genetically engineered potatoes and sludge-eating microbes, but I sought another body of knowledge.

Deb was my chief mentor in all matters girly. When she wasn't fighting on the phone with Dominick, or flipping through the pages of *Bride*, she offered fashion tips and hair-care advice. Nancy, the vice president's assistant, would visit us in marketing for our modeling shows. We'd sashay past the computer consoles in new dresses and suits from Filene's Basement and T. J. Maxx, and she'd clap. "You look mah-va-lous!" she'd drawl, imitating Billy Crystal on *Saturday Night Live*.

Nancy was from Maine, as was Ann, her partner in crime in the executive suite. Like Deb and me they were both twenty-seven, smart, well paid, and underutilized. When their bosses were away, the duo would summon us to a conference room where one of them had staged her death: Ann, prone across the gleaming conference table, a rubber knife sticking out of her power blazer; Nancy, strangled by her pantyhose.

When Ann quit her job to help her husband organize the first Live Aid concert, we thought we'd be bored without her. But Deb got Ann's job, and Deb was replaced by a long-term temp named Ellen. Ellen was the most fun depressed person I'd ever met.

Ellen dragged herself in, wretched and hungover from all-night clubbing, her eyes hidden behind black Ray Bans. It took me days to really see her, to notice her beauty and breeding – her thick, shoulder-length hair flickering gold under fluorescent light, those good bones and perfect teeth, the boarding-school diction. After graduating from Wellesley, Ellen had worked in advertising until she was "downsized," an expression I picked up from her. She had a headhunter on the case and résumés at every ad agency, but for now she was slumming with us. Fellow English majors, we peppered our personal narratives with allusions to William Blake and Virginia Woolf. Both of us were merely posing as secretaries, impersonating helpful young women as yet another challenge on the road to the Better Elsewhere. SPIES IN THE HOUSE OF GIRL, I typed into her computer one day.

It took a month for Ellen to tell me what was haunting her. She and her girlfriend – the woman she'd left her husband for – had been raped at knifepoint that fall, by a neighbor who'd been watching them make love through his window. Then she and the girlfriend, whom she'd known since college, broke up. The expression "post-traumatic stress" doesn't communicate the abandon with which Ellen was trying to drink and dance away these memories.

Wendy, a cheerful Californian who worked downstairs in the lab, was the only married gal in our quintet. Her husband, Todd, headed up the kitchen in one of Boston's major teaching hospitals. At lunch in the cafeteria, whenever Wendy opened a thermos of Todd's homemade minestrone, I asked the nearest geneticist to clone an identical husband for me. Hope, circa 1985, was scented with bay leaves and garlic, with white beans and ziti floating along like little lifeboats.

On Fridays our five convened at fern-strewn Back Bay bars to drink peach daiquiris and sing along to the Pointer Sisters, "Voulez-vous couchez avec moi, ce soir?" One night we thrashed around on rum punch to the Pretenders. Deb broke up with Dominick on the phone, and somehow, Ellen and Wendy ended up making out. In the morning Wendy wasn't sure what had happened and asked me to report what I'd seen – Ellen putting her hand down Wendy's blouse as though she were reaching in a pocket for a theater ticket.

Weeks passed in a calm disorder like a sleep-tousled sheet. Ash Wednesday came and went and although I wasn't Catholic, I gave up fear and insecurity for Lent.

BULBOUS SPRING

Getting accepted to graduate school puffed me up with so much hubris that I did the unthinkable – I invited my mother to visit. For Mother's Day, no less.

Spring in New England is a glandular thing, full of bulbs and roving pollens and the color pink. I treated us to lobster and strawberry daiquiris, which my mother inhaled like an anteater. We marched the Freedom Trail arm in arm, marveling at seventeenth-century gravestones beside historic churches, whiffing up the salt of the harbor. We saw movies at the Brattle Street Theatre, browsed the poetry at Grolier's, and strolled through Harvard Yard, wondering what important ideas might be fermenting there.

I wanted to believe my mother was cured. She did not rifle through my journals and letters, did not ask me in public if I was menstruating regularly, and I did not have to call 911. Not for a minute did I sink into the deep, inconsolable despair I was habitually sucked into at the sight of her. The optimism in my voice never felt false.

Cheery optimism, of course, was being modeled from the top down. That May, the fortieth anniversary of the end of World War II, Reagan refused an invitation to visit Dachau and opted, instead, for the Bitburg cemetery where forty-nine SS soldiers were buried. Finally forced to give a speech in Bergen-Belsen, he spoke of "hope" emerging "out of the ashes." The leader of the Western World would only walk on the sunny side of the street.

Then one day when we were on the sunny side of a street near my apartment, I was struck hard by a random flying object. We were having a good time, not even in the ballpark of our usual conversations about nuclear holocaust, the camps, the Boston Strangler, and the odds (one in twenty-five thousand) of dying in a plane crash, when a baseball hit me in the leg. We'd been so busy getting along that we hadn't noticed we were near a playing field where some middle-aged men were enjoying an after-work game. One of them got me ice from the corner store and I limped home. When I woke up my shin had swollen up like a third knee.

My mother didn't say, "I told you so," but I wondered what odds I had defied to validate her worldview. Was this little mishap a reminder that what goes up must come down? Self-doubt, faith's doppelgänger, moved into my head like an uninvited relative. I tried to keep her in the cordoned-off room where I store old family photo albums and the ghosts of ex-boyfriends, but now and then, as the year advanced, she escaped.

It was around this time that a study came out proclaiming that a woman past the age of thirty had as much chance of finding a husband as getting struck by a meteor or kidnapped by a terrorist. "You've got less than three years," my mother said. "Bring me some grandchildren."

## HEDONISM'S DOPPELGÄNGER

After my mother left, I got my financial aid package in the mail. Now that I knew exactly how much money I did not have, I put an ad in the *Boston Phoenix* for a housemate. Of the half-dozen people I interviewed, I chose Judy. She was quiet, easygoing, and self-effacing. I was concerned about her girlishness – she was twenty-one and looked fifteen – but I liked her. She had a pale, flat face, gray eyes like chips of flint, and a blond ponytail. She was, by her own report, "low maintenance." "You won't even know I'm here," she said.

It took her half an hour to move in. She owned almost nothing: some silverware with wooden handles, a teapot, and a dozen stuffed animals that she arranged on the bed our landlady lent her. In the bathroom, she installed her Listerine, her Bonnie Belle Ten-o-Six lotion, and her Clearasil, and I felt like I was back in college.

True to her promise, I didn't see much of Judy. I was only home to choreograph my aerobics routines and sleep. I swam at Spy Pond with my girls and danced to Reggae on the grass, indifferent to troubling rumors about AIDS-carrying mosquitoes. There were parties, concerts, fireworks displays, and all-night bouts of Truth or Dare. It was the last summer of fun for our posse. Wendy and I were going back to school; Ellen had gotten herself engaged to a scientist from work; Deb had ditched Dominick for an unctuous young pilot who was in training out in Oklahoma; and Nancy's new beau – an Iranian away on business – was determined to get her cloaked in black before Ramadan. I was putting off the moment when I'd have to reacquaint myself with my brain. I read only one book all summer: Laurie Colwin's *Happy All the Time*.

Judy's life seemed to feature sleep. The only people she saw were Pauline, the airline stewardess she nannied for; Pauline's young daughter; and Pauline's additional summer help, an au pair named Brigitte. Judy was so low maintenance that I sometimes forgot I had a roommate.

Eventually, though, the gloom emanating from her room began to smell. I had to avert my gaze when I passed her door. I remembered a recurring nightmare from childhood when I'd dare myself to look into a scary room – a bathroom, with a shower curtain trembling like something alive, or a parlor that had been boarded up for years – and a malevolent force took shape and chased me outside, over snowdrifts, past police bedecked in riot gear, and bombed-out buildings. The terror would wake me to a bedroom gone strange in shadow.

The bathroom we shared began to frighten me too. Her Listerine presence evoked memories of the cleaning solvents in hospitals: my mother's psych wards. As the summer got hotter and muggier, Judy upped her shower quotient to half a dozen a day. I wondered if she was trying to wash away a traumatic memory, to disinfect her soul. Once, when I was waiting to get into the bathroom, I remembered being led up the stairs of our Cleveland apartment building by my grandfather when I was six, watching while he stopped at each step to wipe off a drop of my mother's blood. "See what your crazy mother did to herself?" he said.

I tried to give her a pep talk once. I told her I thought she'd get out of her "slump" when she went back to Northeastern and finished up her education degree: a plan that was vaguely in the pipeline. "I'm sure you're right," she said, smiling weakly, and that was the end of the conversation.

On the Saturday I moved out, Judy set her alarm so that we could eat our cereal together. We had never shared a meal, and I was touched that she'd made this gesture. I had been out the night before at a clambake where I danced barefoot in the moonlight to steel band music, and even though I was groggy after only four hours' sleep, I could see that Judy was as close to happy as I'd ever seen her. She was packing her few belongings to move to Pauline's; tonight would be her last night in the apartment. "I'm pampering myself," she said. "I've got a bottle of wine, and I'm going to make myself a roast."

She asked me how to turn on the gas oven and I showed her, glad to see she was moving beyond her repertoire of Cornflakes and Campbell's soup. She even gave me a gift, her wood-handled flatware. "I won't need this at Pauline's," she said. I read this generosity as evidence of her renewed faith in the future; wherever she was headed, there was nicer silverware to be had there.

We hugged, and she left to take a bag to Pauline's. I wondered if, years later, I'd even remember her name.

Wendy and Todd arrived with the U-Haul trailer. It was in the mid-nineties and so humid that our hands perspired as we lugged my boxed books and futon downstairs. While we struggled with the futon frame I lost my grip, and we broke the window of the front door. We had to drive to the hardware store to replace the glass.

By now it was lunchtime, so we stopped at the grocery store and I went back into the apartment to rinse the grapes and make sandwiches. The phone rang, startling me. My service was supposed to be cancelled already.

It was Brigitte, Pauline's au pair. Her voice was high and frantic. "Thank God you're there," she said. "Judy's on her way home and you have to wait for her."

In between lapses into French and gasps of sobbing, Brigitte explained how Judy had told her, days earlier, that she planned to kill herself the night I moved out. She would seal the kitchen shut with masking tape and turn on the gas. Then she would take a bottle of sleeping pills and wash it down with a bottle of wine, just in case.

"But Judy seemed happy this morning," I said.

"That's only because she finally has a plan."

I didn't want to believe her. I was moving, I explained; my friends were outside waiting for me; I didn't know what I could do. I asked her why she'd waited this long to tell me.

"I thought Judy was just talking, trying to get attention, but I looked in her backpack today and she had everything: the pills, a bottle of wine, and masking tape. She's really going to do this! I'm so scared!" In between sobs, Brigitte went on to explain how according to Judy's plan, I would be the one to find her body – the roast! – when I came back to clean the place on Monday. "Look in her room if you don't believe me. She left suicide notes."

I ran into Judy's room, opened her underwear drawer, and there they were, beneath some honeysuckle-scented sachets: sympathy cards, white and floral, with people's names written on the envelopes. I opened the one to me. In her neat, girlish hand, she apologized for being a burden and enclosed a poem she'd written about her misery. Black water flowed into stagnant pools, and clouds clogged the sky beside an indifferent moon. Perhaps I was merely in shock, but I felt like I was watching myself read these notes, watching myself decide what to do.

I pondered the odds of the events of the last few hours. What if I hadn't broken the window? What was the likelihood that I'd be there to get Brigitte's call when I was supposed to be long gone and the phone was supposed to be dead? And, it turned out, what were the odds that my landlady, whom I turned to for advice, would be a psychiatric social worker?

Todd and Wendy sat on the porch with me and the landlady waiting, eating grapes. When Judy returned, I followed her upstairs reluctantly to play my part in a script I knew by heart. I felt something finally, a compassion for both of us, jailer and jailed, as I barged in on her in the bathroom to watch her take one last shower, making sure she didn't try to cut herself with the razor. There is no dignity accorded to the person who has stepped across the sanctioned border of mental health. She hadn't finished buttoning her shirt when the police began to lead her away in restraints. "Wait!" I cried. "At least let her look her best." I buttoned her up and put a comb through her wet hair while they held onto her wrists, and a familiar guilt washed through me as she cursed me, telling me she'd never forgive me for interfering. "You have no right!" she shouted again and again, and as she was half-carried to the squad car, thrashing and kicking, the sorrow I'd tried to keep at bay all year bobbed to the surface like a giant beach ball.

As Todd and Wendy and I drove to Northampton in a ragged hallucination of late August heat, I wondered how it could be that on the same night while I had danced barefoot on the beach, Judy was staring at the same moon in a dark room planning a foolproof way to off herself. What did this juxtaposition mean? I thought of saturnine Ellen and perky Wendy kissing. I thought of my mother in her spy-movie trench coat stalking me to the high school stadium while I did can-cans at halftime. I thought of Ronald Reagan avoiding the camps, hiding from reports of sex and germs. I thought of how the simplistic, jingoistic rhetoric of the cold war seemed to perpetuate a bifurcated world of secret doubles and shadowy others, a habit of mind in which someone else was always the repository of what we found unacceptable in ourselves.

But I was en route to a place nicknamed the Happy Valley by the locals and I owed it to my friends to salvage the weekend and have fun. I chalked up my recent obliviousness to a solipsism I could and would cure – something else to add to the home-improvement project that was myself.

### DATING FOR DUMMIES

I stayed high on endorphins all fall. I needed money, so I got myself hired to teach five aerobics classes a week at the Northampton Y. After school, I jogged through cornfields, took naked dips in hidden oxbows of the Connecticut River, and then lay out on a blanket reading James Joyce and writing. I was where I had wanted to be for years and I'd never been so happy.

But sometimes I'd lie awake pondering the year's near misses. What if that baseball had hit me in the head? What if I'd been gone when Brigitte called, and I had been the one to find Judy dead? And what if it was true you could get AIDS from someone's saliva? One night before I moved I'd broken my boy fast with Lawrence, a musician who wrote surrealistic poetry. While we were going at it, he told me about his torrid love affair with a male musician in San Francisco back in the bathhouse era. Was the danger itself an aphrodisiac? Was I attracted to trouble? I vowed to mainline respectability and stability, if I could find them.

Enter Cam, a handsome thirty-three-year-old visiting Frost scholar at Amherst College. Cam arrived for our dates bearing roses. He wore tweed jackets, preppy sweaters, and designer jeans. On the rebound from his failed marriage to the anorexic depressive he'd met at Yale, he was eager for uncomplicated fun. He'd cook us a tasty dinner – bluefish, salad, wild rice – and then, on his command, we'd dance to his favorite Prince tape, his arms slicing the air around him. My new friends thought he was a dreamboat but my alarm bells went off when, on our first date, he presented me with a gift-wrapped pair of red Calvin Klein panties. It wasn't just his presumption that irked me, but that everything we did felt prescribed. I grew to dread the bucolic weekends he planned for us picking apples and carving pumpkins; I couldn't stand the pressure. If the slightest thing went wrong – it rained, or the restaurant ran out of lobster – he was utterly bereft. And I resented being typecast as his ex-wife's foil. The more he looked to me for *joie de vivre* infusions, the more I wanted to bring up my mother's breakdowns, my suicidal ex-roommate, and the paper I was writing on the doubling motif in *Finnegans Wake*.

As a corrective to Cam, I'd light a candle in my window and wait for Jimmy. Jimmy was a twenty-four-year-old housepainter and fry cook who lived with a poet in my MFA program. He would climb through my bedroom window in paint-splattered jeans with the tiger lilies he'd plucked from someone's yard. Sometimes we talked, but mostly we kissed and pretended "just kissing" wouldn't hurt anyone. Unconsummated lust hung in the air. We were a storm building – warm tropical wind colliding with a cold front from the north.

Then Hurricane Gloria came whipping up from Cape Fear, and Governor Dukakis declared Massachusetts a state of emergency. UMass closed, and over half the students went home. Sandbags were flown in to protect the rivers from flooding. Evacuation shelters were set up in the schools. This was my mother's brand of disaster scenario, and she called hourly to ask if I had boarded up the windows yet and stocked up on candles and water. I imagined the house lifting itself off like Dorothy's, hurling me through wind, rendering me into a random flying object.

I realized while I was standing outside in a cornfield in the eye of the storm that my two gentleman callers were both sides of my identity duking it out. Would I become a professor in tweed, or resume a life of financial uncertainty in spattered jeans?

I also realized that I was a corrective to Jimmy's girlfriend. "You're not afraid of your appetites," he marveled one night while we ate the shrimp cocktail he'd brought us on my window ledge.

I broke up with both of them on my twenty-eighth birthday. Claudia had always told me, "Rudolph Steiner says that when you're twenty-eight, your angels go away. After that, no one will bail you out." The next evening, I walked into the State Street Fruit Store and Jimmy's girlfriend, weak from hunger, fainted into my arms. What were the odds of *that*? I brought her home for pasta. When she saw my last spread of roses and purloined tiger lilies intermingled in one vase she cried. "You're lucky to be so loved," she said, and I cried too. I sent my confession in a letter some weeks later.

I spent the rest of the year in atonement, going to weddings. I never once caught the flowers.

# 14

# And There Fell a Great Star

And it fell upon the third part of the rivers, and upon the fountains of waters;
And the name of the star is called Wormwood: and the third part of the waters
became wormwood; and many men died of the waters
Because they were made bitter.

  The Revelation of John 8:11

What is history? Is it a theory? I no longer live in the place where I and those
who look like me first made an appearance. I live in another place. It has another
narrative.

  Jamaica Kincaid, "In History"

I was leading the cool-down in AM Aerobics when someone announced
that the space shuttle Challenger had blown up in the sky. Not only were
seven talented people struck down in their prime, but school children had
to watch their beloved teacher, the one civilian crew member, explode
on live TV. It was too awful.

   That night, I forced myself to watch Reagan's State of the Union
and immediately wished I hadn't. After he asked us to pause to mourn
and honor "the valor of our seven Challenger heroes," Reagan implored
us to "go forward America and reach for the stars." There it was – an
infomercial for Star Wars. Reagan was using the death of the Challenger
Seven to legitimize the nearly trillion dollars we were spending on a
program inspired by a bad sci-fi flick he'd starred in.

   By now it seemed that every public event – the release of the Iranian hostages on Inauguration Day in '81, the wag-the-dog invasion of
Grenada in '83, this mission to the stars – was timed to provide content
for the Great Communicator's next speech. And just as planned, after
this one his ratings soared, despite rumors that NASA felt pressured to

launch in dangerously cold weather – frozen O-rings be damned – so that Reagan could deliver yet another triumphal American tale in this State of the Union address.

I had just decided on my own triumphal tale for 1986. Claudia had called from Seattle with an appealing invitation: she and her boyfriend were traveling to Europe that summer and wanted me to sublet their apartment. I knew what I would do: I'd bill myself as a freelance "physical fitness specialist from Boston" and teach around town, transformed, at last, into the serene, fit, confident creature I'd first gone west to become.

Although presenting myself as *from* Boston was a bit misleading, I actually did possess the rest of that credential: my reward, on paper, for enduring a weeklong course with some boisterous jocks at Springfield College. I could calculate target heart rates; lead a snappy routine of aerobic dance moves, calisthenics, yoga stretches, and guided relaxation; pinch an inch with skin calipers to measure your fat; even resuscitate you from cardiac arrest (*Annie, Annie, are you all right?*) although I'd never tried this on an actual human and hoped I never would have to. I pictured the posters Claudia would put up in advance of my arrival with the extravagant promise, GET IN THE BEST SHAPE OF YOUR LIFE, blazoned across the top.

I also applied to the writers' conference in Port Townsend, this time as a fellow. Raymond Carver would be on the faculty again and I was determined to get in his section. I needed a letter of recommendation and I knew just who to ask: Tamas Azcel, my advisor. "Aim high," he said often, encouraging me to reach for the stars.

The call came at the end of April – I was one of two fellows selected, and I'd been awarded a scholarship to the conference. I was high on this achievement until that evening when, perhaps as a corrective for too much joy, my mother phoned with terrible news. She had just learned that my father was dead and that my grandmother, as suspected, had Alzheimer's disease. I hadn't intended to go to Cleveland that year, but I took the first train I could get.

As much as I'd dreaded the visit, when the cab dropped me off in front of my grandmother's red brick house, I felt oddly comforted by the familiar: the cooing mourning doves in the front-yard oak tree, the money-tree bushes lining the driveway, the backyard flowering magnolia tree, even the yellowing Formica kitchen floor.

"Tell your mother the house is going to blow up if she doesn't stop smoking," my grandmother called to me by way of greeting. I was relieved that she knew who I was. She sat on her overstuffed blue chair in her pink duster, sifting through old utility bills from the seventies and drinking, then discarding, endless cups of tea. The year 1986 flickered in and out of her radar and I tried to keep up. Sometimes I was me at thirteen on my way to school, sometimes I was my sister hyperventilating beneath a table during a family quarrel, and sometimes I was my mother returning home from her triumphant debut piano recital just before America entered World War II.

My mother waited until my grandmother was napping to hand me the file with her correspondence from Social Security about my father. "You won't believe this," she said.

It turned out that my father had been dead for a long time – since December of 1980, my first winter in Seattle, when I was living on unemployment in the Ballard duplex with Joe. And now I knew: after romanticizing him all these years, still half-believing he would return to save me from my mother, or that I'd find him in Mexico, or that he'd come looking for me (after he saw my name on the *New York Times* bestseller list), he was to remain my imaginary father, my creation. I thought of all the unsent letters I'd written him during his life and after. I thought of how much space he had occupied in my psyche. I had spent an unhealthy chunk of my life having an intense conversation with a dead guy.

My mother's detective work had uncovered that he had not been in Mexico, or Europe, but in the capital of Boozehound America, New Orleans. In 1979, when I was writing my senior honors thesis on Tennessee Williams, my father was like a character in one of Williams's plays, drinking himself to death in a rented room for transients on Napoleon Street. I should have known.

I held his death certificate in my hand and tried to glean the story behind the words: *marked fatty liver, cardiomyopathy, chronic pancreatitis*. I found out later that he'd been standing on his balcony, opening a beer at 10:30 in the morning when he dropped dead of a heart attack at the age of sixty, having never become the big success he'd abandoned his family to become.

I told my mother I needed a nap and went upstairs to the den, a small room with a sleeper sofa and a green hatbox from the 1930s on an antique Chinese table in which my grandmother kept old photos. I wanted to contemplate the news in private. Outside I heard birds singing, the coo of those mourning doves. I opened my journal and wrote the date, May 2, 1986, and tried to write. Nothing came.

What I'd carried with me all these years, the most persistent of my stories about my father, was that he had left us to do something more important than be our father. I had few memories of him but the one I treasured most was of climbing the attic stairs to visit him in his study when he was writing. I had always believed that even if he changed his name to elude my mother, I'd open a book someday and recognize his voice. His were the potato rhythms of the American heartland, flavored with the paprika of his Hungarian gypsy ancestors. I liked to think they were my rhythms too.

And yet, in the end, all that my father had in his possession were his portable typewriter, five brown suits, a passport, and a six-pack of beer. He'd been with us when he published his one novel, at the age of forty; he was supposedly at work on what would be his masterpiece when he left. What had happened with this manuscript was anyone's guess. All I knew was that he had resisted the gravity of home, family, love, and community for a solitary flight to the stars only to crash-land below sea level in swampy Louisiana, unloved and unmourned, where he would linger in perpetuity not on the American lit syllabi across the lands, but in an unmarked pauper's grave.

A year into my MFA program, barely scraping by on a first-year fellowship of $2500 and my YMCA wages, I still believed that a true artist must relinquish all materialistic urges in the service of that higher calling. And despite my persistent desire to find love and family and security, a part of me still believed that such longings were a sign of weakness I needed to transcend, just as a part of me had always been proud of my father for refusing to be a conventional postwar father – indeed, I loved the idea, if not the reality, that my father had descended from a nomadic, restless, transgressive people. The gypsy identity softened the blow of his abandonment and, in turn, made *me* sound more interesting than I was. I had even played that Hungarian gypsy card when I first met Tamas Azcel. He himself was a Hungarian who fled the Communist takeover of 1956, and I sometimes wondered if it was our shared "homeland" more than the quality of my work that made me one of his pets.

But I would later learn that the Hungary gypsy story was just a story. After meeting another of my father's abandoned children in the 1990s I would discover that he was of Swiss-German Mennonite origin, the descendant of five generations of Indiana chicken farmers. He had told my mother he "worked his way through college in Indiana plucking chickens," but he hadn't told her they were *his parents'* chickens! And though he started college at Purdue, he completed his education in California on the GI Bill. The biggest revelation to me was that my father was a veteran of World War II – something my mother never mentioned. Maybe she knew, but maybe he somehow kept this a secret so that he could deprive her of his GI benefits, or maybe when they met in Los Angeles – she a twenty-two-year-old olive-skinned beauty just out of the mental hospital, he the dapper man in the white suit (like Faulkner's) who at twenty-nine was already a veteran of two marriages, a war, and a master's degree program – he decided to rewrite his biography to impress her, slipping in just enough facts (chickens, Indiana) to give the fiction the stuff of real life. In the end, the most enduring fiction of my father's career was the one he fashioned of his life.

And this fiction had been passed on to me. I had identified with his path, despite my feminist critique of it. Why did my life choices still seem so dialectical, with family and its sacrifices at one pole and creativity and its sacrifices at the other? I wrote in my journal: "Is this my fate too? To be buried by the state with no evidence of ever having family or friends?"

I sifted through the photos in the green hatbox in search of some record that I'd ever crossed paths with this man: my father holding me in his arms in our apartment when I was a baby, my mother and father standing in front of one of his paintings. I felt a pressure in my chest, but nothing more. I studied a picture of my grandmother in a plaid skirt wheeling me in my stroller through a park. I could not cry for her either, my Grandma Anna whose past was eroding like the silt on a riverbed: *Annie, Annie, are you all right?*

I set the photos aside and switched on the news. There was a story about a candlelight vigil: Clevelanders of Russian descent were grieving their loved ones who had been hurt or killed in the recent Chernobyl disaster. I stared at the broad faces and cheekbones of these mourners holding candles, singing and weeping. They had the short torsos, broad shoulders, and wide faces of the women in my family: peasant bodies built for work. I had often thought I'd go to Russia one day to trace my grandmother's roots, perhaps with her by my side, but I saw from the map that she was from the area where the worst radiation had settled.

And that's when I began to cry. For these strangers, whose family members resembled mine. For my grandmother, whose parents were born in Minsk and whose memories of them, their stories as Jews in the Old Country, their stories of the land, had turned to mishmash. For my father, who had left his home to pursue ambitions that never bore fruit and whose ancestral memories would never be passed on to his children. And for our ravaged earth, storied now with the scars of cold war overproduction and the toxic aftermath of the nuclear age.

I imagined the geography of Belarus and the Ukraine: ice-carved valleys of snow and pine-cool forests fragrant with mushrooms laid to waste by the cooling towers of nuclear power plants, the eroded soils of collectivized farms, the crowded city buses, the ugly factories. According to Adi Roche, author of *Children of Chernobyl*, almost 2,200,000 Belarussian people were subjected to permanent radioactive contamination by the explosion. Of the country's forests and farmlands, 25 percent became a nuclear wasteland and only 1 percent remained unharmed. And yet the Politburo wrote forty secret protocols to conceal the dimension of the disaster from the public. One, for example, authorized that the so-called acceptable level of radiation be raised by a factor of fifty. In this way the Russian leadership was mirroring a move made by Ronald Reagan, who set out early on to reclassify documents about nuclear testing and nuclear plant safety that had been opened in the Carter years, thus re-concealing information on public risks to human health and enabling the Nuclear Regulatory Commission to abandon some of its most important safety regulations without the knowledge of the people who lived near the plants. In addition, as Carl Pope wrote in *Sierra* in 1984, Reagan authorized the Environmental Protection Agency's toxics chief, John Todhunter, to increase the pre-Reagan rate of the "risk of cancer from exposure to toxic substances" of "one additional case of cancer for every million people exposed" by a "hundred fold." In Gorbachev's case, had he let the public know the truth of the devastation and relocated the millions who should have been evacuated, and not the four hundred thousand that he did, it would have cost him his career.

Countless thousands of children became afflicted with, or were born with, leukemia, lymphoma, thyroid cancers, deformed limbs, and the whole range of cancers and ailments that weakened immune systems bring. Because many of them were radioactive to the touch, they were abandoned, or exiled into makeshift orphanages in Belarus, without medical facilities, toilets, or hot water.

Imagine having to abandon your home in a forced evacuation. You are sick, vomiting, dizzy, and have to decide what to carry with you when in truth, everything you own, even you, yourself, are contaminated. You, your home, your family are now the carriers of death and suffering. All that gave you comfort brings unthinkable misery.

I wanted to discuss the news with my grandmother, but Chernobyl would have baffled and upset her and perhaps added to her conviction that the house was going to blow up. She also seemed to think her husband was still among us. When I asked her if she could name the year and the current president my mother laughed and said, "I think she'd rather not think about *that*."

My mother was in surprisingly good spirits. She was taking her medication and had resigned herself to a responsibility that would have been daunting even for someone without a history of mental illness.

With the present and the future indecipherable texts, the three of us spent the weekend enjoying a half-invented version of the past. Grandma showed me her treasures – Cleveland teachers' glowing reports of her and her daughter and her daughter's daughters – the testimony that at one time we were all destined for the stars.

The folly of that summer's get-solvent-quick scheme did not hit me until I arrived in Seattle a few weeks later and met my first class of aerobics students – all three of them. With the money I'd spent on ads and studio time, I would need three times that many students just to break even. If I didn't recruit a lot more fitness enthusiasts, I'd have to find an actual job.

After three days of plastering the city with posters, I took a day off with a friend from the MOM-era: a tax attorney named Jerry. A veteran of financial trouble (he was one of the many lawyers MOM fired and locked out without notice) he had survived a spate of recent disasters that made my concerns seem trivial. Two years ago his wife had given birth to twins who were born several weeks premature with serious physical problems. The babies showed up before Jerry and his wife could get on a new health insurance plan and the bills – for which they were 100 percent responsible – came to over two hundred thousand dollars. They had yet to find a subsequent provider that was willing to cover the costs for the babies' preexisting heart and kidney problems. Under the strains of these pressures, the couple had separated, and Jerry had filed for bankruptcy.

"Heck, it's only money," he said. "Let's have fun."

Claudia had loaned me her bicycle for the summer, Jerry had packed a picnic, and after we crammed the bikes into his Saab station wagon, we were off. We took the ferry to Vashon Island, where I'd once day-dreamed of becoming a back-to-the-land homesteader with Joe. Soon I was soaring downhill past a cedar-tree-lined beach, inhaling the salt air and with it a glimmer of the glorious summer days ahead.

And then I hit a bump in the road. The front wheel of the bike *fell off*. I careened over the handlebars and was airborne for a minute, flying past a field of blue lupine, feeling the wind on my neck. I wasn't wearing a helmet because I thought I'd be too hot. I landed on my head.

An hour later an emergency room nurse was plucking gravel out of my face and my hands. A doctor was asking me who the president was and I said, "I think I'd rather forget." The nurse cut a gauze tent under which the doctor seamed my face and scalp back together. A numbing solution, cold as metal, dripped into my ringing ears. The doctor explained that I was getting a lot of stitches on my face and I would look "a bit beat up" for some time. "Wait as long as you can before you look in the mirror," he said.

Beyond the threats to my vanity, the real problem was my brain: if it swelled much overnight, it would need to be pried surgically loose from my skull. I would have to stay in the hospital so they could watch me. Plus, when I'd landed on the asphalt, I had also managed to scrape off the first few layers of skin on my palms. If I touched anything, I could get a staph infection. Gauze bandages held my fingers together, and until they healed, I would not be able to use my hands to cook, eat, or bathe.

Having just heard Jerry's story about going bankrupt over medical bills, I refused this care. I had no idea if my UMass student health insurance kicked in through the summer, and if it would cover an out-of-state emergency room visit, let alone a stay in the hospital. And even if they paid 80 percent, I had no way to pay the rest.

"I can only let you go home if you can guarantee you'll have people with you every minute," the doctor said.

"We've got it covered," Jerry said.

I could not imagine asking for this much help from anyone, not even my sister. Who could I burden? With Claudia gone and Joe off with a new girlfriend to Alaska, I only had Jerry and Neal. Neal had already played nursemaid when Ethan and I visited after Mexico; what had I ever done for him? I'd only been in Seattle for three days and instead of getting its citizens into the best shape of their lives, I was in their care, an invalid.

After Jerry got me home, Neal brought over soup and sandwiches and fed them to me. To pass the time, we invented a game called Fact or Fiction. We would ask each other questions, then either make up lavish lies that sounded like the truth, or tell true stories that were so strange and packed with coincidence as to seem fictitious. "What was the most embarrassing thing that ever happened to you?" he asked.

"Well, one day I was in my apartment in Northampton taking a shower," I began, inspired by a whiff of my body odor. "I was scrubbing away, and somehow I lost my balance and fell through the wall into my neighbor's bathroom where he was sitting on the toilet playing 'The Girl from Ipanema' on his accordion." I started laughing; I've never been a very good liar.

"I would believe it if the guy was playing 'Hey Jude,'" Neal said. "But come on, 'The Girl from Ipanema'?"

We sang the song, which I had always secretly liked.

The falling-through-cardboard-thin-bathroom-walls story was one of those urban legends I'd picked up in Boston. And I actually did have a neighbor in Northampton who played "The Girl from Ipanema" on his accordion. But perhaps the most potent fact in this dopey fiction was that very soon I would have to get naked in front of a man who was not my boyfriend. I was already embarrassed.

A few days later, it was Jerry who led me to the bathroom, covered the mirror with a beach towel so I couldn't see myself, and drew me a bath. As he unwrapped the gauze from my arms, legs, and skull I felt like a mummy being brought back from the dead. I lowered myself carefully into the tub, trying not to gasp as my wounds came in contact with water.

As I bent over, Jerry carefully lathered my hair, avoiding clumps of dried blood, and then rinsed pitcher after pitcher of warm water over my head. I thought of Jerry's toddlers getting washed by their father, and of the public baths for women in Orthodox Jewish ritual, and of the baptism I might have had if I'd remained a Christian. I closed my eyes.

"I'm not going to try to get the tangles out because you might start bleeding again," Jerry said, patting my hair gingerly later with a towel.

"That's okay," I said, looking down so he wouldn't see my tears of gratitude. "I've always wanted to be a Rastafarian."

In my bedridden days I tried not to picture the puffball above my right eye where a dozen wire stitches zigzagged up into a nest of scabrous dreds. But one day when I was ambulatory again I couldn't stop myself: I *had* to look. I made my way to the dresser mirror and stood there for several seconds beholding the bride of Frankenstein: her red lips protruding like grapefruit sections, the black narrow slit of an eye peering blankly out of the bandage on the right, creating the effect of someone permanently, grotesquely, winking.

Several days later, the scabs fell off my face and turned to purple blotches that looked, from a distance, like radiation burns, or Kaposi's Sarcoma lesions.

Since I had literally shed my skin, it made sense to keep going. I walked into the salon at the Bon Marché and asked the stylist to hack off the hair clumps and give me a perm. Why I did this, I still don't know. What is it about our culture that bullies us and beats us down until finally, after months or years of seeing something as ugly and vulgar, it begins to look pretty? My friend Robin Hemley used that same word, *bullying*, to describe the way our current revival of Bigger-Is-Better makes him feel like he should be driving a Range Rover. What is it that makes the outsized, the synthetically shiny, and the hideous start to look the way things *should* look, and why do we capitulate?

The chemical treatment burned my wounds and the stink made me queasy, but I was resolved. I bought a pick to fluff up my stiff curls and marveled at how small my face looked under all that hair, how well the wiry tendrils covered the scars on my forehead.

Thus transformed into Every Woman, circa 1986, I followed my hair out the door to the nearest temp agency. In the strangest déjà-vu of all, I found myself a few days later in a typing pool with Barbara, my supervisor in MOM's office until she was fired and I got her job. I was worried she might resent me, but she did not even recognize me. I, who had tried to reinvent myself at every turn, had finally succeeded. I hadn't written myself into a cheerful, revisionist version of my past, I'd written myself out of the story completely.

Even Port Townsend was a bust. The conference staff had lost my paperwork; they had no place for me in the Carver workshop and no housing even though, on the phone, I'd been promised a single. It was as though I'd never applied in the first place. At the last minute, I was placed with a chain-smoking roommate. My first night there, I came down with a violent stomach flu and spent the better part of the week vomiting. I missed the conference almost entirely.

On the day I finally emerged into the world, the conference director told me she was looking forward to my reading, which was scheduled for four that afternoon. A reading? All I had with me was the second draft of a story I'd hoped to get advice on in the workshop: a not-ready-for-primetime player if there ever was one.

And so this was how it was to be: instead of a triumphal return to the West as an emerging literary star with great quads and perfect skin, I would survive a summer of head wounds, projectile vomiting, and the public humiliation of a lousy reading. I was living proof that what goes up – rockets, the human ego – must come down.

Meanwhile, back at the ranch, Ronald Reagan was not in the best shape of his life either. One day, when questioned by reporters about the U.S.-Soviet talks on nuclear weapons, he paused, momentarily unable to speak. Nancy whispered his cue: "Tell them we're doing everything we can," and Reagan delivered the line. But he would never again sound as convincing and winning as he had the night he comforted America over the loss of the Challenger Seven.

That summer his symptoms of Alzheimer's, though not quite as advanced as my grandmother's, were forcing his wife to write cheat-sheets to help him remember the names of world leaders and members of the Cabinet.

Those U.S.-Soviet talks resumed in October, when Reagan and Gorbachev met in Iceland for a summit. Gorbachev pushed hard to negotiate the most massive weapons reductions in history and Reagan wondered if the apocalyptic Chernobyl disaster had been the catalyst for the Russian leader's new pacifism. In *Dutch: A Memoir of Ronald Reagan*, Edmund Morris remembers Reagan telling him that "Chernobyl means 'Armageddon' in the Ukrainian Bible." Actually, Chernobyl is Ukrainian for Wormwood, a name that Revelation applies to the "great star" that descended from heaven, "burning as it were a lamp" and falling into a third of the earth's rivers, whereupon "many men died of the waters, because they were made bitter." I know Morris's opus is half fiction, half fact, but I believe that a star falling from heaven would capture Reagan's imagination, as it did mine.

Whether or not Chernobyl, the greatest ecological disaster in human history, was Gorbachev's motive to disarm, he came close to getting Reagan to sign a unilateral nuclear disarmament treaty. Imagine what the world would look like now if nuclear weapons had been obsolete since that summit. There were moments of great progress in their talks but Reagan would not let go of his dream to be able to launch or sabotage first-strike weapons from space, to turn our share of the hemisphere into one big gated community with a shield that could zap intruders like an electric fly swatter. The year that had begun with an explosion above the horizon would end with the threat of many more to come as the superpowers played a high-stakes game of fact or fiction.

In *Murder in the Air*, the 1940 movie starring Ronald Reagan, our hero has to protect a wonder weapon from some wicked enemies who would want to steal it from America. This technological marvel is called an "inertia projector"; it disarms enemy planes by dismantling their electrical systems. "It not only makes the United States invincible in war," one line from the film begins, "but in so doing promises to become the greatest force for world peace ever discovered." In Orwellian terms, war is peace. As conceived by Reagan, Star Wars was a "nice" weapons system: it killed missiles, not people. Garry Wills points out that space, the final frontier, would also be the landscape where Reagan's blind optimism put a literal lid on all our problems and fears. Space would be the biggest movie screen ever.

Don't laugh. As I conclude this chapter, Son-of-a-Bush is planning to blast Son of Star Wars, the multibillion-dollar millennial sequel, into a theater near you.

# 15

# Postcard from the Happy Valley

## *My Dinner with the Ollie Norths*

My friend Bill and his lover are coming to dinner; until then, I'm trying to write. The problem is that I'm distracted by Fawn Hall, who
is testifying before the House Committee on Foreign Affairs on TV.
She is one scary babe, and the fact that we're the same age and have
the same big hair is almost as unnerving as the pride in her voice as
she explains how she operates the shredding machine day and night to
keep Democracy safe from the KGB. It's all coming out now, how this
secret covert agency outside the CIA funded a war with Nicaragua that
Congress never authorized, and then said it never happened. Meanwhile
we are selling weapons to our sworn enemies in Iran by way of Israel
– possibly to Hezballah terrorists – so that Reagan can coax them to
release seven hostages in Lebanon while making public statements that
we will never do business with terrorists.

I was right all along; apparently the country really *is* run by Reagan's
rich friends, the shady arms dealers, former military men, and Pentagon
consultants (those guys who gave us the submarines and aircraft with
six-hundred-dollar toilet seats and nine-thousand-dollar wrenches) who
make up the National Security Council. Constitutionality, democratic
accountability, and congressional oversight: this administration has rid-
den roughshod over all three. And now they are presenting themselves
as patriots, and the public is cheering them on.

I don't know what depresses me more, that unelected right-wingers
are running the country and waging wars, or that Fawn Hall will never
have to work again. She'll be offered her choice of TV movie-of-the-week
deals, and if she ever writes her memoirs, every trade press in America
will be bidding for them.

I turn off the TV, but I keep seeing Fawn Hall's head in a cartoon
bubble, taunting me, as I try to work.

The narrator of "Germs," a musician named Ivy Black, is making her way through the game-show circuit – *The Wheel of Fortune, The Price is Right* – to finance a rock musical, *Latex Love*. I want to write a seriocomical social novel that engages with the big issues of the day, but all I've got are notes: all concept, no heart. I haven't located my heart in weeks. As I try to write a scene of Ivy's band shopping for latex body suits, I picture the people in my workshop critiquing it solely in terms of marketability. I imagine someone asking, "Who would play Ivy in the movie? What about the actress who played Fawn Hall?"

In *his* movie-of-the-week deal, Ollie North, no doubt, would play himself.

Yesterday I caught some of his testimony. To talk about lying, he performed himself as a straight arrow. He was decked out in his Marines Corps uniform like a Boy Scout with his big-eared, Opie-from-Mayberry head and his dozen medals proclaiming his allegiance to the flag and his membership to what Barbara Ehrenreich calls "the warrior caste," the hard macho elite that is so *in* right now. As David Denby will point out in "Ollie North, The Movie," in *The New Republic*, "pathological liars, terrorists, and military dictators are sincere too" and "North is a classic authoritarian personality – charismatic, self-dramatizing, a dreamer who dreamed himself and was blessed with the physical equipment and the skill to act the role." In this time of rabid superficiality, dishonesty, greed, self-centeredness, and self-promotion, Ollie's *rendering* of genuineness stands in for the real thing. As of today, Ollie-mania is sweeping the country like the swine flu. In a matter of hours, he has become an American icon.

It was North who got the "neat idea" to "use the Ayatollah Khomeini's money to support the Nicaraguan 'freedom fighters.'" He named his secret program Project Democracy. North has admitted that since February of 1986 he sent Reagan at least five memos seeking approval for the arms deals and for funneling the profits to the contras, and though Reagan has said, "I just didn't know [about it]," one of North's colleagues, Marine Lieutenant Colonel Robert Earl, has testified that Reagan simply said, "It's important that I not know." *Newsweek* has interpreted this comment to mean that "the president was urging a continued cover-up."

A dozen years from now, Bill Clinton will be impeached by Reagan's congressional disciples for urging a continued "cover-up" about some consensual snogging with an intern. Yet selling guns to terrorists and raising millions to wage a secret war and lying about both aren't impeachable offences. I will never understand this.

After four hours, all I've written are the words: "Ivy Black gets mistaken for Fawn Hall in the studio of *The Price is Right* and decides to grow out her perm."

Bill calls about dinner: "Will Chardonnay work?"

"Don't forget our deal," I say. As usual, we're both worried about money and have agreed to pool our leftovers.

"Fret not," he says. "I promise no vulgar cash will sully my palms."

Bill often quotes the bird from T. S. Eliot's *Four Quartets* who says, "Human kind cannot bear very much reality." When we're together, we drink sherry and talk like characters in an Oscar Wilde play. Bill, who is getting his PhD in art history, used to say that he lives only for art. But lately, since Jeffrey entered the picture, he has been pining for his former income as a financial consultant in Boston. I like to remind him how miserable he was then. "Besides, Jeffrey can't reasonably expect someone living on a $5,000-a-year teaching assistant's stipend to supply him with French champagne and pink Ralph Lauren shirts," I always say. "Ah, but love is expensive," Bill sighs.

Jeffrey doesn't work because he is planning to write a gay utopian novel in the lush style of Edmund White, with New Age themes. He hasn't started yet, but he will, any day now. Until then, perhaps as research for the novel, Jeffrey brings home random men and has sex with them in Bill's bed while Bill teaches summer school. Bill's roommate is an unwitting voyeur to all of this, as am I once he asks for advice. Soon we will tell Bill what's what so as to protect him from HIV. Jeffrey and Bill don't use condoms because "Jeffrey says that's like eating candy with the wrapper on." Bill will say: "Jeffrey thinks he's like Nietzsche's Superman and the rules don't apply to him. Don't you love self-confidence like that? It's so sexy. Jeffrey says only people with low esteem get AIDS."

Now Bill is saying, "Jeffrey thinks you're really hot, for a straight woman."

That's all it takes for me to put my condemnation of Bill's lover on hold. I set the table wondering who would play me in my movie-of-the-week deal.

The sight of Bill and Jeffrey in my doorway is a shock. They are dressed like twins, with the same knee-length, plaid Golfing-Republican-Man

Bermuda shorts, the same sleeveless Marlon Brando in *A Streetcar Named Desire* wife-beater T-shirts and – I can't believe it; I will never believe it – Ollie North haircuts.

Two years ago, I didn't even own a TV. Now there is no escaping the thing, even when I turn it off.

For one long minute I take them in, the twin Ollies. Recently Jesse Helms – archenemy to all homosexuals and artists – said that he is just "so proud" of Oliver North, that Ollie is his personal hero. If Helms had his way, he'd send every gay man in America to an internment camp. And they are taking fashion tips from their enemy's hero.

Or maybe they're being playfully subversive. After all, wouldn't it be an incredible assault on Ollie's apple-pie-manhood if the gay men of America all decided to claim his look for themselves? "You are both *too* funny," I say.

"Ollie North is *sooo* cute!" Jeffrey says.

"It's the hottest look in town, love," Bill explains.

When we sit down to eat, I'm in for another surprise. Reaching into a big shopping bag, they pluck out a whole array of yuppie-yummies: the good Chardonnay Bill promised, duck paté, pesto-flavored crackers, roasted peppers, brie, crusty pain de campagne, Perrier. With the last item the slip from Bill's credit card comes fluttering to the floor. The cost of their contributions to our potluck is more than my weekly grocery budget.

"When I promised I wouldn't spend money," Bill says before I can protest, "I meant *actual* money."

We decide that my leftover pasta doesn't fit the menu. I can eat it tomorrow by myself.

As the three of us spread out the goodies on my wobbly kitchen table, I feel like a character in a play, perhaps by Oscar Wilde. I picture ladies in sequined drop-waist dresses and jeweled handbags, a roomful of champagne-swillers laughing at something arch that the charmingly foppish Jeffrey and Bill say in unison in their rented tuxedos. I'm the only one at the soirée who isn't drunk and isn't amused. But who am I to criticize, I wonder, as I push a tendril of my chemical shag behind my ear, pile up my plate, and smile and smile and smile when what I want to do is cry and scream and cry?

# BOOK IV
# New World Disorders, 1987–1989

The huge sums that the Western superpower threw into the Cold War arms race and global power rivalry were largely borrowed. In its rapid transition from being the largest creditor nation to by far the largest debtor nation in the world, the United States piled up debts of unprecedented magnitude. . . . Meanwhile, citizens were informed that for lack of funds the richest nation on earth could do nothing about shamefully neglected social needs. . . . Cities deteriorated, and the best solution offered to mounting crime, drug-traffic violence and gunfire in school halls and classrooms seemed to be more prisons.

    C. Vann Woodward, "Them and US: An American Looks at European Perceptions of the New World," *Times Literary Supplement*

Before we get carried away by the mounting backlash against multiculturalism, we ought to reflect for a moment on the system that the p.c. people aim to replace. I know all about it; in fact, it's just about all I do know, since I – along with so many educated white people of my generation – was a victim of monoculturalism.

    Barbara Ehrenreich, "Teach Diversity – With a Smile"

The language needed to describe unity is itself divisive, each word an island proclaiming its difference from every other. Words tumble out singly, one after another; compared to the infinity of stillness they are crude, noisy things – which is why the name of God cannot be spoken, why "the tao that can be told is not the eternal Tao," why silence is the truest mystic state."

    Alix Kates Shulman, *Drinking the Rain*

# 16

# How I Survived the Crash

Be not made a beggar by banqueting up on borrowing.
   Ecclesiasticus 18:33

STRUCTURAL INTEGRITY

When the stock market reached its peak, my mother came to town to buy me a bra. "A woman's breasts are her most attractive feature," she said on the phone, "and if you don't have adequate support, your breasts will sag and your back will hurt."

This was a lecture my mother had delivered often. No matter how shabby her K-Mart stretch pants and polyester blouses, she never skimped on foundations. Our bathroom was always crowded with battalions of underwires hanging to dry. As a child, I wanted to remain flat as a desk. The bras communicated to me nothing about beauty or support. What they said was that when it came to my mother, what was private was outside for all to see.

Under stress, I dream I am walking topless outside.

Or that my teeth are falling out. One gets loose and starts to wriggle, and then they all are rolling around the bottom of my mouth, cutting into my tongue.

One of my molars was aching when my mother called to say that she had her ticket. I was two months away from thirty, her age when she got dentures. She never got used to them. She would take them out and forget where she left them, then ask me to find them. One of my strongest memories of childhood is of running into the ladies' room of a diner, bus station, or department store to look for her choppers. It's possible I took up running because I'd been doing it all along anyway, had grown adept at getting in and out of embarrassing situations as quickly as possible.

Stress, for me, is connected to the fear that what is most private about me is outside for all to see.

My mother arrived in August, two days after my abortion. It was hot and she wanted to go swimming, so my roommate and my boyfriend and I packed a picnic and took her to Goshen. I had to make up a reason why I didn't want to go into the water at this idyllic swimming hole, I who have always loved to swim. In the photos from this day, I look as pale as rice and smile strangely.

Of course, I didn't want her to come but I hadn't seen her in fifteen months and if I had waited any longer my grandmother would be too ill to manage with just the neighbor looking in on her. I wanted to give my mother a break, to be the good daughter of her dreams.

By my calculations, a visit at the worst time for me possible would balance the books of daughterly debt.

But it is hard to be a good daughter when you have just had an abortion and you are exhausted and ashamed and furious with yourself for letting such a thing happen again. It is hard to be a good daughter when you have no emotional reserves and your mother smokes in the apartment and demands around-the-clock coffee.

On the second day of the visit, when I was trying to wash out my bloodstained underpants without my mother's scrutiny, she popped her head into my bathroom to announce that it was time. "Let's get that bra," she said.

"Sure thing."

As we walked toward Main Street, I felt like I was being led to a public whipping. I didn't want anyone I knew to see us. I picked a very unhip store, which isn't easy to find in Northampton.

"I need to buy my girl a brassiere," my mother told the saleswoman.

I was doing what I had always done as a teenager, trying to keep a buffer zone of at least a foot between my mother and myself, which is why the saleswoman did not realize I was said girl. "We don't stock many training bras," she asked. "How old is your daughter?" I knew my mother was conjuring up the same prepubescent girl that I was. She had been tagging along all morning, hiding her eyes beneath her hair, crossing her arms defensively across her chest.

"She's right here," my mother said, taking my hand and pulling me toward certain death. I could hear my teeth grinding, could feel the dull throbbing. I cringed as these two women gazed in the direction of my still-swollen breasts to decide on my size.

But it was not my mother's type of lingerie department; even I could see that. Those cheap nylon bras would never provide adequate support. She asked if they stocked Bali.

"I'm not familiar with that brand," the saleswoman said. "What do they look like?"

"Like this," my mother said. And with that she lifted up her top and flashed her.

I ran, crying like a child, from the store.

By now there were more residents of the Happy Valley outside pushing strollers and slurping cappuccino in to-go cups. I bumped into my jogging partner, Pete, who was with his yellow lab, Stella, on his way to a leisurely brunch with the *New York Times* tucked under his elbow. Later he would tell me how he was struck by the look of panic on my face as I fled my mother, who, he said, was right behind me, clutching her handbag. "You never run that fast when we're together," he said lightly.

Later, when my mother's breakdown was in full swing, I found myself thinking: If only I would have let her buy me a bra.

When she got back to Cleveland, she started phoning around the clock. She said I had seemed "aloof" on the visit, which meant that by her accounting, the visit didn't count. I was still in deep daughterly debt. On the two occasions when I didn't answer the phone, she sent the police to my door, who believed they were looking for an underage runaway. She called my professors late at night and asked them impertinent questions about their private lives, including whether they had ever slept with me. She phoned the secretary of the graduate program to ask for my schedule. Wherever I went there were "while you were out" messages waiting.

Even my bedroom provided no sanctuary. All summer, a construction project was underway next door and the workers could see into my third-floor bedroom. The sound shook my very bones. My roommate and I had six fans rigged up to open windows throughout the apartment to suck out hot air, and even their propellers could not camouflage the noise of their work. The windows rattled and I felt the drilling inside my mouth; I heard it even in my dreams, especially after I discovered that I needed a crown on the achy molar.

Meanwhile, the news was full of Iran-Contra and the rising stock market, which was as bloated as I still felt. My mother phoned and phoned, letting it be known that she had crashed hard.

Many Happy Valley friends were on their way down too. One went into hock to follow her boyfriend to California where they paid someone to bully them to walk across burning coals. Another was in love with a dancer who only slept with ballerinas with the bodies of twelve-year-old boys. This friend was short and curvy, with a 34D bosom, a fact about her I knew only because I had seen her underwear hanging in her bathroom. Another friend was divorcing a man who wouldn't sleep with her because she was "too fat and ugly to fuck." She was a beautiful woman: five feet seven inches, a strong one hundred thirty-five pounds from riding her bike two hundred miles a week. Bill was still maxing out his Visa card to please the unfaithful Jeffrey whose high self-esteem required increasingly pricier love tokens.

These friends were the kind of people who work hard, cook fabulous dinners, go regularly to the gym, remember everyone's birthdays, and call their mothers dutifully, but they were still trying to do better, still hoping to make themselves worthy of love.

The one in love with the ballet dancer stopped consuming oil, butter, sugar, caffeine, chocolate, cheese, and alcohol. She lent me a self-help book about how to wean oneself from loving beyond one's means, from overspending in the relationship department. I told her I believed that such a book was part of the problem because it did not address the political-societal reasons for the reader's unhappiness, did not advocate social change, did not promote gender equity. I said that these books were a plot, that they made the reader feel that everything wrong in her life was her fault. Then I opened the book and I read it straight through in an evening, with a highlighter.

In my journal, I began to speak to myself in the second person.

I kept dreaming my teeth were falling out, that I was running topless through Northampton, and that the workers outside my bedroom window were in my room demanding coffee.

I searched for signs of sanity everywhere in the world but could not find them.

BAGGAGE

At the moment my life felt most under siege, I began to fantasize about Keith. In the year since he'd taken my class we had become friends. We had long talks about ecology, metaphor, and the Beatles. I began to think of him as the kindest person I knew. I pictured him in a white shirt kissing me in a stand of pine trees on the grounds of Smith College, where I went on my long runs with Pete. I wondered if I wanted him because he was the age I was before my heart first learned guile and subterfuge.

In the dream, Keith and I made mad love on the banks of Paradise Pond, the water splashing onto our entangled limbs, the moss and sludge oozing between us like extra hands. I told myself my body was still young like Keith's but I had never been young and I needed to know what that was like.

Before and after the pregnancy, I would go with my boyfriend to his parents' small house on a lake and spend hours swimming back and forth, feeling the cool water caress my skin and replaying this same fantasy again and again: white shirt, pine trees, water, kiss, kiss, kiss.

These were my grievances against the boyfriend:

1. He was a smoker. (Which begged the question: Why did you start seeing him in the first place, since you hate cigarettes?)
2. He hated to exercise, and therefore, always insisted he was too out of shape to do any of the things I wanted to do, like go for bike rides and nature hikes. (Which begged the question: Why did you start seeing him in the first place, since you are a fitness instructor and you love the outdoors?)
3. Because of 1 and 2, he, at thirty-three, considered himself old. (At almost thirty, who wants to hear about being old?)
4. On and off, he had suffered from depression, a condition I was not ready to admit I had been fighting for a long, long time. Then I read *The Drama of the Gifted Child* by Alice Miller and began to suspect I was playing out the narcissist's dialectic of grandiosity versus despair with the boyfriend. Perhaps I had been rehearsing this dynamic two years ago, when I chose, of all people to share my apartment with, a suicidal woman. I listed some famous narcissists with depressive spouses: Ronnie and Nancy Reagan; Michael and Kitty Dukakis; Gerald and Betty Ford.
5. My boyfriend had seen me in my deepest despair, a private state not meant for public consumption. He saw me pregnant. He saw me with my mother. He knew the panic I was deflecting while I was busy being a popular teacher or running in the woods. When I charged a new eighties glamour outfit to reward myself for surviving my mother's visit (black poplin jacket with shoulder pads, black slit-up-the-side skirt,

Italian sequined pointy stiletto heels) he frowned and said, "This isn't the real you."

I broke up with him on the morning of my thirtieth birthday. Now, if anyone asked why I was sad I could say, "I just broke up with a decent guy so I could be infatuated with someone unsuitable," and then I didn't have to think about my mother's visit and subsequent breakdown, my father's death, my grandmother's Alzheimer's disease, the best friend whose death I was still grieving half a decade later, the children I was not going to have, and my lifelong worries about money.

I could also add, "I'm sad because our whole country is falling apart," but the truth was I was glad when the stock market crashed. I felt vindicated for being right all along. On the Monday after my birthday, Black Monday as the rest of the country would call it, when the Dow Jones industrial average dropped a record 508 points and $500 billion in wealth was wiped out in hours, I understood that the inside was now outside everywhere and there was nowhere to hide.

Ronald Reagan got on the TV and tried to persuade us not to panic. What America needed now, *Time* insisted, was an intelligent, focused adult. Reagan looked confused and tired, his gaze off-focus, like my grandmother's. His voice lacked its usual bravado. He seemed uncomprehending, disengaged, and resentful that anything significant might be expected of him at this time. It seemed that even he had stopped pretending, that he had stopped believing in his bedtime stories about the health of the nation.

I no longer believed in my own bedtime stories either.

But before I finally crashed, there was the dream and then the fulfillment of the dream. It was not that I didn't get what I wanted but that I did, for a minute.

Keith came for dinner, and we took a walk to Paradise Pond. Among trees on the water's edge we shared champagne, and then I kissed him, and he kissed me back. The moment arrived for us to confess our respective fantasies, and they were identical. But then his blue eyes turned gray and I realized I had frightened him. He explained that he did not have enough experience with women to feel like my equal and that he needed to keep the fantasy inside as fantasy, that he had benefited from being infatuated with me but having me out of reach, out there in the world where role models belong. I realized with a start that he had the integrity and backbone that everyone around me seemed to lack at the moment, including myself, which is partly why I fell for him in the first place. Someone had to be the grownup and I was slacking off on the job.

Ever since my mother's visit I'd been feeling like a preteen in a training bra.

Note to future self, in journal: Remember this season of swooning and self-loathing when you are a professor. Remember that somebody has to be the grownup and leave fantasy in the realm of fantasy. Remember what it feels like to need to be adored, the way movie stars and presidents need to be adored, and understand it as a symptom of feeling empty inside.

Never forget that when your mother was thirty as you are now, she lost all her teeth, probably from the strain of delivering you into this world.

This flash of unexpected wisdom could have fended off the crash, but then the AP wire picked up a story about a sixty-year-old Cleveland woman who was stopped at the airport by security with a butcher knife in her handbag. She was on her way to visit her daughter in Massachusetts. She was on her way to extract her daughter's debts, a pound for a pound.

I fled to a psychic fair, desperate for some distracting good news about my future. The man who read my cards just stared at me for a long minute. Finally he said, "When are you going to stop pretending?" I pretended not to know what he meant, but then I excused myself and ran back to my bed, which had never felt more inviting, even though the construction workers were still just outside the window.

I stayed inside for days. My friend from workshop, James, called to find out what was wrong. He said, "The good news is that you now know that you have more baggage than you thought. The extent that you're freaked out about this young guy and your mother is the extent that you have baggage. It's something finite. At least now you know what you're dealing with. And isn't that a relief?"

This assessment offered the comfort of a medical diagnosis. What I had was nasty and required surgery, but it wasn't fatal. I entered that fluorescent-lit room of knowing and not knowing. It was a good place to bring the big beach ball of sorrow I had carried for so long.

HOW

Accept that the gig is up. Admit that there's nowhere to hide. Your investments were in fly-by-night concerns, your infrastructure was weak, your past debts have caught up with you and it's time to do a sober accounting.

You still owe American Express five hundred dollars for the crown you charged for your molar. Then there's that little black ensemble and the pointy Italian shoes. You have no idea how you will pay these bills. All of your assets exist on paper only and carry interest with them. You have become a debtor nation.

Because there are few physical outlets for your condition, you must cry. But when you are sprawled out on the floor beneath the skylight in your living room, do cry quietly so as not to distract and distress your roommate who is watching *Dynasty* on the beat-up overstuffed chair that was given to you by the boyfriend you have treated so badly. If you are nice to her, she will give you a backrub with her feet. She is very good at this.

Ice cream or chocolate won't help; the movies that depict women being soothed by sweets have it wrong. You don't have to starve yourself, but you do need to feel the texture and shape of your emptiness. You cannot fill this hollow space with anything. Not food. Not sex. Not the endorphin high of aerobics classes. You can't use it as inspiration for great art because this is the place where nothing grows. It is nothing-colored, this blank place, and within it lurks something you cannot see or imagine, ever. It smells slightly sour, like yeast. It is located inside the body beneath the solar plexus, but it is also found outside in the space between the people you know, and sometimes in the weeds and candy wrappers and broken glass of parking lots, and behind the bleachers at stadiums where people cheer for their heroes.

If this is real, and not just a hormonal shift, it will go on for some time. Weeks. Months. Try to be brave, but don't get cocky about your bravery. Keep this private, or you'll lose all your friends. There are some things you don't have to share and this is one of them. If you are lucky you will still be able to go outside and buy a newspaper and even go to your classes and meet your deadlines and get your good grades. You will feel, through the long winter ahead, acutely aware of the cold. Your frozen toes will ache. Your lips will crack and blister. If you are smart, you won't kiss anyone with those cracked, blistered lips. You will not kiss anybody for a long, long time.

You will do your accounts. You will accept responsibility for every bad decision you have ever made. You will calculate exactly how little you have. There is something liberating about this knowledge. You live in a time when you are told every day that you are only something if you have everything, and since you have nothing, you *are* nothing, and this knowledge will free you to be just that. This, you decide, is what Buddhism is about. You start to say you are becoming a Buddhist but that would mean you were trying to ascribe meaning to this state of being, and there is no comfort to be found in any category of meaning and thought, no defining tautology to tease out with that restless, grasping brain.

You can finally put grandiosity and despair behind you when you realize that you and your old stories about who you are and where you are from are just stories, and that they are also really boring. When you accept both of these as true, you can walk into a different room where the music is not so operatic.

It is best to watch, in moderation, the television shows that sicken you the most. *The Wheel of Fortune* is good, especially when it is interrupted by Iran-Contra developments and more bad news about the stock market. It is wise to listen to the president's glib speeches, the ones you used to avoid. Pay careful attention to all that you find repugnant in the world and its leaders and look for their counterparts within yourself. Study your cellulite in the mirror. Reread your worst lines from your fiction until you are immune to them. Imagine the room filled with every man you've ever slept with; listen as they discuss your shortcomings, comparing notes. Imagine a table filled with every meal you have ever eaten, every sugarcoated snack gobbled compulsively, piled up on your tiny card table that passes as the dinner table, piled to the ceiling, breaking the table into splinters. Picture your mother's eyes glazed with darkness and understand how you look when you return that gaze with your frightened eyes. This is what lurks beneath the compensatory smile you fix upon the world.

Relive the worst moments of your whole life until you run out of them. Imagine that you have a quota of tears that must be shed each day. Tell yourself that they are like writing mistakes; you have a finite number of them you are required to make, and after that you can get on with things.

This is how it happens: You go down with the ship without a life jacket. You don't sink. You go over the handlebars without a helmet. You bounce and the scar on your face fades. The Challenger explodes in a fury of flame and Chernobyl rains radioactive showers over your ancestors' homeland but somehow the Earth has some kick in it left. The stock market plummets again, and you hope that this is the destabilizing event that will jumpstart the revolution, but then you realize that harboring hope is another way of refusing to accept what is. You give up hope. It's another abstraction, anyway, and offers nothing you can see or touch or smell.

You keep thinking that the worst that could happen has happened and you have survived, but then there's always something worse. You tell yourself you are getting to the bottom of it. You are that old lady on the commercial who says, "I've fallen and I can't get up." Maybe you will need dentures soon.

Tell yourself that grief is not the same thing as self-pity. Tell yourself that you are crying about more than your smallness and your many failings and that you are still a political and spiritual animal, a citizen of a land you care about, perhaps even a patriot. So what if the people in charge are not on your team?

To survive you must convince yourself that you are more than the sum total of these things: your chemically altered hair, the scars on your body, the stories you have written, your shameful treatment of a man who only wished you well, your pregnancies and their sad conclusions, boy-with-backbone's rejection, your debts. You are more than the sorrows of your parents. More than the desperately positive attitude that until now has kept you from falling. More than your goals. More than memory and longing and loss and your plans for a triumphant future.

More and also less.

One day you'll feel good enough to look out the window again. The annex to the house next door will be complete, and people will be living inside it, looking out.

Outside, by a slimy pond at Smith College, there is an empty champagne bottle buried under dead leaves and snow in the place you sat when you hoped Keith would see your new Bali bra, the one your mother mailed you after she got back to Cleveland and before she tried to visit you with a butcher knife in her handbag. You will find the bottle next spring and throw it into the recycle bin. By then this whole chapter of your life will seem like someone else's story, you will be so over it.

# 17

# White Like Me

People were moving in every direction but it seemed to me, in that instant, that all of the people I could see, and many more than that, were moving toward me, against me, and that everyone was white.
James Baldwin, *Notes of a Native Son*

Any healing will require us to witness all our histories where they converge, the history of empires and emancipations, of slave ships as well as underground railroads; it requires us to listen back into the muted cries of the beaten, burned, forgotten and also to hear the ring of speech among us, meeting the miracle of that.
Susan Griffin, *The Eros of Everyday Life*

Who, if I cried, would hear me among the angelic orders?
R. M. Rilke, "The First Elegy"

WHAT WHITE LIBERAL GUILT?

I don't think I ever noticed how white Northampton is until the day I went to vote in 1988. As I walked down Main Street to the courthouse alongside a pair of lesbian Jewish moms in African batik pants pushing a stroller, past Bonducci's Café where I often stopped for cappuccino and muffins, past stores selling crystals and self-help books, I saw two Chinese Americans in Smith College sweatshirts, but everyone else was white like me.

That autumn I'd been thinking a lot about whiteness. A few weeks before, on the bus home from Amherst, I had overheard this conversation:

"Wanna hang out with me tomorrow? I'm cutting."

"Nah, I've got a calc midterm."

"No you don't. Tomorrow's that Civility Day thing. Every class has to interrupt what they're doing to talk about racism. I'm going to the mall. You should come."

"I'm sure I've got a calc midterm. It's on the syllabus."

"Math's doing this too. I heard my TA talking about it. Like, what does math have to do with racism? Besides, this is, like, the third most liberal school on the East Coast. It's not like there's anything they could tell us that we don't already know."

Then the two women proceeded to discuss, in rapid order, their plans for the summer (travels to Europe, South America); thoughts about graduate school (international finance, accounting), and the boycotter of Civility Day's new racing bicycle: all markers of privilege that being white and upper middle class in America had afforded them.

I listened intently to this exchange because the next day, like all other faculty and grad students at UMass, I would be teaching a mandatory class about racism and multiculturalism to my mostly white students, and I expected some resistance of the "I'm a liberal, not a racist" variety.

Lately I'd been thinking about how some of the most politically progressive pockets of America – places where I had lived or traveled to for all of my adult life – were among the least ethnically diverse. It seemed to me that I needed to *hear* the lecture, not deliver it.

The main point we were expected to make came from an essay published in 1970 by Joseph Barndt, "Setting the White Man Free," about the unavoidable consequences of growing up white in this society: "One thing must be made clear: the term 'white racist' does not apply only to the bigot who consciously expresses his hatred toward Black people and other minorities. It applies to all of us and means that all of us – whether we personally desire it or not – are part of a society and culture that continually and systematically subordinates its minority population. We may not be willingly . . . racists, but we are all imprisoned within a society of structured racism."

My class was an interdisciplinary honors course called Metaphor and Creativity. We were currently examining the ideology embedded in everyday expressions and clichés and my plan was to begin by unpacking the cultural baggage associated with the words *black* and *white*, *dark* and *light*. I had even considered bringing up my childhood friend's pastor who denounced rock music as Satanic because of its roots on the "dark continent," but I didn't want to offend any Baptists who might have slipped in among the Jews and lapsed Catholics and Unitarian Universalists and Wiccans.

But what I really wanted to talk about was more personal even than my youthful brush with religion. I wanted to tell my students about my grandmother. In her cosmology, white and dark had become reversed, and she had left her whiteness behind like the pilled up sweater you donate to the Salvation Army. As Alzheimer's disease erased the last vestiges of her memory, my grandmother had become an African American.

But how could I talk about my grandmother without mentioning her daughter and all our familial sorrow? Ultimately, to get to the part about how my grandmother had changed her race, I would have to share something too horrific for public consumption. That June my mother had tried to kill her own mother, then herself. Now the two were separated by court order and my grandmother was in the care of an African American woman she believed to be her mother. This new chapter in my grandmother's life was all I could think about it, but I couldn't talk about it. I couldn't narrate just a little of my family history without derailing the lesson, which was purportedly about race, and subjecting my listeners to the saga of three generations of white women, their battles with madness and violence, and their confusion about loyalty and love.

Which brings me to my anguish that year, to what haunted every class I took or taught, every conversation I had with friends or students. While Civility Day was intended to help our community grapple with a deeply disturbing outbreak of violence that had taken place on our campus two years ago, an incident that many had denied was racially motivated, I was grappling with my own lifetime pattern of denial. Despite everything that had happened between us, I still could not believe my mother was capable of murder.

But how *do* you comprehend what it is to wish another person dead? How do you comprehend that someone you love is capable of brutality? Is it like acknowledging that the polite kid who sits in your class is the same kid who gets drunk and beats the crap out of a black student with a baseball bat? (This very thing had happened at UMass, the third most liberal school on the East Coast.) Is it like acknowledging that the genial cop who patrols your college town and retrieves kittens from trees ignored the beaten black student's cries for help? (This very thing had happened at UMass, the third most liberal school on the East Coast.) Is it wrong to try to find a connection between family violence (white on white) and racial violence (white on black)? Yes, you say, because one kind of violence is personal and the other is impersonal. One is about individuals, and the other is about groups.

Or, you say, we're comparing apples and oranges. Your mother is your mother, and such a bond is supposed to be sacred, and the relationship between white and black is profane, profane because we can never forget that the white man brought the black man to this country in chains. You don't have to tell me this: to forge a connection between my white family's troubles and the culture's troubles with race I run the risk of denying the systemic dimension of racism and its unique features.

Or I run the risk of sounding like a racist. James Baldwin wrote in a 1960 essay in *Esquire* called "Fifth Avenue, Uptown": "People are continually pointing out to me the wretchedness of white people in order to console me for the wretchedness of blacks. But an itemized account of the American failure does not console me and it should not console anyone else. That hundreds of thousands of white people are living, in effect, no better than 'the niggers' is not a fact to be regarded with complacency. The social and moral bankruptcy suggested by this fact is of the bitterest, most terrifying kind." Not only do I agree with Baldwin, but this statement of his is my response to those "liberals" on the bus who thought they didn't need the Civility Day lecture. It's also my response to the people without money who listen to *Rush Limbaugh*. I want the rich to understand their privilege, but I also want poverty-stricken whites to work with poverty-stricken people of color to change the system, not to fight them over the scraps. We must examine the forces that create institutionalized economic inequality and not let them off the hook; they are the same forces that profit from our prejudices for they keep us from rising up in mass protest.

And yet, astonishingly, as the bottom income groups of our society felt the squeeze from 1980s economic policies that widened the gap between rich and poor, the poorest of whites were often turned on by the hateful, divisive rhetoric of the right. Rather than thinking structurally, the white have-nots were buying lottery tickets, dreaming of joining ranks with those featured on *The Rich and Famous*, and lashing out against those who dared to call themselves the victims of injustice; the richest whites, in contrast, felt that their work for racial justice was done.

As I tried to understand what had happened in my family and what had happened on my campus, I wanted to see what, if anything, the two acts of violence had in common. I wanted to examine the larger forces that pull the cords between mother and daughter and tighten the lynch mob's noose; I was not willing to believe anymore that my situation was particular only to me or that yours was particular only to you. While I was all for taking responsibility for one's individual actions, it seemed to me that a belief in my utter singularity – and yours – got some culpable institutions off the hook.

My grandmother instinctively knew such things. Once, on a bus ride through the Jim Crow South, she caused a ruckus when she gave up her seat for an African American woman carrying a small child. Even though she couldn't stand up to her abusive husband, she could mouth off to an abusive, racist conductor. She helped me see that all struggles for dignity and freedom are related. Long before I'd ever taken a government class it was my grandmother who made me understand that the same white supremacist ideology that had created apartheid in the United States was the motivation for the bombing of distant Cambodians in an undeclared war. "The bastards! The bastards!" she shouted at the political architects of these policies on TV.

Somehow, during her time in the hospital while she recovered from the stabbing, this bastard pool expanded to include everyone white. When white nurses and doctors came to tend to her, she screamed holy murder. Every thermometer, bedpan, needle, and stethoscope became another butcher knife. Only black nurses and doctors could calm her down. The midcareer Malcolm X was speaking through her: white people were blue-eyed devils.

And then, when she moved in with her court-appointed caregiver, Gloria, and her husband and father-in-law, my grandmother began to associate blackness with family, comfort, and love. When Gloria said to me on the phone, "Your grandma loves us as her own," I did not realize at first that she meant it literally. Gloria's father-in-law also had Alzheimer's, and he and my grandmother believed they were twins. They were the same age and in their illness, they had both regressed back to the thirties, to New Deal America, the time when he had been living in the South under the thumb of Jim Crow and my grandmother was on the East Side of Cleveland under the thumb of her violent husband. To their way of thinking, they were in the same place at the same time.

When I visited them that semester in East Cleveland, we went to a Denny's for lunch. Grandma looked calm and cared for while flanked by Gloria and her husband, Pap. "How do you like my mother?" she asked, beaming at Gloria, whose smooth, broad face and unlined mouth showed her to be at least a decade younger than my mother. Grandma asked me who I was, then waved her menu at a nearby booth where a family of standard-issue white American Midwesterners – mom, dad, son, daughter, all overweight and clad in red and blue with baseball caps – were eating burgers and fries. "Isn't that your family over there?" she wanted to know.

## TEAM SPIRIT

Civility Day marked the second anniversary of a riot that had occurred on 27 October 1986, in the southwest residential area, a block of ugly, sixties-era dorms I passed on the way to class every day. The brawl had broken out after the New York Mets beat the Boston Red Sox eight to five in the final game of the World Series. A crowd of somewhere between a thousand and three thousand students spontaneously streamed out of the cinderblock residence halls: elated Mets fans and enraged Red Sox fans.

Imagine coming upon this scene in the night. You're walking across a college quad on an October evening, your books inside your backpack, noticing the last orange leaves clinging to the oak and maple trees around the pond. You feel a touch of winter in the air. Suddenly you see people running and shouting. You smell beer. Picture this moment: hundreds of people shouting at each other, squaring off into two groups, only a foot or two of cement pavement between them. Many of the loudest voices are those of football players. Picture their bulky shoulders as they raise their fists and shout, their faces obscured by the visors of their baseball caps. At first, when you see students running in and out of the dorm, you wonder if there has been a fire. Then you watch some of the young men lift baseball bats into the air and swing. Others flail golf clubs, breaking windows in the dorm. The word "nigger" echoes across pavement and centuries and there you are, watching blood spill and feeling the roiling mass of people rush you, demanding something from you, but what?

And if you are an African American student walking into this scene, you immediately find out that you have enraged a whole lot of drunken white people, even if you don't follow baseball.

The way I heard it in news reports, many of the white Red Sox fans were from rural, white hill towns in Western Massachusetts and many of the black Mets fans were from New York City, although my students said that, in truth, there were black and white fans from each side. A crowd of fifteen to twenty chased one black student named Yancey Robinson until they caught him. They jumped on him, kicked him, and beat him until someone led him away to the campus infirmary. Ten students in total were treated for injuries that night, most of them people of color.

But when the news broke about the fight, university officials and students denied the riot was about race. The administration invited Marty Barrett of the Red Sox and Mookie Wilson of the Mets to campus, and as they addressed the thousand people who had crowded into the UMass Campus Center Auditorium, these athletes said that the tension was only about team rivalry. "I don't think this is a case of white guys thinking that black guys aren't as good as they are," Barrett said. "No way do I think that's what happened. What happened was a flare-up of tension from the ball game."

Frederick A. Hurst, one of three commissioners with the Massachusetts Commission against Discrimination, assessed the brawl quite differently. After interviewing hundreds of students and university officials for his fifty-three-page report, he called the events on 27 October 1986 "predictable, preventable and primarily racially motivated." He said in an interview with the *Hampshire Gazette*, "You don't get mad at a Mets score and chase and beat a black student. That's not a response to a score."

Hurst was also highly critical of university officials and campus police for making a poor showing at the brawl and for failing to come to black students' defenses. UMass Security had told Amherst police that they should be on the alert, but only if the Red Sox won, which might provoke Mets fans – a.k.a. black kids – to take out their frustrations in Amherst. Yancey Robinson, still in a neck brace weeks after the incident, filed charges against the UMass police, claiming they ignored his cries for help during the attack on him. Almost a week passed after the incident before the university administration contacted his parents. Hurst wrote:

> Not until October 31, 1986, when the chancellor sent a letter to the student body denouncing racism and promising to punish the wrongdoers, was a strong message sent by anyone in the administration. By then, denial, one of the subtlest forms of racial intolerance, because it tolerates it, had caused the incident to grow. I later came to suspect, and still do, that denial played a role in causing the incident and still

is the single most important reason why those investigating it have not and could not get to the bottom of it. Denial might even explain past administration failure to prepare for such an incident.

It was because of Frederick Hurst's report that UMass created Civility Day. Hurst wrote that changing racial attitudes was a gradual process but "you can't have it go unattended to at the university. If you do, you can't expect to solve it in society at large." He concluded, "The historical context of the events of October 27 did not occur in a vacuum."

What happened in my family did not occur in a vacuum either. And it, too, had something to do with politics.

Both my family and the participants of the 1986 World Series riot on the UMass campus were affected, personally, by the politics of the 1980s, by an administration that was indifferent to human suffering. After nearly eight years of Reaganomics I understood in a visceral way that a government that does not believe in Aid to Dependent Children or state-funded social work agencies – the kind of agency I hoped would be able to care for my mother and grandmother separately, on Uncle Sam's dime – generally does not believe in Affirmative Action, Head Start, Job Corps, multicultural education, or in any federally funded programs or laws that would aim to rectify centuries of institutionalized violence and poverty. And when a president devalues the importance of federal programs and espouses the importance of local and state control, beware: if it had been up to the local government in Little Rock, schools would never have been desegregated, Jim Crow would continue to be the law of the land in several states in the South, and domestic violence would still be legal in many of those same states. A government that believes that it should be up to the whims of private do-gooders and religious organizations – George Bush Senior's "thousand points of light," George Bush Junior's faith-based charity – to decide if a family of any color deserves a helping hand is a government that is not committed to sending the top-down message that every American has some basic rights. A government that explains away riots and domestic violence as the actions of misguided "individuals" is a government that is not committed to eradicating violence from our streets, our campuses, our homes.

In "Fifth Avenue, Uptown" Baldwin goes on to say that the people who find some consoling value in the fact that white Americans suffer too are the same Americans who point out how "So-and-So, white, and So-and-So, black, rose from the slums into the big time. The existence

– the public existence – of, say, Frank Sinatra, or Sammy Davis Junior, proves to them that America is still the land of opportunity and that inequalities vanish before the determined will." In other words, if So-and-So has made it and you haven't, quit whining and get to work, or go back to Africa/Hoboken/Cleveland. If So-and-So made it, there's really nothing systemically, structurally, institutionally in place to block you from getting there too.

That fall, someone scrawled on one of the buildings at Smith College near my apartment: "NIGGERS, SPICS, AND CHINKS, QUIT COMPLAINING AND GET OUT."

In America just then, our black So-and-So was Bill Cosby, who played a rich doctor on TV. He also happened to be a member of the board of trustees at UMass, Amherst.

One of my friends was at the regents' meeting that took place before Hurst's article came out, when the administration was still denying that racism played a role in the riot. She said that Cosby told them off eloquently (how I wish I'd been there to hear it) and that before he stormed off, he added that his one consolation was that he had more money than everyone in that room put together.


FAMILY BONDAGE

A few years ago, somebody sent me this quote on the Internet, something attributed to former vice president Dan Quayle: "Republicans understand the importance of bondage between a mother and child."

Much of my life history, and certainly my experience with the politics of the 1980s, is summed up in that statement. A president that cuts federal spending on domestic programs while touting so-called family values is a president that has cast you and your family to drift on a sinking ship through your private ocean of internecine terror and violence. Bondage indeed.

What precipitated my family's breakdown was my mother's fears about how she would survive financially as her mother's disease took its toll. My mother, heeding the advice from one of the books she'd read about having a parent with Alzheimer's disease, wanted to protect the house and her mother's savings by making herself her mother's legal guardian. She drew up papers to have her mother sign over to her half the house and half her savings. There was one problem, however; my grandmother wouldn't sign. Half the house, okay maybe, but not her bank account, which was all she had to show for fifty-five years of spousal abuse and self-sacrifice. My mother had never been good at managing money. My grandmother, still semilucid, didn't trust her.

To this day, I have never inhabited the scene of the crime in my mind's eye, never watched that blade pierce my grandmother's flesh or heard her cry out for help as she fell toward the stained linoleum floor, grabbing at the sink where the butts from my mother's cigarettes had trapped the breakfast dishes in gray water. From the window she must have seen the flowering fruit trees in the back yard and wondered, perhaps, how there could be so much beauty in a world with so much hatred. It is impossible for me to picture my grandmother bleeding. When I was a child of six and seven I often threw my arms around her neck to cry into her comforting, soft chest. This flesh that soothed me as a child may have been what spared her life because she had so much padding around her heart, the heart my mother aimed for with the butcher knife.

Then my mother went upstairs to the bathroom and tried to jump. I will never try to picture this moment either. If I do, I don't think I'll recover.

My sister and I would not be informed about the stabbing and suicide attempt until both my grandmother and mother had already been released from the hospital. I never found out who came to their aid or how much time had passed, how much blood they both lost. What pains me most is to imagine them calling for help and no one answering.

What both my grandmother and my mother needed was the help of a government-funded social agency. By the late 1980s, our belief in the primacy of the individual had made us all into Yancey Robinsons, crying for help that doesn't come. After my mother was treated for her own wounds she was transferred to a state-funded mental hospital, but when my grandmother was well again, she was sent home by cab to the empty house. Why? How could that happen? Were it not for the intervention of the neighbor who called us, she would have been left completely on her own.

The irony in all this was that with one stroke of a knife my mother had accomplished what my sister and I had failed to bring about through the scratching of countless pens. All our letters to social workers and family court judges had gone unheeded over the past year as we tried to get the two women legally separated and put under the care of different court-appointed guardians. But once my sister found out about the stabbing through the neighbor, she could set things right.

My mother's actions convinced the state that she was unfit to care for her mother, and a probate court judge assigned my grandmother the legal guardian who sent her to live at Gloria's house.

At first, my grandmother missed her daughter. She believed that she had been attacked by a robber who stole her purse and that her daughter had been kidnapped. My mother was eventually allowed to visit her mother in public places, but not without Gloria as chaperone, and she was forbidden to have Gloria's last name or phone number and address. Soon my grandmother settled into her new life. With no one around to shout at her or beat her, she experienced the only peace she had ever known as an adult. Finally she had the loving family she'd always wanted. My only source of comfort that fall was the knowledge that my grandmother was safe, at long last.

But I had also learned a hard lesson. The state had deigned to protect my grandmother because she was mentally incompetent and old but, ultimately, because she had a savings account. My mother, on the other hand, had no money. She was my problem and my sister's, with no relief for any of us in sight.

When Dan Quayle said, "Republicans understand the importance of bondage between a mother and child," he had inherited a policy for dealing with incompetent mentally ill citizens that had been signed into law by Ronald Reagan. Under new laws established in the early 1980s, you had to have money to get a court-appointed guardian. Because she did not have a nest egg, my mother could not afford to find some responsible person to make sure she took her medication and stayed away from the cutlery drawer. Thanks to the will of government, my mother's problems, and her violence, were now a private family matter. If I wanted someone to look after her, I would either have to move to Cleveland to take care of her myself (meanwhile sacrificing my career prospects and possibly my life) or hire someone to do it on my $6,000-a-year graduate teaching stipend.

I was amazed and frightened beyond measure when the mental hospital released our mother only a few weeks after the stabbing without even calling my sister or me to warn us. My mother, an independent but impoverished citizen, was free to go. The collect phone calls she made from the hospital were increasingly hostile, and what was to stop her from coming after us with a knife? There were no stalking laws yet, and apparently my mother fell into a curious category: she was too ill to be charged for violent crimes, but unless I could prove otherwise to a judge, too well to be institutionalized for her illness. I wanted her placed in a group home (for which the waiting lists were several months long) but state funding for such places had also been cut, and then there was the matter of her violence.

Her competency hearings were scheduled around the time of UMass's Civility Day. My mother, determined to remain a free agent, went right to the top. Unbelievably, she hired the attorney who defended John Hinckley after he tried to assassinate Ronald Reagan. How she paid for him I don't know. Perhaps she still believed the court would give her half of her mother's savings.

This $240-an-hour attorney did what she hired him to do. When I could bring myself to speak to her again she said with an edge of defiance, "The judge says I can live wherever I want. I'm thinking I'll move in with you."

THE GREAT WHITE HOPE

My roommate and I were watching *Dynasty* when we saw the commercial attacking our governor's prison furlough program; the juxtaposition between the beatific Krystal in white fur and angry dark-skinned people in prison was so unsubtle as to be almost funny. Shot in black-and-white, the ad showed an endless stream of prisoners, mostly black, leaving jail in fast-forward time through a rapidly revolving door. The camera angles gave the effect that these men were coming out of the TV and marching straight toward us, toward our apartment in Northampton where we sat on our white living-room carpet. Dangerous men like Willie Horton, who had raped a white woman, while out on furlough, were headed our way, with the hundreds of other escaped prisoners "still at large." If our governor, Michael Dukakis, became president, who knew how many more black criminals would come after us?

Maybe I'm still too idealistic, but I believe government is meant to be a force that encourages a culture to flourish and its populace to work together toward a greater good. George Bush, in contrast, closed the gap between himself and Dukakis in the polls by fomenting fear and prejudice and division, by appealing to the worst in the American mind. Over *Jaws*-like theme music, the ads closed with the line, "America can't afford that risk." The strategy worked. Once Willie Horton became the sign and signifier of the Democratic party, Dukakis's unfavorable ratings doubled from 25 percent in July to 50 percent, according to the *NBC News–Wall Street Journal* poll.

The way my roommate and I saw it, George Bush rose to power on the back of a black man (as would his son, a dozen years later, when the Bush-appointed Clarence Thomas helped appoint him in the contested presidency). Were we surprised when race riots broke out in Los Angeles a few years later under Bush's watch?

As children, we need to believe that the world we live in is just and good. We can't survive without believing that we are safe and the world will be kind to us. If we are lucky, some of this faith lingers as we become adults.

If I found it hard to believe that my mother was capable of killing, it's no wonder that most Americans distance themselves from the killing our government does in the name of democracy in distant parts of the globe, or in the killing it turns its back on in the districts where black and brown-skinned people live. We believe in our government's goodness and innocence, and our own; Lewis Lapham has pointed out that a belief in our inherent goodness and innocence is part of the American national character. And so we construct two governments of the mind – the good one that passes legislation like the Voting Act of 1963, and the shadowy one that starts coups, in say, Chile or Nicaragua. Or Watts. Or Amherst. Or Los Angeles. We acquire dual citizenship. We compartmentalize.

My grandmother never stopped believing that the world's bigots ("the bastards") would "drop dead" in her lifetime and that the children they'd bred would know better. But she would only live to see this happen on the personal level, not in the nation she had such high hopes for. After she moved in with Gloria my grandmother finally felt loved and cared for. She learned to compartmentalize, to trust her new family, but not the government.

"Pretty girl so nice," my grandmother said, stroking my hair when I visited her at Gloria's house. She was clean and happy, and sat smiling on the easy chair in the living room. George Bush, the spokesman for the "kinder, gentler America" came on the TV and my grandmother frowned. "Buncha crooks and murderers," she said. "Is he the one who took my pocketbook?"

AMEN

On Civility Day, when my students told stories from their lives about race, I came very close to bringing up my grandmother. Oh, I was tempted: I'd even practiced my imitation of her shouting "The bastards!

The bastards!" her arms flailing at Richard Nixon or George Wallace or Henry Kissinger on TV. I found words forming in my head, but I was afraid if I got started I would cry.

Somewhere in the conversation, I asked them to write down some adjectives about themselves. After the white people in the class shared some of their responses – "optimistic," "messy," "addicted to caffeine," and "a big fan of 10,000 Maniacs" – I asked why none of them had written the word "white." "Those of us who are white don't really think about our whiteness," I said. "We think we are the universal human, which in itself is a racist assumption. And we don't see the privilege this so-called lack of a race affords us."

Or, as Manning Marable says, "White people have the luxury of never having to talk about being white."

We had a good, honest discussion, which was more than I'd hoped for given my lack of experience. I don't know if we made any in-roads toward changing the world, but I know that the class changed me.

A few days later, about three thousand of us turned out for the Hands Across UMass rally, a little more than the number of baseball fans who had manhandled each other two years before. One of my students had suggested that our class go together to this rally and we did. We stood in a line holding hands around the campus pond with the other marchers – black, brown, white, leather-jacketed, down-parka'd, big-haired, bald, green-mohawked, and skateboarded – shouting "Hey, hey, ho, ho, racism has got to go," and singing "Amazing Grace."

It had been a long time since I'd been at a rally. I had forgotten what it was like to shout and sing and join hands with others. The last autumn leaves were falling but it was warm and the sky was the undiluted blue of some team's colors, I wouldn't know whose. Some of the ducks in the pond turned their heads toward us, alert to our serenade. A few weeks later I would hear them flying south for the winter and the pond would be empty, the grounds white with snow. But today our campus felt vibrant and full of color. And although I hadn't brought her with me into the classroom, as I marched with my students, I felt the presence of my grandmother. As I linked hands with friends and strangers, she was leaning into my shoulder, egging me on.

# 18

# Last Postcard from Cleveland

*Family Values*

Empires rise and fall; so do families, and so do theories of law and aesthetics.
  Lewis Lapham, "Notebook Omens," *Harper's*

My mother has sold the family home. We have come to Cleveland on a ruse, ostensibly to help her move into the apartment she found nearby, but actually to save her life, and ours.

Mira and I have enlisted the assistance of our mother's social worker to convince her she needs to move into a supervised setting, a group home that she just got accepted to despite a certain violent incident we are afraid to mention. We don't have money for movers or U-Haul vans so we have reluctantly drafted my sister's boyfriend and my friend from school, Michael. Our mother has known Mira's boyfriend for years, but she has never met Michael, so we have given him an alias, Jim, and have turned him from a New Englander into a Chicagoan. Our mother doesn't need another man's name in her address book.

When we arrive, our mother is wearing only a thin, stained nightgown on a below-zero day. She has not brushed her hair or bathed in weeks and has lost her false teeth. The floors are black with dirt, the kitchen counter pocked with cigarette burns, and the toilet near the side door is backed up with shit. The house smells like raw sewage and cigarettes. The realtor is expected tomorrow, the new owners of the house in two days.

But my mother has no intention of tidying up for strangers. She has lured us here on a ruse as well.

As the four of us confer about what cleaning supplies to buy, my mother says, "Boys are not welcome here. You'll have to go, gentlemen." The boyfriends try to convince her that they are there to help, that they have driven a long way to help, but I suddenly am afraid for them. What if she tries to hurt them? What if she has a gun? Has anyone checked the cutlery drawer? Mira's boyfriend has an aunt in Cleveland, and we urge them to go there where it's safe. "I'll try to calm her down," I whisper to Michael/Jim. Call us in an hour."

The moment the boyfriends pull out of the driveway, our mother yanks the phone from the kitchen wall and says, "We're going to stay in this house, the three of us."

"But it's not yours anymore," I say, as if she could listen. "The realtor is coming soon, and so is your social worker."

"No one is making me move," she shouts.

As my sister tries to fix the phone, our mother breaks a bottle and lunges at her. They fall to the ground, wrestling, my mother holding the broken bottle to my sister's jugular artery while I stand in a trance, screaming but immobile, like in one of those nightmares when your feet are glued to the ground and the bear gains on you and then he is there, all jaws and teeth. My mother is prepared to murder my sister, then me, to keep us with her.

I have floated above the living room. I am near the ceiling, watching myself at thirteen doing sit-ups on the carpet while our mother pounds out Tchaikovsky and our grandfather calls me a "whooore" for wearing hot pink hot pants and my sister hyperventilates beneath the sideboard, pretending to be a panting dog. Grandma is on her blue chair eating chocolate-chip ice cream and swearing at the TV.

The bottle is at my sister's throat, but I cannot move from my post above the curtain rods. I am useless in this emergency, shocked into paralysis. But something happens, something I am the first in my family to see. I *finally* get it. I finally comprehend that the situation is hopeless. I have no choice but to abandon all plans and schemes that include our mother being cared for, recovering, and being a mother. I have to give up.

We are all going to die here anyway.

My sister holds on even as the broken bottle looms only an inch from her neck. I scream and scream, still stuck, still floating above where no one can see or hear me.

But we are saved, anyway. The boyfriends return, enter the house, and my sister and I outrun our mother to their cars as she follows us barefoot through snow, flailing the broken bottle. All I can think about is that she might memorize Michael's license plate and find a way to track him down and kill him. And I'm worried about her getting frostbite in the snow.

We call the police from a pay phone, then have a long day ahead of us filling out paperwork with various social workers downtown. When the police and social worker come and get her at the agreed-upon time, we go back to the house to say good-bye to our mother. We say we are sorry but it is for the best. She doesn't listen, so I write it down. My tears fall and blur the ink but I want her to have some record, some piece of evidence of what I am trying to say, a document that will contest whatever spin she gives this horrific memory in the future. I write that I love her, but I want her to get help, and I can't help her myself. She yells, "This is just a family dispute. My daughters are mad at me about money. They want my money." The policemen shrug and take her anyway.

That night we are at the house again: my sister, the boys, and me. We sift through all the possessions we have stored over the years in attic trunks, in the green hatbox in the upstairs den. Here are all the letters I wrote home. Photos. School memorabilia. Letters from Patti. Clothes from childhood: a beaded purple Turkish vest my sister and I once shared, my faux-fur coat from the seventies. Mira's paintings. My first stories and essays. Newspaper clippings about my high school journalism awards. Then there's the furniture. The pale yellow side tables from China that our mother promised me. We have the two vehicles and are ready to haul off what she doesn't want for herself. We have even promised one of the beds to Gloria, who has taken in another Alzheimer's patient. Our plan is to bring it to her tomorrow when we visit our grandmother.

Suddenly our mother is at the door. She lets herself in. This is not a dream. It is really happening, although in dreams for years to come I'll relive this scene in a prisoner-of-war barracks, the old basement apartment, every place I lived in Seattle, my college office, and most terrifying of all: the home I share with my husband and two sons. Our mother is opening the front door. "Hold the door against her," I scream to Michael, while I frantically gather our coats. "She's here, Mira," I call upstairs to where she is gathering mementos. "Hurry! She's here!"

We will find out later that the doctors found it convenient to believe her story that this was just a family dispute about money. They were short on beds.

This is it. We have a minute to take what we can hold in our arms as we leave this house, this house that will live forever in our memories and dreams, our stories and our bodies. We can't think about it; we can only act on instinct.

My sister takes the handful of old photographs of family members she was sorting when I called to her. From the living room where she could have died today she removes and carries away one of her paintings. It is titled "Help is on the Way," an irony that does not escape us even in our haste. I only want one thing: my mother's address book. It has the names of my friends, professors, old boyfriends, and everyone else she has ever called in the middle of the night to accuse of raping and kidnapping me: all of my lifelines, my every contact. That's all I will have from my past to carry with me. After I get back to school, I won't even have that. I'll burn it, watching the names in my mother's hand fly up in charred curls.

We run again into the snowdrifts on the driveway, with our mother chasing us. Mira gets in her boyfriend's truck and heads back to Chicago. Michael drives his Isuzu pickup and I sit beside him, shaking with cold. We crank the heat but I can't get warm.

As we flee the city, the smokestacks behind us, the Cuyahoga River snaking along beside us like a tired old companion hissing, *Remember me?* I make a decision that will change my life. I am never coming back. I give up. I can't help my mother and in fact, my presence seems to make her even crazier. This is it. I'm done.

The Big Eighties are almost over. These are my values now: *Every woman for herself*. This is what the me-first decade has taught me.

And yet, ironically, for the past ten years, this is the message I've heard, from Ronald Reagan to Dan Quayle to John Hinckley's lawyer to my mother's Catholic social workers: *Families need to stay together. If you girls don't help your mother, nobody will*. What none of these people understood, even the psychiatric social workers, is that the family members are not the people who should be tending to the psychotic person's needs. They have been traumatized repeatedly and are scared and scarred. And they are often in denial that the ill relative could harm them. The family members can only see their way clearly through the dynamic when they are apart from it. Moreover, the disturbed person seems to go deeper into her psychosis in the company of the family; the family is often the subject of her most dangerous paranoid obsessions.

No, what my family needed was not more bonding (or bondage) but a well-funded mental health system that was free, not only for our mother but also for my grandmother, my sister, and me. We needed free medical aid. We needed practical advice free of the sentimental platitudes that help no one and only contribute to useless guilt. We needed well-paid social workers that weren't overburdened and cynical. We needed free legal services. We needed our mother to be assigned a legal guardian whose wages would be paid by the government and not our mother's meager Social Security and welfare pittance.

Across America, as families eroded and watched their security vanish, as the families from the lowest 20 percent of income got poorer still, we all needed not only a safety net but a safety valve: a drop-in crisis center on every block, a place to alleviate the pressure, a place where people were authorized to step in and intervene before a woman stabbed her mother, tried to jump out a window, or tried to cut open her daughter's jugular vein with a broken bottle in a "family dispute over money."

Meanwhile, Dan Quayle was quoted as saying that he lived in a country full of "happy campers."

As we leave the city I know that my decision is final: a part of me will love her always, but I will never speak to or visit my mother again. If I want to live, I must live apart from her. If I will be plagued with a lifetime of guilt for abandoning her, so be it. If she ends up homeless, which she very well might, so be it. This is one story that offers no possibility of transformation or redemption. The only thing left for me to transcend is my old Pollyannaish belief that I could live well without money. All that's left for me now is to get a good teaching job and hope the family I create won't perpetuate the bondage of the old.

Here are my family values now: If you are lucky, and have a good one that nurtures you and cares for you, treasure it with all your heart for all your days. But if you don't, be sure to get out while you can.

# 19

# The Bastille Day Blues

One way or another rigidity came to characterize thought on both sides of the partition.

    Susan Griffin, *The Eros of Everyday Life*

The residents of La Maison had been pleading with her for days, but the mother superior of the Sisters of Fidelity would not budge. If she was acting as our jailer on Bastille Day, on, of all things, the *bicentennial* Bastille Day, *ça c'était normal*: it was merely her job. It didn't matter that the two hundredth anniversary of the Declaration of the Rights of Man and the Citizen and all its attendant gaiety – dancing and swilling champagne al fresco, singing the French songs we'd learned in grade school – was the main attraction luring us to Paris that summer, inspiring at least one of us to rack up extra grad school debt. *N'importe quoi* that our American professor had volunteered to give the nun who worked the door a holiday and buzz us in herself. La Maison had its rules and, *donc*, we had to be in before midnight or we would be homeless that night – a disaster that had befallen many of the women already. A resident would be late trying to get back from the opera or a concert because the Métro stalled or the crowds slowed her down and *voilà*, lockout. The next morning when the convent doors opened at precisely 7:10, we would find her curled up on the sidewalk, her bag beneath her head, her cheeks streaked with tears.

    Perhaps for the regular college-age students who boarded at La Maison during the school year, those from strict Catholic homes at least, an *in loco parentis* policy was expected, but as I reminded the mother superior one day after lunch, Wendy, Mary, and I were older than many of the nuns. Nonetheless, if our safety was her primary concern, she could rest assured that we would have a male bodyguard on Bastille Night: the handsome Eugene, who, on our study date to bone up on the subjunctive (men were allowed only on the ground level, and never after dark) had charmed a smile out of the mother superior when he praised the beauty of the courtyard roses. "Non," she said again. "But do you *want* us to sleep on the streets?" I asked. No answer. "Among the drunk and the . . . sick?" Over lunch, our professor had told us that when she pressed the mother superior about her recalcitrance she had whispered that she was only protecting us from contracting *le* SIDA – AIDS – which she apparently believed was spread most rampantly after the witching hour. The epidemic was her new justification for a rule that had been in place for nearly half the century.

"*Écoute*, all the beds will be empty that night," I said in my halting French, but Mother Superior told me that she had faith in the moral fiber and conduct of her *jeunes filles*, and that I would be proven wrong.

"We shall see," I tried to say, but it came out as, "We will look."

That spring, without the foreknowledge that I'd be barricaded in a convent, I had decided to prepare for my foreign language competency exam on location. Certainly, history had brought me here – the revolution, the bicentennial, and the current democracy movement in Europe – but also my romance for all things French. Given my usual aversion to groups and tendency to conk out by eleven I was an unlikely candidate to be the spokesperson and instigator of this particular mass revolt. Still, there was the principle of the thing – our rights as adults, our rights to be the witnesses to something newsworthy. Without planning to or relishing this role, I was now the Robespierre of a Left Bank convent.

At that moment, one of the resident *jeunes filles* bumped into the mother superior with her lunch tray, spattering yogurt on the sister's crisp white blouse. "Ce n'est pas grave," she said soothingly to the flustered young woman. "Heureusement, c'est seulement blanche sur blanche." It's only white on white. I happened to shift my gaze to the bulletin board area behind the serving line, at the montage of posters that passed for art in La Maison. There, shining down on us, were tableaux of kittens peering into fruit bowls, young girls clutching puppies: a treacly shrine to the virtuous *jeune fille*. I understood in one glance that no amount of reasoning would penetrate *this* fortress, not a celebration of democracy, not a lecture about sexism and the infantilization of women, not the threat of a large-scale rebellion. There was nothing more to say.

The American Christian Right and my banished mother had stalked me to Paris. I might be the spokesperson for enlightenment values, but I was also a teenager trying to climb out the window to freedom.

I fled to my language class where I hoped to stir up an outraged, "Ce n'est pas possible!" from a few of my peers.

The democracy movement had brought a diverse group of people to Paris that summer. We did not know that the Berlin Wall would come crashing down that fall, but we knew revolution was stirring when, in my class alone, students from the United Kingdom, Italy, Spain, Puerto Rico, the United States and West Berlin elbowed up to students from East Berlin, Austria, Romania, Poland, and Beijing. Our instructor, Marie-Hélène Naveau, loved to stir up political debates. She had been a student activist in the May 1968 uprisings and her father had fought with the French Resistance. Intense and provocative, she goaded us to argue with each other, to spar and bleat and refute. But the first topic that got us all talking at once was not democracy or Bastille Day or the politics of a Bastille Day curfew. It was sex.

Madame told us that she was thirty-nine, divorced, the mother of a young child, and ready to start dating again. We all took her in: her shoulder-length black hair and bangs, her shapely dancer's legs, her mischievous eyes. She smiled gravely, then posed the question: Should she bring a man home for the night? Was she free to pursue her own life? Each of us was to offer a frank opinion.

A murmur of shock swept through our rectangle of twenty like a Molotov cocktail at a demonstration. I admired Madame Naveau for her boldness, especially since we had among us: a priest from Vietnam and two shy nuns on loan from the Marcos regime. While the stunned searched for a response, Wendy, a plump, blond kindergarten teacher from Milwaukee, cried, "Bien sûr!" She had confided in Mary and me over wine that she hadn't had sex in years and was hoping for a romantic adventure that summer. She added that in her work she had seen that happy mothers made better parents.

"I think children should be taken from mothers who do such things," a young man shouted, rapping his gold signet ring against the table. It was Tim, a recent graduate of Notre Dame: a diminutive, androgynous-looking fellow with bulging blue eyes, grandfatherly spectacles, a high-pitched voice, and a tic. He looked like a young, highly caffeinated Gary Bauers.

During our why-we-came-to-Paris introductions Tim had explained he was there to join the followers of the archbishop Marcel Léfèbvre, an archconservative who did his sermons with his back to the congregation, in Latin. Many of the Léfèbvre priests and devout parishioners were followers of Jean-Marie Le Pen, the leader of the neo-fascist Front National. You could see them clustering around the Left Bank church of St. Nicolas du Chardonnet on Sundays selling pamphlets and monarchist insignia, including portraits of the "martyred" Louis XVI. For some of them the counterrevolutionary tradition was still alive. They remained the King's loyal subjects, scowling in scorn at the likes of Hume, Locke, Pascal, and unruly heretics from the New World like Thomas Jefferson – all those blasphemers who turned otherwise good Frenchmen into free thinkers. This brand of human was a revelation to me, like so many other things that summer. If I had not expected to be locked in at night, or to debate sexual morality in the City of Love, neither had I predicted I would meet a monarchist. A monarchist from Indiana.

"People who think the way Wendy does should not be permitted to work with children," Tim added.

I tried to leap to Wendy's defense, opening my dictionary to the French for "prig," "chauvinist," "patriarch," and "zealot," but all I managed was a stammering, "You are a crazy man!" in a crazed voice that made me wince.

My love affair with all things French began in third-grade French class, when our teacher instituted a tasty tradition called La Table Française: a monthly feast of croissants, French cheeses, sausages, and pastries. How she found such goodies in white-bread Ohio is still a mystery to me, but she infected me early on with the conviction that France was the culinary capital of the world.

But alas, if the expression "white on white" evoked the mother superior's construction of the feminine, it also described our meals at La Maison. Everything was white. Stale white baguette, curdled hot white milk, white radishes, white brie, white overboiled cauliflower, white yogurt, and when I was lucky enough to find a hot vegetarian meal in the cafeteria, creamy white potato soup. Except for one prepaid all-group lunch at the Hotel de Paris presided over by Jacques Chirac (then mayor of Paris), and one prepaid farewell dinner out, I never had a decent meal in Paris. I was always starving.

At La Maison our meals, like our hours, were strictly regulated. We went through a cafeteria line, and there were rules about how much you could have of what. You could take one meat and one vegetable and salad and one fruit but never two veg at any one time. I didn't eat red meat and even though it would have cost them less to give me an extra stalk of broccoli instead of a serving of pork, they wouldn't make concessions for my diet or anyone else's, even the elderly woman keeping kosher. My vegetarian lunch might be one side plate of white radishes and a piece of dried-out baguette from the morning, and one banana (you couldn't take two fruit either). Dinner might be boiled potatoes and an orange (ah, color!) and a small piece of white cake. I got desperate for protein, but we only got fish on Friday. I could have cheese, but that meant passing up dessert: their one specialty.

The young women they hired to work the line were the enforcers of these rules, and there was no reasoning with them. The worst of them was a red-haired, smirking, pasty girl of about twenty that Wendy, Mary, and I nicknamed the Sadist. She worked the breakfast shift. One morning, when one of the Italian women complained that her hot milk had lumps of what looked like mucus skimming on the top and that the bowl was lined with flakes of dried-out milk scum, all the Sadist did was laugh maliciously. When we told her she was *méchante*, evil, she laughed again, and we suspected that she had spit inside the dirty bowl herself. The Italian girl fled the cafeteria in tears.

Under normal circumstances, I would have walked out with the Italian in solidarity and offered to treat her to a real breakfast. We lived next door to a patisserie that sold exquisite croissants, *pain au chocolat*, and pastries filled with apricots, strawberries, apples, and prunes. On mornings when the residents couldn't face the milk scum and stale bread, they dined at this bakery instead. I longed to join them, but I couldn't. Once again I had miscalculated and – oh, how this story was starting to sound like an old song from my youth stuck on replay – I was broke.

I had financed this trip with a student loan that I'd been told would be deposited into my checking account that July. Whenever I went to an ATM, however, my card was rejected. I made a panicky long-distance phone call to the financial aid office and found out that the person who'd handled my papers had misspoken; my money wouldn't come until October. I did not have a Visa card so I couldn't even wrack up some high-interest debt. After I bought my books, I had less than a hundred dollars to live on for the month. I couldn't afford to miss one of La Maison's meals and I certainly couldn't spring for a hotel, even a no-star hotel, if I missed curfew. Here was irony for you, here was progress.

Talk of liberty rang through much of the globe and I was trapped in a nunnery.

Jail — the Bastille, the convent, and also the mental prison of rigid ideology — became that summer's multilayered theme; I did riffs on it in my journal. Sometimes I sat outside and sketched the abutting residential buildings that adjoined the chapel, the black iron balconies that no one was allowed to climb onto: black jailhouse stripes against white sills. Deprived as I was of sensual satisfaction, I gathered fallen rose petals from the courtyard, silky shreds of blood red, orange, pale pink, and salmon, the only color within view, and I'd imagine saying to the mother superior, "So, do you ever think about the fact that flowers are the sex organs of plants?"

When I'd moved into my room, I'd been disappointed at first not to have a balcony overlooking this pretty garden. Instead my room faced the city: the school across the street and, off in the distance, the top half of the Eiffel Tower. Once I realized how cut off I would be from the city because of the curfew and my lack of funds, I came to cherish this view. As time passed I kept returning to a line of poetry from Linda Gregg: "What if the world remains far off?"

Solitude was another theme. Not having money made it difficult to socialize. Mary, a graduate student from Notre Dame who was in Paris to get fluent enough to read Hélène Cixous' "écriture feminine" in the original French, was always inviting me to drink wine and swap graduate school horror stories. Wendy wanted to hit the nightclubs and listen to torch singers' renditions of Edith Piaf (a losing proposition anyway since nothing really got going until after eleven). Eugene, who lived in a residence without a curfew or a cafeteria, was always inviting me to join him for a dinner out. I could never accept these invitations. My one big extravagance was to see Spike Lee's *Do the Right Thing* with French subtitles at a matinée, but I passed on the popcorn.

And so, to entertain myself on the cheap, I walked. I had bought one small bottle of Evian water earlier in the summer and I would refill it with tap water from the communal bathroom and then set out: to admire the glamorous women pushing strollers through the Parc Monceau, to see Jimi Hendrix's grave at the Montparnasse cemetary, to watch school children playing in the place des Vosges, and to stroll along the Seine into Notre Dame and watch the sun set through rose-colored windows.

Sometimes I brought Mary or Wendy or Eugene along with me and we talked, exchanging life stories as we roamed. It was near the Panthéon that I learned that Mary was questioning her faith as a Catholic because she could not reconcile the Pope's views on women with her feminism. Wendy was complaining about the blisters all our walks were giving her when she told Mary and me, in Les Jardins Luxembourg, that she often cried herself to sleep over being single and alone. But of all the confessions exchanged in motion, the most stunning came from Eugene.

He and I were passing a café on a small street off the boulevard St. Germain when we saw the café owner shouting at his wife. Something about this abusive man reminded Eugene of his father. He told me then that he was gay, and that his parents were paying a psychiatrist to "reprogram" him straight, although so far all this man had succeeded in doing was compounding Eugene's feelings of shame and guilt. He had no support from anyone anywhere on this issue; his family and friends were all strict Catholics. Even here in Paris he couldn't be "out," at least among our seemingly friendly group of American students. The undergraduates from his alma mater – our sponsor for the study-abroad program – were all virulent "fag-haters. They beat up suspected homos at my school," he said. "Or shun them."

I saw a little of what he was up against when I went jogging in the Luxembourg Gardens with Claire, a student from our program who said that the sight of men greeting each other in the traditional French way – kissing each cheek – nauseated her. She was from a wealthy Catholic family in Virginia with a father who raised ponies for polo and grew tobacco, and as far as she knew, she had never met any homosexuals. Eugene made me promise I'd never tell.

Eugene was gorgeous. He had close-cropped, wavy, auburn hair, a ruddy complexion, and big hazel, green-flecked eyes with long eyelashes. Wherever he went, women fell for him; with his sexuality so cleverly hidden, he gave off few signals to indicate he was off-limits. I think even Claire had a thing for him.

Early in his time in Paris, someone approached him and tried to convince him to sign with a modeling agency. He was deciding. He could imagine creating a life for himself in "gai Paris," modeling suits by Yves St. Laurent by day and dancing at the discos at night. Like me he had arrived in Paris with high hopes about *la vie bohème*, but they were countered with the conviction that he would be repaid for this life by burning in eternal flames. The result was a tortured soul.

Eugene treated me to a drink one night – "Pour courage," he said – *his*.

He was about to make a foray into the club scene for the first time. His pale peach-colored cotton shirt, open to expose his chest hairs, brought out the red in his cheeks. He looked embarrassed, scared, and happy. The lock clicked behind me as I said good-bye at the stroke of midnight, and I begged him not to contract *le SIDA*.

Gradually, in language class, we crept up on that dicey subject occupying much of the world: the struggle for human rights and freedom. One day Madame asked us to give five-minute reports on the most pressing issues in our respective homelands. I was curious to hear what the ambassador from Beijing had to say – it was only a month since the massacre at Tienanmen Square. The reports from the press were confusing and conflicting and no one knew exactly how many people had been killed and how many were students. The ambassador spoke, instead, on China's policy of only allowing one child per family to curb population growth and the common occurrence of aborting girl babies. Perhaps that important subject was risky for him to broach, but I wondered how he could see it as the most timely one.

Stupidly, I raised my hand and asked about student participation in the democracy movement in China. He pretended he didn't understand my French. It was only then that I realized that this ambassador was very much "on duty," even though he appeared to be just another student in Paris. There was another Chinese person in the class, a woman whom I presume would have been obliged to report him for saying anything critical about the government's role in the tragedy. This was my first encounter with Communist censorship, and what surprised me was how much it surprised me.

When it was my turn to describe America's biggest problems, I didn't know where to start. "La droite," I began. I didn't have enough vocabulary to say that although George Bush seemed more intelligent than his predecessor, I was scared he would start a war against one of his former arms-and-drug-running thug cronies from the CIA era so as to counteract his "wimp" image. "La difference entre les riches et les pauvres," I added, giving a simplified version of my usual spiel about how I believed that America needed to adopt a government more like France's under Mitterand: a socialized democracy. I ended by lamenting that it was a sad irony that while other countries were looking to our Bill of Rights to inspire their own reform movements, some of us were in danger of losing our voice and our rights thanks to the power – I didn't know the French for "lobbying efforts" – of a minority of religious. I didn't know the French for "fanatics," but "madmen" would do – *fous*.

Tim's forehead was pulsing overtime and I knew he wanted to challenge me, or perhaps attempt a French proximity of "commie-pinko," but he waited until the circle came to him. Then he held forth on the evils of abortion and affirmative action and the forces of political correctness, and I doodled my repudiations in my French journal. Tim made many a guest appearance in that notebook.

As, of course, did the nuns. Back at the convent, our war with them was escalating. Many of us regressed into childlike behavior, faking smiles and saying, "Bonjour, ma mère," with so much obvious insincerity that I'm surprised she remained civil to us at all. The Italian who'd been served the disgusting hot milk bowl one morning told a story, speaking loudly so that the mother superior would hear, about a nun she'd had in Catholic school in Milan who beat her for taking the clothes off her Barbie doll at playtime. "I was just changing her from her dungarees to her evening gown," she said, "and they thought I was playing doctor with my dolly." We all laughed raucously.

Only once did we get away as a group. The weekend before Bastille Day, several busloads of students from the Institut Catholique went to Normandy for a prepaid trip to Mont St. Michel. To our astonishment, the Institut had arranged to house all of us at another convent, and although it was a Saturday, our curfew there was two hours earlier than in Paris – ten PM! We all returned to the city feeling grumpy and depressed. I found myself getting grumpy and blue a lot that summer, and then I would chastise myself for having such unrealistic expectations, for forgetting how lucky I was to be in Paris when most people at my income level had never been anywhere, and then I'd feel bad about feeling bad, which depressed me.

Depression, and its antidotes, was one of Madame Naveau's favorite topics. The ever-elusive pursuit of happiness, she reminded us, was meant to be a by-product of democracy. "So what do you do when you are sad?" she asked. Most people opted for two-word sentences – I eat, I drink, I walk, I pray – but I felt compelled to try to explain my multipronged attacks on misery at La Maison, a combination of writing, walking, and talking to new friends. One of our exams was to listen to and try to reproduce these words in correct French, and then translate: "Le bonheur suppose sans doute toujours quelque inquietude, quelque passion, une point de douleur qui nous éveillé a nous-même. Il est ordinaire que l'on ait plus de bonheur par l'imagination que par les biens réels." My rough translation of this was that happiness could not exist without its companions, worry and pain, and that the happiness we create in our own imaginations is always superior to that of real life.

Now and then Madame asked us to say what we disliked most about Paris. Many spoke of the cruelty of French civil servants, and Wendy said that she had noticed that if you are carrying heavy bags and need help, the men won't lift a finger if you aren't young and thin and pretty. She glanced with envy at the thin and beautiful Elisabetta, a college student from Pisa. "Being in Paris makes me feel old and fat and ugly, and that makes me very sad," Wendy said.

To counter the negatives, Madame Naveau assigned us to go to an appealing public place each week – a café, a park – to write a poem or a short story. As I did my homework, I imagined the other students doing theirs, and felt a kinship with them: the ambassador from Beijing, who went to the Louvre on his days off; the slim Elisabetta, who treated herself to ice cream; Anna, the sophisticated booking agent for the Polish opera, who danced away the blues at the discotheques; and those sweet, shy nuns from the Philippines who only giggled when it was their turn to speak.

Sometimes I would stand outside La Couple, the famous café, which was only a maddening few minutes from the convent: so close, yet so far. From the pavement, I would picture myself sitting inside at various moments in twentieth-century history: World War I, the '20s of Gertrude Stein and Josephine Baker, World War II under German occupation, the revolutionary late sixties of Madame Naveau's youth. I examined the characters near me and tried to imagine myself in their places: geezers in caps drinking brandy; young couples playing the choreographed, delicately nuanced, lip-pouting dance of the date; a woman in her mid-forties in a soft white linen suit, obviously waiting for someone; a sharp-chinned poet scrawling into a notebook. Were they happier than I was simply because they were French and such café life was a normal part of their day? Did they take pride in their citizenship?

Were my fellow students in Madame Naveau's class proud of their homelands? Was Tim? I wanted to ask him, but we were so far apart in the cultural divide that I could not imagine having a civil conversation with him. Which is why I was so surprised when one day, as our group filed out of class, he said to me, "Madame Naveau is an excellent teacher."

I turned to him, noticing again how young he was – almost ten years my junior. "I don't agree with her on anything, but I like the way she makes us talk."

"That's true," I said. "She's making us learn." I thought back to the times Tim's remarks had provoked me to wrestle with the language to fire something back. Madame Naveau had known exactly what she was doing, getting us to goad each other as she had. Nonetheless, one of the reasons I liked Madame so much was because she was in my ideological camp, and I could not imagine being so generous about a teacher with zealous right-wing views.

It made me cross to see Tim, my sworn enemy, behave better than I would in his shoes, and this depressed me too.

Finally, the week of Bastille Day arrived. On July 13, the day before the big night, Madame asked us to summarize what we had learned from the assigned readings.

Part of the trouble with understanding the French Revolution, she had warned us, was to know what, exactly, one was celebrating. Although I had been taught that the storming of the Bastille freed hundreds, the article we read said that the vast fortress held only seven prisoners on that night. And in the period of violence and horror afterwards known as the Terror, some historians say only one-tenth of those executed (by guillotine or drawing and quartering) were members of the aristocracy; Robespierre, the Jacobin leader who came to symbolize the most radical and bloody phase of the revolution, ordered the deaths of thousands of undistinguished "enemies of the people" until he himself was executed in July of 1794, a date that some people – the counterrevolutionaries, in particular, like Tim's mentors – believe is the occasion that should be commemorated.

In only one decade, France moved from being an absolute monarchy in 1789 to a constitutional monarchy, to a democratic republic, then an ideological dictatorship under Robespierre, then a corrupt state with only one party, and then a military dictatorship under Napoleon by 1799: ten years of mob scenes and bloodshed and panic and chaos.

Even the famous column on place de la Bastille, where many in our group had plans to gather the next night, was erected not, as I always thought, to commemorate the 1789 surrender of the prison but the July revolution of 1830 that ousted the autocratic Charles X. The monarchy had returned after Napoleon's defeat at Waterloo and would continue to reassert itself at least as the model of governance for France's emperors. Charles X was replaced with the "citizen king" Louis-Philippe, but he would later have to flee in the revolution of 1878, and his throne would be burned beside the place de la Bastille column. Ultimately the French would choose to celebrate the 1789 revolution mainly because it was milder than the ninety years of upheaval and violence that came afterward.

But as we discussed this history in class, most of us agreed that despite the near-century of bloodshed that followed the 1789 raid of the prison, the spirit behind the Enlightenment-inspired Rights of Man and the Citizen still had a fresh sound to it in 1989. We did not know that by November, the citizens on both sides of the Berlin Wall would be given government permission to tear it down (and sell chunks of it for kitschy souvenirs) but we did know that some of the people gazing at each other from across the parallel tables in our rectangle would not have been able to meet as recently as a year before.

Our conversation shifted to what we were going to do on Bastille Day. Joaquim, a jolly Spaniard who had rented an apartment for the summer, invited us all to a party, but in the rush after class, I didn't get his address. Besides, I had a revolt to lead.

I was right and the mother superior was wrong. On the night of July 14, almost every bed in the student halls at La Maison was empty. It would have been nice if we had broken out of the cliques defined by our mother tongues and mixed more; it would have been great if we could have been organized enough to stage an en masse walkout during our wretched cafeteria no-extra-frills-despite-the-holiday dinner. But as in many grass roots movements, we started small, spreading the word through small groups of three or four. After talking to as many of the residents as we could, Mary and Wendy and I had gotten almost everyone to agree to either stay out all night or spend the evening with a friend somewhere else as a show of solidarity. The nun whose duty it was to buzz us in and write our names in the book would have nothing to do.

After dinner my trio joined Eugene and Claire in front of the convent and headed toward the Seine in search of outdoor parties. Eugene confided in me that he had completed his portfolio and had already signed with a modeling agency. He would not be going home with his peers; he was staying in Paris indefinitely. "If I'm going straight to hell," he said,

"I might as well enjoy myself until then." He was in excellent spirits for someone contemplating hellfire and damnation. I was too.

It was warm and clear that night, and we felt euphoric as we walked down the wide boulevards admiring the beauty of the city. A big party was underway on the quay near the Pont D'Art, and Eugene and I implored the others to dance. Wendy joined us at once, and then Claire, then Mary. Eugene bore his status as the token male with good humor as he twirled us around one by one to tunes by the Rolling Stones, Roxy Music, David Bowie, Lou Reed, the Beatles, the Sex Pistols, and the Pretenders: all my favorites. It wasn't that late yet so there was plenty of room, and the people who had sponsored the party, a bar who had hired a DJ, were friendly and welcoming.

We spotted some of the other residents of La Maison there on the river and they joined us. Soon we were all one big body, pulsing and flapping: American, French, German, Italian, West African, Japanese. You didn't need to be anybody special or have a centime to your name to be in our posse. We had been sprung from the coop and it was glorious to be us that night, feeling the summer night wind on our skin as we threw up our hands and hooted.

And then Claire made an observation. I couldn't hear her so she pointed. A lot of young men were dancing together and a few were bumping and grinding with a bit too much vigor for her taste.

"But *we're* dancing together," I shouted in her ear. "Women with women. Does it matter?" The truth is, Eugene and I had sussed out it was a gay party as soon as we arrived and tacitly agreed not to mention it. In fact, our growing gang of La Maison residents provided the *only* women until some strangers joined us as the evening wore on. I had thought for a few overly optimistic minutes that Claire knew where we were and just didn't care, that she was letting go of old prejudices in the spirit of revolution.

"They're queer!" Claire shouted. From the look of horror and betrayal on her face you would have thought she had just walked in on her brother and boyfriend taking part in a vigorous group orgy. "I'm going to be sick," she said. And that was it. We had agreed to stick together so we couldn't let Claire leave without us. We had to go.

After that, as the night unfolded beneath a cloud of smoke, jeers, songs, and sweat, I remembered why I hate the Fourth of July in the States. When we tried to proceed along the Seine, we were trapped in near standstills in thickening crowds, easy targets for firecrackers thrown by random marauders toward the feet of passersby. We couldn't see anything. When we stopped near the place de La Bastille, we could not make out the inscribed words we had come to recite daily as our mantra: *liberté, égalité, fraternité*. Near the column was the newly erected Opera-Bastille we had been assigned to read reviews of in French class. One critic had described it as resembling "a hippopotamus in a bathtub." All we could see were the shirtless backs of the drunken men in front of us.

By midnight the non-Maison residents had grown weary. Eugene had never recovered from the Claire Inquisition, and he slipped away without saying good-bye, perhaps to return to the gay party. Claire, who did not have lockout to contend with in her dorm, left sometime around one to go to sleep. Mary and Wendy and I had six hours to kill.

It was fun, at first, to wander at night without the usual hurry. All summer the pressure of our curfew and the set meal times had made it difficult for me to linger anywhere without looking at my watch. We competed with each other to see who could walk the slowest, and I made a game of scrounging up change I found glinting under streetlights, performing the part of the street urchin. We followed the Seine down the Right Bank all the way to the place de Gaulle, admiring the Musée d'Orsay across the river, imagining it as a train station a century before with fashionable women rushing past in hats and gloves and bustles, and, on our side of the river, the palatial complex of the Louvre and the adjoining walled-in garden of the Trocadéro.

The hours passed and before we knew it we had, without intending to, strolled to the Arc de Triomphe, one of those must-see monuments we'd all been meaning to get to for weeks. By now we were cold, hungry, and utterly exhausted. We were sick of Paris, sick of being the foreigners. And I was sick of being poor. We stared down at the flame lit for the unknown soldier who had died for *la patrie* in World War I and thought, "So what?" We weren't interested in the conquests of war. I said that I thought those "big, manly half-naked dudes" lurking from the sculpture frieze were grotesque, that the Roman ghosts reinstated by neo-Classicism, this fascination with gladiators and clawed-up men, left me cold. Mary quoted something in French from Hélène Cixous, but we were sick of speaking French. Then, in English, she agreed that this place "wasn't much of a girl thang." And the Champs-Élysées and all the other giant streets shooting out from this triumphant center like the spokes of a giant wheel weren't either. We envied Claire for having a room to go back to, and we wished we'd brought sleeping bags. We sprawled out on a bench by the arch and rested our feet, laughing that we should write to the tourist guides to report that five in the morning was the best time to get a good look at the Arc de Triomphe. We finally had the city and all its (dis)contents to ourselves: historic monuments festooned with empty liquor bottles, party streamers, coke cans, used syringes, used condoms, and McDonald's wrappers. *Enchanté*!

As dawn broke over the partied-out city, we rousted ourselves and prepared for the long walk back to the convent. We were done. We had *been* done. We slunk along the Champs-Élysées, to the place de la Concorde, and along the Seine until we crossed back over to the Left Bank, found the boulevard St. Germain – Wendy's blisters were bleeding by now – and dragged ourselves down the boulevard de St. Michel for the home stretch in silence.

But just before we arrived, too weary to smile our fake smiles at the nuns before we collapsed in bed for the entire day, I decided to do something wild. I went into the bakery next door whose fragrant odors had always filled me with self-pity, plunked down all the centimes I had scavenged throughout the night, and bought myself a *chausson aux pommes*. I was half a franc short but the baker was mercifully generous in the spirit of the revolution: let them eat pie! The buttery pastry was light and flaky, the apples tart but sweet with a trace of lemon. Long-deprived taste buds had a party in my mouth. I have never eaten anything more delicious. When I close my eyes now, as I write these words, I can still taste it. Yum.

During my square-off with the mother superior in the basement, the words *blanche sur blanche* had taken on the sheen of symbolism, suggesting to me the false images of girlhood that were being nourished inside the convent walls. But perhaps the color scheme that best depicts the epistemologies I was party to inside and outside La Maison is black and white. All I know is that every utterance I heard seemed to be informed by the most rigid, dualistic thinking, and all choices on offer seemed absolute and irreconcilable. All matters, from the trivial to the monumental, were posed in the form of the dilemma. If I wanted protein in the form of cheese, I couldn't have dessert. We could go out on Bastille Night, or we could get to sleep before 7:10 AM. Eugene could be himself, which meant loving men, if he was prepared to burn in hell; or he could retain the love of his family and his God, but live a lie. Mary could be feminist or a Catholic, but not both. Instead of Communism, Russia could now embrace the free market system in its totality, which would soon mean more hunger, homelessness, increased crime, prostitution, an attempted coup, and that great Western import, the Mafia.

As time has passed I have come to better understand why we didn't hear from everybody in French class on the subject of politics, even from the students who did not have snitches from home beside them at the seminar table. And I have somewhat of an inkling as to why the students who groaned the loudest over Madame's creative writing assignments were those from countries behind the Iron Curtain.

Early in my teaching career I would become the first-year writing instructor of a brilliant young woman named Kristina, who grew up in Ceauşescu's Romania and had to wait until she was nearly twenty-three to be permitted to come to the United States. If I prodded her, she could describe vividly all she had endured under Communism – her parents' expulsion from their house and land in the country, their cold winters with inadequate heating rations, their perpetual hunger – but only when the two of us were alone in my office. When she wrote a memoir for class, she chose the universal moments her teachers had taught her were the only occasions worthy of artistic expression: the death of a cherished grandmother, the birth of her younger brother. When I urged her to move beyond what I called the "Hallmark card sentimentality" of publicly sanctified, predictable, generically rendered abstractions, she told me that she really didn't know how to use her imagination in an idiosyncratic way. It would appear that her creativity itself had been collectivized by the state. The personal and quirky and original were transgressive, taboo.

In *The Eros of Everyday Life*, Susan Griffin writes about the way cold-war politics reified a kind of dualistic thinking that trapped all of us into worldviews of reductive, binary oppositions that made it impossible to see or accept the truth about life on either side of the Iron Curtain. She says, "The ambiance of the divide was stifling. The effect was to polarize the social imagination. Dissident thinkers of every kind found it difficult to criticize either China, the Soviet Union, or Marxist theory for fear of being used in any fashion to aid or abet the witch hunt." When my thesis advisor, Tamas Aczel, had talked about the horrors of life in Hungary under Communism, I had suspected him of being quietly pro-Reagan, although I'm pretty sure now that he was not. I knew a little about the Stalinist purges – I'd been assigned *The Gulag Archipelago* as a high school senior – and I had no desire to live in the

USSR. I thought of the Politburo as a bunch of humorless, murderous old generals, with torture methods not unlike those of the Nazis, but I also believed the East and the West were shadowy doubles of one another like the characters in Conrad's *Secret Sharer*. It seemed to me that each side was guilty of a version of the same crimes they accused the other of committing: The Evil Empire versus . . . the Evil Empire. I couldn't pick one system, in its absolute form, as superior to the other. I believed there needed to be a sort of Hegelian synthesis between the two, which is why I was so enamored with European forms of socialized democracy. I believed (and still do) that every citizen is entitled to decent shelter, food, clean air and water, health care, and education, and I admired (and still do) countries like France and Western Germany and Great Britain and Scandinavia that guaranteed all citizens their rights to these basic elements of survival: rights we were losing in America in 1989, rights that have all but disappeared today.

But while I could see how the two superpowers were in many ways alike, I could not recognize the similarities between Tim and me, even as we vilified the other with similarly clenched jaws.

What I did comprehend was that there was something about the times themselves holding my imagination – and that of my colleagues – in a kind of vise. Even in the creative writing workshop, where that autumn we would shake our heads in disbelief over the fatwa against Salman Rushdie and the editors, publishers, and distributors of *The Satanic Verses*, no one seemed sympathetic to my frustration when I said that there were things I, as an American woman, was forbidden to say in fiction. "You're lucky to live and write in the most progressive country on the planet," someone said. But then a professor would pronounce a story with a bleak ending "unsellable" and I would remember a piece I'd read some time ago by Joyce Carol Oates in which two writers, one from Poland and one from America, compare the difficulties of getting published in their own countries and both agree that the question, "But will it sell?" is a form of censorship too.

The politics of the white, male dominant culture were at play in our workshop critiques, although few would admit it. "Your male character is too unlikable," someone would say. "That's male bashing. A story with a feminist agenda won't sell." I could not make the student critic see that *he* had a political agenda. But I wasn't very good at talking to people who did not already agree with me. I, too, was trapped inside the mindset of the polemicist. I'm still trying to break free.

A few years ago I met Sidney Piburn, the editor of Snow Lion Publications and friend of the Dalai Lama. I told him I was writing a book about taking politics personally, and I asked him to explain the Buddhist perspective on the presidential election of 2000 and on politics in general. "On one hand," I said, "if you subscribe to the Buddhist notion that you must devote your life to alleviating the suffering of all sentient beings, a life of political engagement makes sense. But political engagement to me means passion, and Buddhism to me means detachment from strong emotions. It's hard for me not to hate the people who want to drill in Alaska and cut education spending and start up Star Wars again and countless other wars. I hate the people who hate."

"Yes," Sidney said. "And then you can end up thinking you have to hate half of America."

I've been thinking about this line ever since. I don't want to think that to work for justice and peace that I have to hate half of America.

The most moving moments in my life have been those instances when I felt not division between myself and others but a transcending unity: my night in the forest at Camp Patmos, my four-hour meetings at the Salal. My favorite times in French class were not when we debated or when Tim and I squared off but when, as a group, we recited poems by Apollinaire and sang the songs of Jacques Prévert. And although I quickly fell prey to an us-against-them mentality at La Maison, I would eventually wonder what had happened in the red-haired cafeteria worker's past that made her so mean. Beyond the details of her particular life story, I came to suspect that much of her behavior could be explained by class resentment. The Italian girl she was most cruel to was always bursting into the room eager to show us the pretty dresses she had bought at the boutiques.

I read somewhere once that in adolescence our moral reasoning tends toward absolute, black-and-white, either/or scenarios. When I teach first-year college students, one of my tasks is to move them away from reductionism and essentialism toward more nuance and complexity. It's more difficult to do this when the culture itself is stuck back in high school as well. During the Reagan-Bush years it often seemed to me that the country was being run by prom court. Prom court with guns.

When the Wall finally came down, America would be forced to face the intricate networks of a complex, changing New World order. And when war broke out in the former Yugoslavia and the news was full of terrifying expressions like "ethnic cleansing," we would learn that abandoning communism cold turkey in countries that had never known democracy would lead to near economic and social collapse. While we had divided the planet into two, we had not accounted for the forces of religious fundamentalism and nationalism that rejected both superpowers as devils or murdering imperialists. We would have to look beyond the dualities and isms of the categorical systems we'd been taught since World War II. The left would have to embrace the horrors of the regimes they'd felt reticent to criticize for fear of giving the right more ammunition, just as those on the right who had armed guerilla rebels and paramilitary troops in Afghanistan and Pakistan to help them defeat communism would have to accept responsibility for the creation of the Taliban (who were so warmly welcomed into Reagan's White House) and those fundamentalist hijackers who turned airborne Americans into suicide bombs. Perhaps one lesson we have yet to learn from the tragedy of the Pentagon and World Trade Center attacks is the suicidal course we set forth on when we divided the world into only two.

Someday I would like to look up my old classmates from Paris and do a more systematic comparison between life before and after 1989 on either side of the great divide. For now, when I think of what East and West had to teach each other at the table, only these tidbits have stayed with me:

That when they have the blues the skinny Italian, Elisabetta, eats *gelatto*; an American named Tim prays; an ambassador from China talks to his wife; a Polish opera buff dances all night; and Wendy-from-Milwaukee cries, especially if she's been hauling luggage without male assistance.

That although equal doses of people from East and West disapproved of Madame bringing men to the apartment, she most certainly would.

That the French, for all their talk about *liberté et égalité*, have strangely hierarchical ways.

I know my account of the French Bicentennial is mostly a story about behaving badly while on vacation. I know I've been too hard on the nuns. But if you can put these faults aside, I ask you to savor this victory with me. Picture the stars dappling the surface of the Seine. Listen to the sound of pranksters' firecrackers, people shouting the seconds, the whoops and calls of bodies dancing. It is midnight, the moment of lockout. Somewhere in that throng of thousands, three American women from the Midwest link hands and jump into the air, and I am one of them. Soon we are going to be hungry and tired and short-tempered, and we'll all catch whopping colds, but it'll be worth it. "Vive la Revolution!" we scream. "Vive la Resistance!" Above us, pinwheels and roman candles light up our faces and the famous river and the famous monuments – all in dazzling, promiscuous color.

# Afterword

Of course the people don't want war. . . . All you have to do is tell them they are being attacked, and denounce the pacifists for lack of patriotism, and exposing the country to greater danger.

    Hermann Goering, *At the Nuremberg Trials*

Chanting among them, I see that politics and spirituality, those seemingly discordant airs, can merge into a single harmonious song whose tune I hope one day to carry on my own.

    Alix Kates Shulman, *Drinking the Rain*

# Déjà Voodoo

The scouts and trail bosses who served as Reagan's economic, spiritual, and foreign-policy advisers (many of them now attached to President Bush the Younger) haven't brooked the insult of a new idea in twenty years.
Lewis H. Lapham, "Notebook: Civic Lesson," *Harper's*

The smell of pumpkin pies baking drifted up from the monastery kitchen into the meeting room where I sat talking to the monks of Dai Bosatsu Zendo. With Thanksgiving a couple days away and the legal dogfights in Florida showing no signs of abating, I had come to spend a day in the same community where, two decades ago, I had watched young monks weep at the news that Ronald Reagan had been elected.

The morning meeting had started with some good-natured grumbling about the temperamental furnace, which seemed to make no headway against the cold November wind that blew a thin dusting of snow down from the ash and yellow birch trees lining the Beaverkill River. I was thankful for the layer of polar fleece I was wearing under my cotton robe.

At Dai Bosatsu Zendo, news tends to come via snippets heard over the car radio during short drives to town for groceries or other supplies, or a day late via the *New York Times*. The monastery's one computer provides Internet access, but most of the monks are too busy chanting sutras, sitting zazen, and doing chores to get on line.

Jiro Osho Fernando Afable, the assistant abbot of the zendo, asked us if anyone had more news.

"I heard a story on NPR that said that according to an exit poll people who call themselves 'religious' tended to vote for George Bush," said Entsu, a thirty-four-year-old former community-college professor of bioethics, member of ACT-UP, and advocate for the homeless in Syracuse.

"Did any of you vote for Bush?" I asked. They all shook their heads no. Kigen, who took his monk's vows after spending over fifteen years practicing law in Manhattan, had confided in me earlier that he hadn't voted since he moved to the monastery a year ago, shortly after he turned forty. "I used to vote even at primaries, but back then I thought I'd run for public office someday, so I thought I had to."

Entsu said he had voted for Nader. "I'm still a registered Democrat, and I wouldn't have voted for Nader if I lived in Florida. If I knew it would be close."

"I'm worried my son might have voted for Bush," said Sally, a fiftyish Japanese woman with gray bangs and a pageboy who used to be married to an American businessman. "He's twenty-two. He doesn't understand why I'm here; he just thinks it's because I'm old and crazy. He doesn't understand the importance of being pro-choice; he doesn't understand what segregation was like. He thinks happiness is money. He just wants to maintain his 3.9 average and get a job right out of college for eighty thousand dollars a year."

"What's being fed to young people over TV is that values, like everything else, are a commodity," said Tendo, a very pale-skinned artist and musician from Athens, Georgia, where the band, the B-52s, got their start. The day before, he had reminisced with me about his college years in the early eighties and all the great music in Athens. I thought back to the Ballard days with Joe, how we slam-danced above Vicki and Glenn, plotting our transcendence from the mainstream American business world. "Nobody's thinking. Media literacy needs to be taught in college. That's something I've thought about a lot lately. When you come here you are forced to derive your own self out of the routine of no labels, no products. If you derive identity out of what you consume – whether it's ethics or Rice Krispies – you aren't going to have anything here. Nothing at all."

"I have to admit something else," Sally said. "Bush Senior got my sympathies when he stopped bombing in Desert Storm. I sometimes think he should have just finished and won the war. He would have been reelected."

"But he did win the war," Tendo said. "His oil quota from the Gulf was maintained."

"But I think we would have considered it a true win if the common people in Iraq had been protected from Saddam," Sally said. "We made no headway there."

"George Bush Senior was a war criminal," said Entsu. Earlier he'd read from a text called *The Way of the Tea*. One line warned that a man "at fifty" is "a criminal" if he has lost his Buddha nature.

"That's right," said Tendo. "And so was Ronald Reagan. The invasion of Grenada, Panama, Central America: those were technically illegal. Only Congress can declare war. These guys were war criminals just like Pinochet. And we live in a national security state, not a democracy."

Tenring, a young monk seated to the right of Jiro Osho, spoke for the first time. "No one's said anything about Clinton. We had a monk here from Haiti whose life got much worse under Clinton. No one talks about that."

"I wonder what ever happened to Baby Doc's money," said Jiro. "His wife took all the money and ran." Some of us listed off some of the bloodiest places where we'd launched air strikes or sent our advisors through the two Clinton administrations, a time of so-called peace and prosperity: Haiti, Somalia, Bosnia, Rwanda, Iraq, the Philippines, Sudan, East Timor . . . I was sure we'd forgotten some, and I vowed to look them up at home.

I had also visited the monastery in 1992, right after Bill Clinton was first elected. Everyone I spoke to then was as enthusiastic about this sea change as Buddhists ever get. Would any of us ever be this optimistic again? Reaganized, then Clintonized, the United States could now boast weaker trade unions, zero job security, low wages, and increasingly volatile, global markets. Most of the goods we rely on in the Land of the Free are now made in the hot, wet places where Vishnu or Buddha reign, and children do the work. And who could have foreseen that a Democrat would be the one to hammer the last nails in the coffin of the welfare state? Or that a Democrat would allow Congress to reintroduce the idea of funding Star Wars?

"I'm glad only one of them will win," Sally said. "I've lived in Europe and seen what coalition governments are like. I really think America has the best form of government in the world."

Tendo said, "If you like a country that was set up by landowners and managers. It was set up to be this way back in the writing of the Articles of Confederation."

Sally said, "Okay then. When you talk about democracy, is there really one that meets the standards?"

Everyone laughed. "Ancient Greece?" said Tendo.

"Still, give a republic a set of civil rights and then you can watch it slowly evolve into a democracy," said Entsu. "You have to be patient. That's one thing I've learned from political activism. And from Buddhism. You have to take the long view."

"Well, it's not at all surprising that the race was a tie," Sally said. "We live in a deeply divided country. The social pendulum swings back and forth between times when issues matter and times when individuality and money and consumerism are all that people care about. It's really wild to think about how it's going to swing now."

"Now when Ronald Reagan was elected I thought the worst could happen," said Tendo. "I was eighteen and I was sure he'd start a war. A nuclear war. This election, though . . . I don't think it will really change our life here. Our institution is in place. And the choice . . ."

"One has horns and one has a tail," said Genshin, a young commercial artist from New York City who was halfway through a *kesai*, a three-and-a-half-month-long residency. "A choice between Exxon or Microsoft."

"I was driving by a Wal-Mart," said Tendo, "and I thought, that's it. That's America. A network of distributors for retail outlets."

And that's how our meeting ended, with this image of the united Wal-Marts of America in our heads as we chanted the closing sutra: "However endless the Buddha's way is, we vow to follow it."

When I was signing my Visa bill, Kigen, the monk who had once dreamed of a life in politics said, "If you're a Buddhist, you're committed to alleviating the suffering of all sentient beings. You are alive and awake and are in search of the truth. The last thing the government wants is a nation of Buddhists. In that way, a life like ours here at DBZ is as radical as it gets."

Entsu had something else to offer to me too, as I left him in the kitchen where he was supervising the preparations for the upcoming Thanksgiving feast. "I've studied many religions, read Buddhist texts in Japanese, and I still think the U.S. Constitution is the most enlightened document every written."

I think so too. But we have some work to do, you and I.

As I write these words, the politics of the eighties have been revived with vigor. Members of the Reagan and Bush administrations are back, running the country as Bush Junior's advisors and cabinet. Reagan's trickle-down economics has been reinstalled without debate, with tax cuts for the rich in the face of rising national debt. Star Wars is back, along with draconian budget cuts for education, the poor, a brutal assault on the environment, and a rigidly dualistic you-are-with-us-or-you're-not way of relating to the rest of the world as we fight not Communism now but terrorism. The language of the cold war is back too, as Bush tries to sell the nation on one war after another, most recently a "preemptive strike" against Iraq, that cost, per *day* over a billion dollars, the entire amount it would have taken to prevent cuts to education in 2003. The language is being manipulated again, Orwellian style, to obfuscate the truth about our eroding civil liberties as a result of the Patriot Act. Once again those who dissent are accused of being unpatriotic, even treasonous. Liberals are the rusty relics of a bygone era, and some – writers, academics, and other cultural critics speaking out against the Bush administration – have even made it back onto government blacklists.

And yet, I believe that the general populace is wiser than it was in the 1980s, more compassionate toward human suffering here and everywhere, more alert to internal threats to civil liberty and democracy. As someone who took what I have come to think of as a decade-long sabbatical dedicated to self-improvement and study, I know it is possible to learn from past mistakes and make better choices for the future.

I have also come to see that no one can transcend the values of her time. Not in a Buddhist monastery, a ghost town of artists, a Mexican courtyard, or a convent in Paris. Our choice is to be passive, and hence complicit, or to resist. We are all citizens, even when the people in charge are not on our team.

# Source Acknowledgments

Portions of this book are based on the following previously published material. I am extremely grateful to the editors of these journals and am particularly indebted to Anne Fadiman, whose meticulous and inspired editing of *The American Scholar* excerpts made the whole book stronger.

"Blood Memories." *Bellingham Review* 24, no. 1 (Spring 2001).
"Blurred Vision: How the Eighties Began in One American Household." *Prairie Schooner* 74, no. 4 (Winter 2000).
"The Come As You Are Not Party." *The American Scholar* 70, no. 3 (Summer 2001).
"How to Survive the Crash." *Del Sol Review* 9 (2002).
"In the Courtyard of the Iguana Brothers." *The American Scholar* 73, no 1 (Winter 2004).
"The Paradise at the End of the World." *The North American Review* 287, nos. 3–4 (May–August 2002).
"Postcard from the Monastery." *Confrontation: A Literary Journal of Long Island University* 52/53 (Winter/Spring 1994).
"Voodoo Economics: Soul Work in the Age of Reagan." *The Iowa Review* 30, no. 1 (2000).

IN THE AMERICAN LIVES SERIES